D0284901

Framing American Divorce

❖ Framing American Divorce ❖

From the Revolutionary Generation to the Victorians

NORMA BASCH

UNIVERSITY OF CALIFORNIA PRESS

Berkeley · Los Angeles · London

University of California Press
Berkeley and Los Angeles, California

University of California Press, Ltd.
London, England

First paperback printing 2001

Library of Congress Cataloging-in-Publication Data

Basch, Norma
  Framing American divorce : From the revolution-
ary generation to the Victorians / Norma Basch
      p.   cm.
  Includes index.
  ISBN 0-520-23196-1 (pbk. : alk paper)
    1. Divorce—United States—History—19th
century. 2. Divorce—Law and legislation—United
States—History—19th century. I. Title.
HQ833.F73   1999
306.89'0973'09034—dc21   98-33947
                                                CIP

Printed in the United States of America

08   07   06   05   04   03   02   01
9   8   7   6   5   4   3   2   1

The paper used in this publication meets the mini-
mum requirements of ANSI/NISO Z39.48-1992
(R 1997) (Permanence of Paper). ∞

To Shelly

Contents

Illustrations

Acknowledgments

This book has been a long time in the making, and it is my great pleasure to offer thanks at last where thanks are due. At a time when assistance to scholars is diminishing and the National Endowment for the Humanities is imperiled, I begin with thanks for the funding that made this project possible. My research was supported by a National Endowment for the Humanities Fellowship, an American Council of Learned Societies Fellowship, and an NEH–American Antiquarian Society Fellowship. I am grateful also to Rutgers University for providing me with a research assistant, Maire Vieth, who lightened my load significantly.

Because archives are pivotal to scholarship, I want to thank the county clerks of New York County (New York City) and Monroe County, Indiana (Blooomington), who afforded me an opportunity to dig into dusty legal records amid the press of contemporary courthouse business. I am especially grateful to Joanne Chaison, Georgia Barnhill, and members of the American Antiquarian staff, who went to great lengths to guide me through the society's extraordinary cache of nineteenth-century ephemera.

Teaching and writing are not mutually exclusive activities, and I owe a debt of thanks to both the undergraduate and graduate students on whom I tried out my material. The most critical forum I faced, in the sense of being both exacting and important, was the NYU Legal History Colloquium, where I first tested the unorthodox structure that underpins this book and discussed the problems and possibilities it posed. My thanks go to Bill Nelson, John Reid, and the colloquium participants.

Dirk Hartog, Mary Kelley, and David Konig read portions of the manuscript, and Mike Grossberg, Nina Dayton, and Joyce Appleby read it in its entirety. I deeply appreciate their cajoling me into making changes, saving me from making mistakes, and offering suggestions that I often ignored. Their magnanimity gives real meaning to the phrase "a community of scholars." Jan Lewis, my Rutgers colleague, read and commented on virtually every version of the manuscript I managed to write. Not only did she address my raw efforts with perceptivity and generosity, but her readiness to buoy me during times of doubt attests to the glories of friendship.

Chapter 1 was adapted from "From the Bonds of Empire to the Bonds of Matrimony," in *Devising Liberty: Preserving and Creating Freedom in the New American Republic,* edited by David Thomas Konig, with the permission of the publishers, Stanford University Press, © 1995 by the Board of Trustees of the Leland Stanford Junior University. Chapter 4 appeared in an earlier version as "Relief in the Premises: Divorce as a Woman's Remedy in New York and Indiana, 1815–1870," *Law and History Review* 8 (1990): 1–24.

I have many reasons to be grateful to Monica McCormick, my editor at the University of California Press, not least of which is her unwavering enthusiasm for the way I "framed" American divorce. I am grateful, too, to Alice Falk for the care with which she copyedited the manuscript. My deepest gratitude goes to Shelly, my intelligent general reader, my indefatigible proofreader, and my longtime sparring partner.

❖ Prologue ❖

On a bleak day in the early spring of 1879, a somber young woman boards a train in Boston to begin the first leg of a journey to Indiana. Dressed entirely in black and wearing a heavy black veil, she looks as if she is in mourning. She is traveling with her little girl, her elderly father, a female friend, and her friend's brother. When the group connects to a sleeping car in New York and the train begins to roll westward, she cannot bring herself to contemplate the ordeal she is about to face. She focuses instead on the changing landscape, noting how the frozen hollows of the New England countryside have given way to the blooming rhododendrons of the Alleghenies. The train reaches the banks of the Ohio, and uncouth westerners begin to occupy the seats vacated by reserved easterners. A rapturous bride and groom come on board and sit entwined in each other's embrace. As the woman in black bitterly recalls the elation of her own wedding day, the purpose of her long journey begins to press in on her. Neither the open prairies nor the raw villages of the midwestern landscape can divert her from what lies ahead. She feels as if she has been called to a deathbed and wants the end to be over. Yet she dreads the prospect before her so much that she is grateful for each and every stop the train makes.

The woman in widow's attire is Marcia Hubbard, the central figure in William Dean Howells's novel *A Modern Instance*. She is on her way to defend herself against her husband Bartley's fraudulent suit for divorce in an Indiana courtroom. Her father will act as her attorney and her friends will serve as witnesses. The novel will reach its climax when the pathologically jealous Marcia finally understands that the careless and self-indulgent Bartley has left her for good and is ratifying his decision by accusing her of desertion in a distant legal jurisdiction where he anticipates a swift and uncontested decree. Marcia's arduous trip westward, then, represents a quest for the honor and revenge that a unilateral Indiana suit would have deprived her of. But when her outraged father follows his cross-petition for a divorce that establishes Bartley's guilt with a demand for Bartley's indictment for perjury, a pitiful moan escapes from Marcia's lips. The hard edges of the law seem ill suited to provide an appropriate ending for this once-impassioned union.

Marcia and Bartley's plight would have been familiar to contemporary readers. Growing numbers of real-life Marcias and Bartleys were entering American courthouses to put formal ends to their failed marriages. A few spouses actually participated in migratory divorce, making the trek westward to more lax and hospitable jurisdictions. Howells's depiction of the Hubbards' marriage, then, should be read in the context of a rising divorce rate as well as a national campaign to roll back divorce. Howells, moreover, used the novel to explore divorce both literally and metaphorically, representing it simultaneously as a legal procedure and a cultural symbol. Thus while he demonstrated the problematic nature of fault divorce, with its dubious but unequivocal assignment of guilt and innocence, he read divorce in general as a signifier of national moral decay. Every facet of the novel suggests that neither the stuffy decadence of the East nor the raw depravity of the West can provide an environment that will sustain the safety, order, and harmony embodied in traditional marriage.

What Howells exploited so deftly, however, was the way divorce resonated with Gilded Age readers. Outlining his plan for *A Modern Instance* in 1881, he noted: "This subject occurred to me years ago as one of the few which are both great and simple. We all know what an enormous fact it is in American life, and that it has never been treated seriously." Although he was not the first American novelist to seize on the narrative possibilities of divorce, he developed them with more finesse than had his predecessors and, realist that he was, with more respect for legal detail. For Howells, who had first entertained *The New Medea* as his title, the Hubbards' Indiana suit stood as a distinctively modern American instance of an old and tragic story. "I feel that I have a theme," he averred, "only less intense and pathetic than slavery."[1]

Howells's sense of the deep impress of divorce on nineteenth-century American life provides a fitting start for this study. It serves to suggest that divorce is a theme that resonates deeply for novelist and historian alike. My subject, too, is divorce, and it has long struck me as one which is both great and simple in the sense that it telescopes a profound and still-evolving cultural transformation into a single, dramatic legal symbol. That transformation consists of nothing less than changing the rules for marriage. In the nineteenth century, when the new rules were first put to the test throughout most of the nation, divorce derived its symbolic punch from its capacity to undermine the contract of marriage, and marriage was (and is) a metonym for the social order. Divorce thus implicitly rocked the foundations of the social order. In a century that elevated the concept of contract to unprecedented heights, marriage was a contract unlike any other. It was the simultaneously private and public contract that defined the obligations between husband and wife, bound their union to the political order, and shaped constructions of gender. The source of harmony and stability in a shifting, competitive world, it was the irrevocable contract that made all other contracts possible. As one scholar has put it, marriage was for bourgeois society "the all-subsuming, all-organizing, all-containing contract."[2]

Divorce took away marriage's irrevocability, bringing it closer to other contracts. The so-called divorce revolution of our own day is a by-product of this unraveling, the culmination of some two centuries of debate over and experimentation in the dismantling of indissoluble marriage. Admittedly, when we read backward from the present, the early part of the drama recedes and flattens out before the meteoric rise of divorce in our own time; but when we read forward from the late eighteenth century, we can see how the dismantling took shape and gathered momentum in the face of daunting obstacles. We can also see how competing narratives about divorce emerged, diversified, and changed.

If these narratives from the past tell us anything, it is that divorce was a vital and capacious subject. Then as now, it inspired accounts that linked legal changes in marriage to the collective fate of the nation and thus collapsed the rhetorical separation of private and public life. Every aspect of legalizing divorce altered the boundaries of individual marriages, and each and every suit for divorce, in turn, was suffused with collective meaning. The counting of divorces, which began tentatively in the late eighteenth century, represented an effort to bring some quantitative precision to what contemporaries sensed intuitively: divorce was assuming a place in the life cycle, taking a tenuous position between the time-honored rite of marriage and the inevitable occasion of death. In Howells's day, when divorce was "an enormous fact . . . in American life," the counting was already under way on a comprehensive, national basis. The numbers pale, of course, by today's standards, but it is the perception of their significance that matters here.[3]

My aim in this book is to map out the web of perceptions, beliefs, and attitudes that coalesced around divorce during the formative stage of its legal development, roughly 1770 to 1870. In particular, I want to traverse the elusive connections between the implementation of divorce as a precise legal form in a specific institutional context and the emergence of divorce as a viable social option and a vibrant cultural symbol. If there is an overarching story to be told here, it lies somewhere between the almost silent legitimation of divorce in the post-Revolutionary era and the militant contestations it elicited in the wake of the Civil War. You might say that I am trying to understand the processes whereby an Indiana divorce suit could become both a trope for moral decay in an important Gilded Age novel and an emblem of personal liberation in the lexicon of radical feminism. Let us turn, then, to the outer boundaries and internal contours of this study and to my deployment of the term *framing*.[4]

PERIODIZATION

In the tumultuous years between the onset of political independence and the aftermath of civil war, Americans shaped the foundations for divorce as a legal institution. They debated the basic ground rules, honed them into statutes, tested them in the courts, and even tried them out in their best-selling works of fiction. It was a process that began precipitously with their collective divorce from Great Britain and then proceeded in fits and starts into the states and territories of the expanding nation. In the end it transformed the world in which women and men lived from a virtually divorceless one, in formal legal terms, to one that granted divorces in the civil courts for specific and limited grounds.

It is important at the outset not to distort the nature of the transformation. Broadly construed, divorce was hardly a new phenomenon; its roots ran deep in the Judeo-Christian tradition and the folkways of Western culture. Its early modern contours were shaped by the Protestant Reformation, which, in the course of rejecting marriage as a sacrament, moved the dissolution of marriage into the secular realm. Relying on its primary meaning, I use the term *framing* here to suggest that the creation of American divorce law was an act of re-creation, a putting together or encircling of many old and familiar components.

Ironically, the inherited components included the canon law provisions for annulment and separation established by the Council of Trent. They were, of course, the source of the problem of divorcelessness, an essential part of the Counter-Reformation, and uncongenial, to say the least, to a Protestant cast of mind. But they nevertheless contributed to the legal foundations for American divorce, because they continued to structure matrimonial litigation in the English ecclesiastical courts. They made their way into a newly independent legal system that still relied on English customs, English forms, and English legal idioms, even as it moved in dramatically new directions. Similarly, the expensive and cumbersome mechanism of parliamentary divorce, the principal English departure from the canon law provisions for marriage, was transposed in the American setting into legislative divorce.

There were also a host of Protestant continental models on which to draw, in addition to much older Roman, Anglo-Saxon, and early Germanic models. In fact, learned debate about divorce was played out in competing accounts about the long history of divorce in the Western world. Americans, moreover, were not entirely lacking in precedents of their own. Puritan jurisdictions had provided for divorce in early America, and elsewhere local communities had endowed customary dissolutions of marriage with a large measure of legitimacy. Native American tribal customs also encompassed forms of divorce, which white observers either denounced for their "savagery" or upheld as sensible indigenous models to follow.[5]

What was distinctly novel about American divorce and therefore controversial was the growing particularity of the law that came to frame it. To anticipate the argument that follows, the clean and simple lines of the earliest divorce provisions—terse lists of those sins or faults that warranted dissolving the bonds of matrimony—became cluttered with substantive and procedural refinements, particularly as divorce moved out of the jurisdiction of state legislatures and into the civil courts. What began as a single (albeit thorny) question about appropriate grounds became a progressively complex set of questions about both grounds and procedures. In part, this was a result of the readiness of women and men to use the law—or, as critics asserted, to abuse the law—along with the willingness of the legal profession to serve their needs. In any case, both litigants and their lawyers were determined to take the law to its outermost limits. As legislators and jurists responded, defining and refining divorce with ever greater specificity, they rendered its moral premises ever more ambiguous.

When critics of divorce exploited its moral ambiguities with devastating effectiveness, it was because the legal system afforded them ample ammunition for the task. The rise of divorce mills—lax jurisdictions granting divorces to nonresidents on the flimsiest of pretexts—pointed to striking statutory variations among states, and therefore to the absence of any uniform principles to serve as grounds. Those asserting that the average divorce was a dishonest and hypocritical affair had only to point to the adjudication of divorce within states. In an adversarial proceeding designed to determine the guilt or innocence of a spouse, notice to the allegedly guilty spouse was often inadequate, proof of guilt dubious, and the vital element of fault little more than a hollow legal fiction.

It is in the context of such criticism that my use of the term *framing* acquires its secondary, idiomatic, and uniquely American connotation of rigging evidence so as to ensure a fraudulent outcome. Critics claimed that either one spouse unilaterally framed the other, as in *A Modern Instance,* or they both colluded in the framing by agreeing on the appropriate fault and on their respective guilt and innocence. The critics had a point. Most complaints contained elements of framing that ranged anywhere from outright perjury to a creative stretching of the truth. This is not to say that litigants perjured themselves casually; rather it is to point out that for those who were committed to securing a divorce, the statutes often gave them very little choice. Because each ground defined a wrong committed by one spouse against the other, a suit for divorce resembled a tort, and litigants framed their accounts accordingly. Nonetheless, despite heated criticism from many quarters, the framing went on largely because there was little support for the apparent alternatives: to move closer to a no-fault system or to return to a state of divorcelessness.[6]

A different but closely related kind of framing also went on. Divorce, after all, was a story that dictated certain narrative elements. There was a victim (the plaintiff), a villain (the defendant), a wrongful action (the fault), and a resolution (the decree). But contested divorces, which presented two versions of the same story, set off doubts about which version to believe and implicitly invited jurors and spectators to create versions of their own.[7] Contested suits were especially affecting when they focused on the wife's adultery because they raised the possibility that she was wrongly accused. Newspaper editors learned to exploit the pathos of the accused wife's suffering by providing readers with detailed coverage from the courtroom; and where newspapers led, sentimental fiction followed. Law and literature coalesced in these genres to create a popular divorce lore that resonated across the nation. By the middle decades of the nineteenth century, then, women and men were beginning to make sense of divorce and assess its long-term consequences by reading divorce stories, both real and fictional.

At the same time, despite state-by-state variations, the law itself began to display broad and irreversible contours. By the 1870s, when antidivorce sentiment coalesced into a national movement to roll back divorce with a tough, unified federal code, the legal framework for modern divorce was already firmly in place. Divorce would remain within the jurisdiction of individual states, and despite the legislative tinkering that accompanied the movement for restrictions, it would retain its basic lineaments until the advent of no-fault in the 1960s. More important, the very idea of divorce had acquired a dynamic, extralegal life of its own.

SCOPE AND METHOD

The chronological margins of this study have been set by the legal and cultural configurations of divorce; its internal contours are more problematic. To explore the framing of American divorce in the multiple contexts I have outlined raises questions about scope and method. As the foregoing summary suggests, the ensuing chapters are not so much a legal history of divorce per se as a series of essays that collectively probe the interplay between the legal culture and the larger culture. In making this distinction, I disclaim responsibility for the comprehensive, state-by-state coverage of American divorce law; but this should not be read as a disclaimer about the place of law in my analysis. On the contrary, law is central to my conceptualization of the issues. I view it as the template within which shifts in social values were at once generated and contained. In the decades under consideration, the principal paradigm for dissolving a marriage became increasingly law-centered. As Americans came to view and pursue divorce in new ways, it was because of the law, or even in spite of the law, but always with the law now as a critical referent.

And yet law is by no means the whole story here. For one thing, in so protean a subject, the sources often elude tidy distinctions between the legal and the nonlegal; for another, the sources that can be brought to bear on the subject are virtually boundless in their multiplicity. "The divorce question," as Victorian Americans came to call it, preoccupied moralists and reformers of every conceivable stripe. The divorce process, as we will see, affected women and men of every class. And the divorce story, with its diverging accounts of the same marriage, engaged the popular imagination.

Given the prominence of divorce as an issue in the nineteenth century, the sources available to the historian are too much of a good thing. At first glance, they serve to obscure rather than to illuminate. Printed trial reports, original file papers, legislative debates, legal treatises, statutory revisions, newspaper accounts, essays, sermons, speeches, novels, dramas, anecdotes—all these texts, to borrow a term from literary theorists, are not only overwhelming in their volume but daunting in their diversity. What is more, drawing on them with an eye toward capturing the insights generated by crossing disciplinary boundaries carries the risk of trading the rigor of a more bounded inquiry for a dubious eclecticism. Nonetheless, this book rests on the premise, more intuitive than theoretical, that the collective promise of such sources is at least as great as the problems they pose. Embracing them en masse demands cutting them down to manageable size and shaping them into an intelligible structure. I address the first problem here by resorting to samplings, and the second by organizing the samplings under three rubrics: rules, mediations, and representations.

Part I (Rules), the only section to take up the eighteenth century, consists of three chapters that proceed chronologically and consider a variety of discourses about the basic rules for divorce. I begin in chapter 1 by investigating national independence as a prototype for divorce, thereby anchoring its legitimation in Revolutionary political culture. Chapter 2 explores the tensions unleashed by refining the rules—both grounds and procedures—in the crucible of legal experience, and chapter 3 charts the explosive role played by gender and religion in the great divorce debates of the 1850s and 1860s. What links the disparate discourses in this section together is their concern with long-term consequences: they all look primarily to the future.

Part II (Mediations) takes up how individuals engaged with the rules in the courts of New York and Indiana, the conservative and liberal ends of the divorce spectrum, respectively. New York permitted divorce only for adultery from the late eighteenth century through much of the twentieth, while Indiana developed grounds and procedures so elastic as to become the first divorce mill of the nineteenth century. Chapter 4, which focuses on the remedial dimensions of the divorce process, looks at women coming to court as plaintiffs; chapter 5 does the same for men. The cases I consider here serve to contrast the immediate, specific, and palpable nature of litigation with the general, abstract, and prospective nature of legislation. They mark a shift in perspective to the quotidian world of individuals who subjected their problems to adjudication by the rules and, in the process, slowly reshaped the rules.

Part III (Representations) charts the spiraling imagery of divorce in American popular culture. Because the most broadly disseminated images of divorce appeared in the daily newspaper coverage of sensational trials, which editors then collated into pamphlets and sold like dime novels, I devote much of the one chapter in this section to the genre of trial pamphlets. The competing stories generated by these fiercely contested divorce suits turned on emerging tensions between the social freedom of married women and the conjugal authority of married men; they also exposed a troubling gulf between the Victorian commitment to marital duty and the rising ideal of romantic love. As divorce stories found their way into sentimental fiction, the novels explored the very same problems, albeit from a narrowly didactic perspective. I conclude here with fictional divorces, juxtaposing the conservatism of their messages against the subversive themes in trial pamphlets.

This structure allows us to view divorce successively as a legal form, a social option, and a cultural symbol. The taxonomy I have created, however, is neater in the abstract than the particular. As the materials supporting my discussion of the rules in the post-Revolutionary era indicate, I do not always adhere rigidly to my own classifications. Culture, after all, does not compartmentalize itself into tidy discursive boxes. Nevertheless, the tripartite organization I have set out not only suggests the aims of this study; it also constitutes its method. To construct three discrete views that sometimes shadow each other closely but often differ dramatically is akin to changing a camera lens while keeping the camera focused on the same subject. A close-up can reveal a world that is invisible when one gazes through a wide-angle lens. Readers undoubtedly will imagine other kinds of lenses—other types of sources or even entire genres—that I may have inadvertently missed or consciously rejected. Such alternatives only point up the myriad opportunities in such a design, which represents a frankly experimental effort to explore in a legal-historical context the possibilities of shifting the point of view.[8]

Still, a few caveats are in order regarding both the geography and sociology of divorce. Regional variations in divorce law were more pronounced on an east-west axis than a north-south one. While South Carolina distinguished itself by prohibiting divorce for almost the entire period under consideration, it was the only southern state to do so, and

Tennessee, by contrast, emerged to become a relatively liberal divorce jurisdiction. However, there were important north-south distinctions, and my choice of county court cases slights the role played by slavery in the framing of American divorce. As a legal institution, slavery both excluded the women and men in bondage from the rules defining marriage and also influenced the way the rules were applied to the free population. With the abolition of slavery, freedwomen and freedmen inundated southern courts with litigation regarding the status of their marriages. As for east-west differences, "west," a highly relative term in the context of nineteenth-century expansion, could signify any area from western New York to the state of California.[9] Indiana is subjected to scrutiny as a "western" jurisdiction not only because it had enough longevity as a state to permit a chronologically extended comparison with New York, but also because it stood as an emblem of a lax divorce jurisdiction. In fact, I decided to concentrate on the New York and Indiana courts because of the emblematic role played by the two states in public debate.

References to the legal culture and the larger culture reflect professional versus lay components at work in divorce. Given the nature of my sources, the so-called larger culture refers mainly but by no means exclusively to a middle-class marital ideology that was perpetually contested and in flux. I do not use the term *larger culture* to allude to a monolithic consensus shaped under the influence of powerful cultural texts. My principal focus, however, is on the broad ramifications of a specific set of legal constructs—an assemblage of formal, unitary rules at once imposed on and transformed by a profoundly heterogeneous group of individuals, some of whom were inured to a host of customary alternatives. Wife-sale, the folk ritual whereby a husband sold his wife to her paramour or back to her family of origin, is one example.

There can be no denying the new hegemony of the law in defining the boundaries of marriage. The growing sway of formal divorce is perhaps best exemplified by the willingness of propertyless litigants to opt for legal dissolutions of their marriages over customary alternatives. This point is an important one, for it highlights the increasing impress of the law on immigrant and working-class subcultures. It is important also with regard to the concept of a female subculture and notions of female agency, for while women used the law in their own way and for their own purposes, they acted within the guidelines of an androcentric legal system.

As a conclusion to these introductory remarks, I want to acknowledge the rich body of scholarship that has helped me frame this study,
including several recent works on divorce. In deploying the term *framing* in this self-consciously authorial context, I also want to acknowledge
both my struggles with and indebtedness to the theoretical insights of
postmodernism. As for my role in the framing, although I, in contrast to
my nineteenth-century litigants, have endeavored to avoid the fraudulent rigging of my own evidence, readers will discern my biases along the
way; they emerge, for example, in my apprehensiveness about the
woman-as-victim theme, a common thread in nineteenth-century
divorce stories. My use of the term *framing* in describing the historian's
craft, however, is not intended to blur the critical distinction between
fraud and bias, or to conflate history with fiction. Rather I use it here in
an active, ongoing sense to suggest the dynamic, discursive, open-ended
spirit of contemporary historical inquiry.[10] In keeping with that spirit,
and with an eye toward contributing to legal-historical discourse, I have
framed "the divorce question" as broadly and provocatively as possible.

 Rules

Modern American divorce rests on a post-Revolutionary legal foundation that encoded the rules for ending a marriage into short and simple statutes. Not only did these modest statutes lay the groundwork for the reordering of marriage as a social institution but they emerged in an easy confluence with the political reordering of the society at large. In the United States, as in France, where revolution was the handmaid of divorce, the transformations of family and polity were closely connected. These connections inflected thinking about divorce for years to come. Although comparisons between the marriage contract and the social contract punctuated early modern political thought, in the wake of the Revolution they assumed new configurations, which made their way into the divorce debates of the nineteenth century. One consequence of the Revolutionary foundations of American divorce was that analogies between divorce and revolution were never far from the surface of what Victorians called "the divorce question," an impassioned public dialogue about the appropriate rules for divorce.

In this section titled "Rules," I pursue divorce from its late-eighteenth-century origins to its post–Civil War contestations by tracing the interplay between legal changes and public responses. Using a wide-angle lens to capture an overview of divorce, I explore why it was initially legitimized, the ways in which its provisions diverged, and how those divergences set off a national debate that resonated from the mid–nineteenth century into the Gilded Age and beyond.

Both procedural and substantive changes in the law are critical to my discussion of the rules. And yet, because the shifting tenor and terms of public discourse are no less critical, I range here beyond the rules narrowly construed to examine how the divorce question encompassed a good deal more than the rules for ending a marriage. By the 1850s, when access to a divorce decree was becoming ever easier and the number of decrees was rising, divorce served as a lightning rod for deep-seated tensions over the positive and negative implications of freedom. The mid-century tendency to link divorce policy to the long-term destiny of the nation only intensified after the Civil War. In a discourse whose terms were dominated increasingly by conservative moral critics who embraced marriage as a signifier for law and order and deployed divorce as a trope for chaos, debate over the rules escalated into a battle for the very soul of the republic.

Because the tensions radiating from that debate were invariably gendered in either a substantive or metaphorical sense, I track gender in this section even where its presence is ignored or obfuscated. It is worth remembering that fault divorce placed a man and a woman in an adversarial setting that implicitly tested their relative authority. The avoidance of gender—indeed, the censoring of gender—is an important motif in my discussion of the rules. Although legislators constructed the typical divorce plaintiff as male or genderless, at some level they understood that the reality was otherwise. They understood as well that symbolically divorce ran against the grain of marital domination. Marriage, after all, in its indissoluble form was the principal institution through which men controlled women and mediated their relationship to the state.

What did it mean, then, to invest women with the right, however circumscribed, to sever the bonds of matrimony by challenging their husbands as adversaries in a court of law? As the ambivalent responses of woman's rights advocates suggested, the answer to that question was by no means simple, but prodivorce legislators were loath even to raise it. Evangelical critics of divorce, in contrast, responded to the threat they perceived to the gender system by appealing to Scripture and suffusing divorce with shame. In laying bare here how divorce invested women with a measure of independence that both the legal culture and the larger culture obscured or denigrated, I probe the ways in which divorce at once undermined and sustained gender hierarchy.

Finally, there is the matter of the relation of this section to the other two sections of the book. The reader would do well to keep in mind a composite notion of divorce in which the rules evolved in tandem with *an increasing number of individual divorces and a torrent of sensational divorce stories. Although segmenting rules into a discrete section is conceptually useful, it is historically artificial. Indeed, each of the three chapters in this section opens with an individual divorce case not only because such cases humanize and particularize abstract rules for the contemporary reader but because they served precisely the same functions for historical actors. Anyone wishing to defend or critique the rules knew that individualizing narratives made divorce more palpable and rendered arguments more persuasive. But even though the diverse facets of divorce unfolded simultaneously, the sequence I employ here suggests the significance of the rules. I begin by mapping out the increasingly powerful, fault-based legal paradigm that would shape the contours of both how divorces played out and how they were represented.*

ONE

❖ Inaugurating the Rules, 1770–1800 ❖

In 1787 Sarah Everitt petitioned the Court of Chancery for a divorce from her husband William, a New York City butcher to whom she had been married for twenty-two years. The uncontested suit was a simple one with regard to the circumstances of her marriage, which had come to an informal end well before the suit began. The couple's two sons, one a fifteen-year-old apprenticed to a butcher and no longer living at home, the other a thirteen-year-old about to follow in his brother's footsteps, were not a factor in the case, and William, who had previously "absented himself," in the words of the court, from Sarah's "bed and society," was propertyless and insolvent. As a result, the sole purpose in undertaking the action was to bring a legal end to a marriage that was long since over.[1]

The adjudication of the case was swift. Custody, support, and property were not at issue, and neither was the proof of William's adultery. Among the witnesses who came to court was a woman named Mary Moncrief, who not only admitted to living with William in an ongoing state of adultery but who also testified to having a son with him. William, it seems, had embarked on a second union with Mary and was raising a second family while he was bound by law to his first union with Sarah and to the obligations of his first family. In October of 1787, not long after the Constitutional Convention had concluded its affairs in Philadelphia, the court brought his union with Sarah to an official and unequivocal end. Given the redundancy of the decree, there could be no mistaking its finality. The marriage was "entirely and absolutely dissolved and declared to be null and void."[2]

The Everitt case only begins to suggest the world of meanings encapsulated in the legitimation of divorce. Adjudicated in the year the State of New York passed its first divorce statute and the federal constitution was drafted, it not only highlights a chronological convergence between the legal reordering of marriage as a social institution and the political reordering of the society at large, but also points to the possibility of deeper connections between these changes. Furthermore, because the case embodied both legal and extralegal forms of marital dissolution, it alerts us to the diverse ways in which Americans of the post-Revolutionary era both conceived of and acted on divorce.[3] At the same time, the roles played by the parties in this classic but untidy human triangle exemplify the transition already under way. Cast by the law into a sharply adversarial configuration, with Mary set off to the side as a witness, husband and wife were presented in the end with an orderly legal resolution.

Other resolutions were possible. As William's apparently unilateral arrangements indicate, putting an end to a marriage in the early republic did not hinge on the statutory recognition of divorce. Extralegal and customary alternatives filled the void in divorceless jurisdictions, and they continued to flourish alongside the law in jurisdictions that provided for divorce.[4] But if William's simple strategy of self-divorce and pseudo-remarriage was undoubtedly familiar to his contemporaries, the remedy now available to Sarah was something of a novelty. Moreover, if we use William's occupation as the measure of Sarah's social standing, we are bound to be struck by the broadly democratic thrust of the state's earliest divorce provisions. One of the first plaintiffs in the state to sue under the rules of the new statute was the wife of an obscure and impoverished tradesman.

The Everitt divorce serves as a fitting frame, then, for basic questions about the new rules. How did the state come to legitimate the dissolution of Sarah Everitt's marriage? And how did Sarah Everitt, in turn, come to submit her marital difficulties to the disposition of the state?[5] Although these open-ended and interrelated questions about political motivation and individual agency do not lend themselves to conclusive answers, they are nonetheless worth raising, not so much because of the quantitative place divorce would assume in the long run as because of its qualitative place in the context of the late eighteenth century. Moreover, linked as they are to the interplay of the social contract and the marriage contract, they invite us to explore the striking convergence of revolution and divorce in the last quarter of the eighteenth century.

LEGITIMATING DIVORCE

The United States was not alone in recognizing divorce in the age of revolution, a time when the sources of legitimate authority were directly contested and indelibly transformed. The first French Republic, which went from upholding the complete indissolubility of marriage to instituting the most permissive divorce code in the Western world, provides a stellar example of the late-eighteenth-century confluence of revolution and divorce. In France even more conclusively than in the United States, the right to put an end to an unsatisfactory union was an integral part of the revolutionary order, a legal component of the quest for individual fulfillment through a reconfiguration of the family. As the deputy Pierre-François Gossin argued in the National Constituent Assembly, "After having made man again free and happy in public life, it remains for you to assure his liberty and happiness in private life."[6]

In light of Gossin's distinctions between public and private life, we can assume that *man* in this case encompassed *woman* as well. Perhaps, as Joan Landes has argued, the transition from French absolutism to a bourgeois, secular state entailed the silencing of women in the public sphere; but endowing them with the right of divorce empowered them at least symbolically in the private sphere. Petitions to legislatures in the early years of the Revolution indicate that divorce was routinely construed as a wife's legal counterweight to her husband's conjugal authority. The notion that the right of divorce for both wives and husbands was a fundamental freedom that flowed from the new political order resulted in the divorce law of 1792. Not only did that remarkable but short-lived law provide for divorce with the mutual consent of both spouses, but in a provision akin to the no-fault statutes of our own day, one spouse could petition unilaterally on the ground of incompatibility and receive a decree without producing affidavits or witnesses.[7]

The terms on which Americans recognized divorce were rather more modest and, as a result of state-by-state variations, somewhat eclectic. Still, the impress of the Revolution was unmistakable. No sooner, it seems, did Americans create a rationale for dissolving the bonds of empire than they set about creating rules for dissolving the bonds of matrimony. Divorce, of course, had been available in New England before the advent of independence; Connecticut had provided for it on such liberal terms that it granted almost a thousand decrees between 1670 and 1799.[8] By comparison, those states that relegated divorce to a legislative decision after the Revolution instituted a highly restrictive divorce policy. And yet even in such restrictive jurisdictions, a complete divorce with the concomitant right to remarry became a legal possibility for the first time. Though American divorce policy paled before the robust liberality of its French counterpart, it assumed much more radical dimensions in an Anglo-American context. By 1800 fault divorce, as we have come to call it in our era of no-fault, was a legal concept that departed significantly from the parliamentary and ecclesiastical precedents on which it was based. In its gender-neutral approach to fault, in the completeness of its dissolutions, and in the access it afforded litigants, American divorce already diverged dramatically from its principal English roots.

The timing of this development was as telling as its substance. Concern with providing for formal divorce arose simultaneously with the political turmoil of the 1770s. With the notable exception of the Puritan jurisdictions, Britain's North American colonies did not challenge English divorce policy in any collective or sustained way until that time, nor did England attend to those challenges that were in fact made. Throughout the colonial period, the balance of the colonies probably sent no more than a handful of provincial divorce bills across the Atlantic, and these (together with the wholesale disregard of the English rules by both Connecticut and Massachusetts) were largely ignored in the affairs of empire. As Linda Kerber has observed, the Privy Council exhibited an almost studied ignorance on the subject of colonial divorces.[9] As late as 1769, a barrister representing the Board of Trade and Plantations declared the Pennsylvania legislative divorce of Curtis and Anne Grubb to be "not repugnant to the Laws of England."[10] But confronted by a similar Pennsylvania decree three years later, the board found that it represented a dangerous power "rarely and recently assumed in your Majesty's colonies in America." An extended ruling by the Privy Council in 1773 designated "Acts of Divorce in the Plantations" as "either Improper or Unconstitutional." Subsequent divorce bills from New Hampshire and New Jersey were also disallowed and reported to the Privy Council, which instructed colonial governors to void all future provincial divorces.[11]

Thomas Jefferson, a proponent of legitimating divorce, may very well have had this prohibition in mind when he drafted the section of the Declaration of Independence denouncing the British monarchy's refusal to "Assent to Laws, the most wholesome and necessary for the public good." More important, his notes supporting divorce anticipated the rationale he employed to justify independence: "No partnership," he declared, "can oblige continuance in contradiction to its end and design." In one sense, the right to end an adverse marital partnership was a direct by-product of the frustration experienced under an adverse political partnership, for in the wake of independence, those colonies that had been overruled by the Privy Council provided for divorce in new state statutes. Other states followed suit. By 1795 a disaffected spouse could put an end to a marriage in a local circuit court even in the Northwest Territory. Titled "A Law respecting Divorce, Adopted from the Massachusetts code," the simple territorial statute providing for that right highlights the flow of divorce westward with the settlers who spilled over the Appalachians. "Divorces shall be decreed," it declared, "where either of the parties had a former wife or husband alive, at the time of solemnizing the second marriage; or impotency or adultery in either of the parties."[12]

Although the states carved out of the Northwest Territory would eventually expand their statutory grounds to encompass desertion and cruelty, New York continued to adhere to terms very close to those in the territorial statute. Clearly, statutory provisions could vary widely. If the South tended to lag behind the North both in recognizing divorce and in placing it within the jurisdiction of the civil courts, east-west distinctions became even more pronounced, with "western" states tending to render divorce more readily accessible to their restless new inhabitants. This was true even for the post-Revolutionary South. Whereas South Carolina eschewed divorce altogether, the first Tennessee divorce statute provided for adjudication in the state's superior courts; and in addition to adultery and the traditional grounds for annulment, it recognized willful desertion or two years' absence without a reasonable cause.[13] Far more significant than the divergent terms that were being spelled out in state statutes was the wholesale legitimation of divorce itself, especially in those areas that had been officially divorceless. By 1799 twelve states in addition to the Northwest Territory had recognized the legal right of divorce, thereby indelibly imprinting the new rules all over the American legal landscape.

Little attention has been devoted to this quiet but profound transformation. The stunning nature of this legal departure is best appreciated when balanced against late-eighteenth-century English practices. In England female plaintiffs, who were required to prove aggravated adultery (adultery compounded with some other marital offense such as physical cruelty), were all but shut out of the divorce process except for formal separations. Of the 325 complete divorces that Parliament granted between 1670 and the legal reforms of 1857, only four went to women. Inasmuch as a decree permitting the complainant to remarry, as opposed to a divorce from bed and board, depended on securing a private bill from Parliament, men hardly fared much better. In order to secure such a decree a male plaintiff would need to begin with a suit for damages against his wife's paramour in the civil courts, follow it with a suit for separation in the ecclesiastical courts, and then pursue it to completion in Parliament. In contrast to the speedy decree issued to Sarah Everitt, the New York butcher's wife with whom we began, a complete divorce in England was an option for very privileged, very determined, and very patient men who nevertheless had to be prepared for failure at any point in the process.[14]

From both a substantive and procedural perspective, divorce law in the early republic was light years beyond its English equivalent. Moreover, despite striking variations in the particularities of early divorce provisions, there were broad commonalities in the fundamentals, and it is the fundamentals that concern us here. Shared notions about divorce were embedded in three dominant strands of early national culture: an essentially Protestant view of the moral order, a distinctly English legal heritage, and the indigenous political culture of the American Revolution. These three great currents of thought—three discrete ways of looking at the world in general and the conjugal in particular—were by no means prerequisites for the mounting of divorce as a legal institution, nor did they always flow together harmoniously. But their convergence in the United States in the last quarter of the eighteenth century determined the course of American divorce and shaped its internal tensions. That particular historical conjunction ensured that the moral premises for divorce would emanate from the New Testament, the forms for its implementation from the English ecclesiastical courts, and the political foundations for its legitimation from the singular experience of independence itself. Because independence was the catalyst in the process, the event separating English legal traditions from American innovations, it merits particular consideration.

FROM THE BONDS OF EMPIRE
TO THE BONDS OF MATRIMONY

At a tangible political level, independence freed the states to depart from English law, which had channeled divorce along a path so costly and tortuous as to render England virtually divorceless. But that account still begs the question of why states departed from English law in the first place. When viewed instead at a symbolic level, independence looms as a compelling prototype for divorce, and nowhere more than in its most celebrated text. Consider that in letting the "Facts" be submitted to a candid world, the Declaration of Independence at once explained, decreed, and sanctified a divorce from the bonds of empire; and from the bonds of empire to the bonds of matrimony, it was but a short conceptual step.[15]

The principle of comparability that structured eighteenth-century concepts of knowledge only served to enhance the time-honored association of family with state and vice versa. As Natalie Davis has observed of early modern France, all the weighty and contentious issues in the larger political order could invariably be symbolized "in the little world of the family." Reversing the order of the analogy in *The Social Contract*, Rousseau asserted that families are the first models of political societies.[16] Placed in the Anglo-American setting, this common maxim of Western political theory acquired a new and expansive meaning. Jefferson's use of words such as *brethren, consanguinity,* and *kindred* in the Declaration not only exemplifies the easy interchangeability of family and state in Enlightenment thinking but also marks their transfiguration. His language implies that severing the bonds of empire entailed the radical and complete separation of two peoples who were as intimately related as the members of one family. That family, to paraphrase the end of the Declaration, was no more, and the two peoples, once knitted together as one, were to regard each other now as enemies in the war that was already under way. As this imagery suggests, the Revolution predisposed Americans to think of themselves in declaring independence as both dissolving one family and, at the same time, constituting another. The significance of that image is even greater than has been generally recognized. The Revolution not only killed the king, metaphorically speaking; it separated the family.

Admittedly, Jefferson's allusion seems to conjure up a schism between male kinfolk. Still, for Americans of the Revolutionary era, the image of the severed family could extend beyond filial and fraternal bonds to embrace marital bonds as well. As Carole Pateman has observed, the relation of a husband to his wife was as central to seventeenth-century English debate over the political order as was the relation of the king to his subjects. This symbolic legacy from the English Civil War was very familiar to Jefferson and his contemporaries. Framing the schism between Great Britain and its North American colonies as a divorce, moreover, is instructive on two counts: it highlights the interplay between the social contract and the marriage contract and it exposes the role of gender in Revolutionary culture. Pateman cautions that to consider social contract theory without considering the marriage contract, or what she calls "the sexual contract," is to suppress the gendered part of the story of contract.[17] In keeping with her caveat, the Revolutionary deployment of the familial paradigm merits a reading in conjugal terms.

Although a host of scholars have elaborated on the antipatriarchal dimensions of Revolutionary culture, they have focused largely on the filial ramifications of killing the king. Historians have noted that whereas a tyrannical parent-child relationship supported the logic of American rebellion, the bonds of filial affection came to exemplify the post-Revolutionary ideal of union. To be sure, apart from the obvious Freudian appeal of the killing-the-king paradigm, there is a good deal of cultural evidence to support it, as well as flesh-and-blood figures who embody it. It is not difficult to envision George Washington as a humane and virtuous post-Revolutionary father who came to replace the despotic figure of George III. But scholars exploring the centrality of consent in antipatriarchal representations of the republic have projected a more gendered reading of the post-Revolutionary transition by demonstrating that conjugal ties came to supplant filial ties in popular representations of the state. As Jan Lewis has shown, both the hopes and fears for the nation's political order were consistently dramatized in relations between the sexes. The happy and harmonious conjugal union of the brave husband and his chaste wife, she suggests, came to represent nothing less than the happy and harmonious political union of the young American republic.[18]

That the success of both unions hinged on the element of consent provides important clues to the legitimation of divorce, because it underscores its contractarian underpinnings. In a legal as well as a moral context, marriage derived its primary legitimacy from the principle of consent. In the prevailing legal construction of marriage, there could be no contract without consent; if consent were absent or compromised, the contract could be deemed null and void. Of course, in traditional legal terms, once the marriage was validly contracted then the contract was indissoluble, consent ceased to be a factor, and the equality that prevailed at the time the contract was made was effaced by the requirements of coverture. Marriage, after all, was a public, prepackaged contract that was impervious to the wills of the contracting parties.[19] To put it in political terms, one could say that having contracted for her ruler, a wife was consigned to his rule for life. As will become evident, Americans of the post-Revolutionary era were not altogether comfortable with such an image, but neither were they prepared to abandon it completely. Both their discomfort with the traditional legal model of marriage and their reluctance to adopt a thoroughly contractual alternative illuminate the degree to which social contract theory intertwined with their perceptions of marriage and divorce.

Their dilemma was hardly new. It is precisely because marriage in its consensual-but-indissoluble form stood as a far-reaching metaphor for the existing political order that it served as a convenient hedge against incipient political upheavals. A common analogy for the relationship between rulers and the ruled, it was exploited by royalist defenders of Charles I to equate Parliament's rebellion with the ludicrous prospect of a wife divorcing her husband.[20] Gender was obviously central to the effectiveness of the analogy. The figurative use of a divorce by a woman to signify the anarchic breaking of a sacred contract, thereby subjecting the action to ridicule, intimates that domestic rebellion enjoyed less credibility than political rebellion. But it also reveals parallels between the two rebellions in the very grain of Anglo-American political thinking. The advent of the American Revolution turned the thrust of the analogy on its head, for just as divorce could serve to discountenance revolution, revolution, especially a successful one, could serve in turn to legitimate divorce.

The act of legitimating divorce is clearly not the same as the act of legitimating revolution: to assert that it is would be inherently reductive and demonstrably wrong. But since the effectiveness of a metaphor emanates, in a sense, from its wrongness—that is, from its capacity to conflate widely disparate actions into a simple, unitary framework—the correspondences between revolution and divorce could be manipulated into powerful analogies. As ethnographers have long known, charting patterns in such analogies in a specific time and place can help expose a culture's fundamental premises and underlying tensions. Or to put it another way, as Lynn Hunt has demonstrated, recognizing the importance of the family in constituting the political order provides a window on the "collective political unconscious."[21]

It is useful, then, to pursue the correspondences between revolution and divorce in the context of Revolutionary culture. Consider the problem of justification. The framework for a just divorce code, like the juristic rationale for national independence, would need to stipulate under what extraordinary circumstances and for what grievous offenses a dissolution of the contract might take place. It would pivot, also, on an agonizing dilemma: how to dissolve those contracts that had been so seriously violated as to destroy the ends of marriage (the Everitts' marriage presents a good example) without at the same time destroying marriage itself. For Jefferson's contemporaries, the Revolution posed a comparable dilemma: how to dissolve their connections to a legitimate but despotic government without, in the words of an English critic, at the same time putting "the axe to the root of all government."[22]

One solution, as Gordon Wood has observed, was derived from the notion of breach of contract. It consisted in delegitimizing the contract with the duly constituted government by documenting the nature, intensity, and duration of its despotism. Breach of contract, however, was not the only legal construction that suggests striking parallels between declaring political independence and justifying divorce. Equity was another, and it supplied an important modification to the relatively crude concept of breach of contract. Following J. W. Gough's analysis of Locke, Peter Hoffer has argued that both the sequential pattern and the conceptual structures on which the Declaration is modeled were derived from a bill in equity, a form that Jefferson as a Virginia lawyer would have drawn on with some regularity. All the complaints at the core of the Declaration, Hoffer insists, "showed their equitable origins, fitting categories familiar in chancery." Because Hoffer, like Gough, depicts the relationship between the governed and their governors more as a trusteeship that has been violated than as a contract that has been breached, he locates the Declaration's appeal squarely within the purview of the protective and discretionary sorts of justice meted out by a court of chancery.[23]

Marriage, by analogy, could assume the hierarchical characteristics of a trusteeship in which the husband acted as the wife's trustee but could be held accountable for his actions in a court of equity. It is worth noting that given the absence of ecclesiastical courts, divorce in America began as a proceeding in equity in those jurisdictions that maintained a distinction between law and equity. Of course, equity was itself an integral part of the inherited legal system, but it was distinguished, as Hoffer points out, by its distinctly remedial dimensions. Thus divorce entered American jurisprudence with a set of procedures that translated a suit to dissolve a marriage into a quest for a remedy that was not ordinarily available. Accordingly, after spelling out a list of harrowing abuses suffered at the hands of the allegedly guilty spouse, a divorce petitioner typically concluded with a prayer for relief—an appeal, if you will, to a higher and more flexible form of justice not unlike that invoked in the Declaration.

In a variety of ways, then, the Declaration of Independence endowed the women and men of the Revolutionary era with an elegant and eloquent example of how to dissolve a sacred contract. Resting as it did on its purported proof of English despotism counterpoised against colonial innocence, its argument unfolded very much like that of a petitioner in a divorce suit who, lacking a standardized form, piled up and compounded the alleged causes regardless of the statutory grounds. Sacred contracts are not dissolved casually, and the long and arduous route to the decisive stage of separation, ran the argument in the Declaration, was determined by the respondent's cumulative and unremitting guilt. In unmistakably Lockean language, the Declaration averred that severing the bonds of empire was not undertaken for light and transient causes, but only in the wake of a long train of abuses and usurpations to which the petitioner had submitted patiently. So intense and sustained were these abuses, went the narrative, that it was not just the right but the duty of the petitioner to seek a formal dissolution of the union.

The juristic language, the familiar truths, the judicious caveats, the assembled facts—none of these could obviate fully the unbounded possibilities that lay at the heart of the Declaration, which was shaped, after all, so as to justify the right to begin all over again. As Carl Becker long ago observed, the classic philosophy in the Declaration would lose ground in the nineteenth century precisely because it had been used with such stunning success in the eighteenth and might be so used again in ever more radical causes.[24] Yet if fear of endless dissolutions and countless reconstitutions ran just below the surface of post-Revolutionary culture, thereby posing a threat to the legal recognition of divorce, it was assuaged by an abiding faith in the justness of the Revolution.

The connections between the political ideology of a just revolution and the liberating potential of a just divorce code were strong, durable, and deeply rooted; the American Revolution only served to strengthen them further. It is no accident that John Milton wrote his divorce tracts in the midst of the English Civil War, tying the freedom to divorce to "all hope of true Reformation of the state." Nor should we be surprised that reference to the incompatibility between a contractarian theory of government and the principle of indissoluble marriage can be found in John Locke's *Second Treatise of Government*. In the wake of American independence, moreover, at least one wife expressed the belief that the Revolution had directly empowered her to reject a despotic husband. When Abigail Strong petitioned for a divorce in Connecticut in 1788, she reasoned that she was no longer under any obligation to submit to her husband's authority, since "even Kings may forfeit or discharge the allegiance of their Subjects." And when the nineteenth-century spiritualist leader Andrew Jackson Davis advocated greater equality in marriage, he linked his vision of an ideal union to the freedom from tyranny delineated in the "covenant . . . signed by the brave Fathers of our republic and sealed by the heart's blood of Patriots and Heroes." The Declaration of Independence, he insisted, was as "sacred still as the testament of a new-born savior."[25]

The same intellectual premises that supported the right of revolution predisposed Americans to support the right of divorce. Nonetheless, since few sources were as explicit as Abigail Strong's politically charged petition against conjugal tyranny, it is far easier to chart the connections between revolution and divorce at a high level of abstraction than it is to understand their influence on ordinary people. At the same time, instituting the rules in any meaningful or comprehensive fashion depended on the willingness of wives and husbands to come before the law as plaintiffs. It is far from clear how the collective experience of revolution reshaped individual attitudes toward either law or marriage to create support for formal divorce. The persistence of customary alternatives to formal divorce may very well indicate that for countless Americans no such change occurred. Yet while we should not assume that divorcelessness in the pre-Revolutionary era meant that marriages stayed intact, neither should we deny that in complex ways that continue to elude us, independence set the stage for the acceptance of new forms of divorce. Old arrangements were rendered unsatisfactory if not, in fact, obsolete; this was true for litigants like Sarah Everitt as well as for jurists and legislators, although not necessarily for the same reasons.

MARRIAGE AND DIVORCE
IN POPULAR LITERATURE

Glimpses of how Revolutionary ideology opened out to recast understandings about the social order in general and marriage in particular can be found in the burgeoning popular literature of the Revolutionary era. Eighteenth-century writers regarded the whole universe of knowledge and experience as a convenient repository of evidence to be used in treating social problems. Parables and limericks, essays and advice columns, novels and dramas—all expressly and self-consciously didactic—redefined the ends of marriage and, in so doing, approached the appropriate bases for divorce. As *The Emigrants,* a 1793 epistolary novel championing the right of divorce, put the case for proselytizing through fiction, "perhaps it is the most effectual way of communicating moral instruction, for when the vices and follies of the world are held up to us so connected with incidents which are interesting, it is most likely they will leave a more lasting impression than when given in a dull narrative."[26]

The range of moral instruction that informs this literature illuminates the connections between government and marriage at a distinctly anecdotal level. This is precisely the level where analogies between the social contract and the marriage contract were commonly deployed, where the issues of conjugal power and female subordination were directly confronted, and where the problems of how to constrain sexual unions in a democratic political context were regularly addressed. Insofar as much of this literature concentrated on distinguishing the truly harmonious unions from those that were spurious, uncaring, despotic, and mercenary, it focused in both a social and political sense on securing a more perfect union. Union, as Jay Fliegelman has observed, was the critical word in the Revolution and after, and liberty was equated regularly with the freedom to chose one's bond.[27] Still, allusions to marriage invariably contrasted the hollow forms that chained an incompatible couple together with the silken bonds of mutual affection. Given the prevailing political assumption that some bonds could be legitimately dissolved, support for divorce was at least implicit and sometimes even explicit in the sharpness of the distinctions.

Few writers were as ardent in extolling the right to end an unhappy marriage as Tom Paine. Paine, who was separated from his wife and had personal experience of the constraints of English divorce law, dramatized the contrast between a loving and loveless union in a little fable about Cupid and Hymen in the *Pennsylvania Magazine.* In his tale, Cupid, the god of love, prevents Hymen, the clerk of matrimony, from legitimating a wedding of convenience in Arcadia, where marriages were always made of better stuff. Although Paine does not use the fable to advocate dispensing with Hymen's formal services, which would be tantamount to espousing free love, he wants their role to be regarded as subordinate to the affective contributions of Cupid. "'Tis my province to form the union, and yours to witness it," asserts Cupid, hero of the tale and Paine's avatar of marital values, and "besides you are such a dull fellow when I am not with you, that you poison the felicities of life." The message is clear. Hymen might "chain couples together like criminals," but the only laws that ought to be binding on them were the universal "laws of affection."[28]

A few months later, assuming the persona of an American savage considering all the follies in a typical Christian marriage, Paine carried his theme of marital fulfillment to its logical conclusion. He alleged that not one in a hundred unions bore any relationship "to happiness or common sense," and without the freedom to end their unions, spouses simply doubled each other's misery "by way of revenge." Concluding with an innovative gloss on the union of Adam and Eve, Paine used the story to develop the claim that since God made us all in perfectly matched pairs, it was our duty to find the partner we were destined to have and to consummate the perfect partnership, presumably even if that took more than one try.[29]

Insofar as Adam and Eve were traditionally offered up as the embodiment of the one-flesh doctrine and hence as corroboration for God's support of indissoluble marriage, Paine's reading of Genesis was uncommonly bold. But although few contemporaries would venture as far as he did in advocating an open-ended quest for Edenic happiness in which the sons of Adam and the daughters of Eve were perennially free to seek the perfect partner, the theme of the perfect partnership was popular in more secular form. "On Marriage," for example, presented a handy neoclassical version in which Jupiter broke Androgyne, the perfect whole person, into two incomplete and unsatisfactory halves, leaving every man and woman thereafter with the need to find their other half. This bifurcated, essentialist version of the perfect partnership, which constructed women and men so profoundly different as to render them tragically incomplete on their own, serves to illustrate that gender differentiation was one of the important hallmarks of Revolutionary culture. At the same time, in projecting a complete complementarity between the sexes, it invested women as well as men with the need to search for the perfect partner. If we move away for the moment from reading gender as a metaphor for power—admittedly one of its most compelling rhetorical functions—we can see that this late-eighteenth-century rendition of the androgyne legend framed the perfect partnership in intimate and egalitarian terms.[30]

Intimate and egalitarian constructions of marriage were persistently qualified and inevitably undermined by references to order and subordination. For those who had already chosen their partners, practical advice on sustaining the partnership could be rendered in a distinctly political idiom that imbued men with a potential for tyranny and women with a penchant for rebellion. Men, declared an essayist for the *Boston Magazine,* should not be tyrants to women, because tyrants produce rebels, and rebels when they prevail become tyrants themselves. No one was better positioned to appreciate those sentiments than the members of the Revolutionary generation, who were preoccupied—if not obsessed—with redefining the relationship between the rulers and the ruled. Contract, however, was the basis for obedience as well as dissent, and men remained the rulers in the marriage contract, albeit with some limitations. Men should rule women, conceded a writer for the *Columbian,* but not with a "rod of iron." Another essayist counseled the husband to be not "a barbarian" to his wife just because he knows that she is his property, and the wife "to let thy gentle bosom be the pillow where all . . . cares may be forgot."[31]

In the face of unremitting despotism, however, dissolution of the union remained an option. As the cautious advice of the Matron, a columnist with a persona like that of Ann Landers, indicates, within the still-hierarchical relation of marriage, certain kinds of behavior went beyond the pale. Considering the problem of an innocent young bride who had contracted a venereal disease from her worldly husband, the Matron held out hope for the union only if he would confess and agree to be treated. But if he failed to accept blame for his wife's condition—or, even worse, accused her of infidelity—she advised the young woman to "summon up all her fortitude and leave him."[32]

Advice on appropriate conjugal behavior had its limits, for the ultimate fate of a marriage, according to popular counsel, was determined more by the choice of a mate than by any other single factor. That was the key to the perfect partnership and its most egalitarian component. Both sexes exercised freedom of choice here, and both staked their futures on making the right choice. Both, moreover, were susceptible to making tragic mistakes. Examples of those who had chosen foolishly, who had married for the wrong reasons, or who had simply misread the true character of a prospective partner punctuated the literature on marriage. "The Bad Effects of an Imprudent Matrimonial Connection" chronicled the fate of a woman who fell victim to a money-seeking libertine. The consequences of her mistake were devastating. Her profligate partner, who "had a taste for social company," expensive diversions, and the pleasures of the alehouse, and who showed very little inclination to hard work, squandered all her money and was never to be seen at her side.[33]

Profligacy and licentiousness, adultery and seduction, bigamy and desertion—these were the misbegotten fruits of the wrong choice, and popular advice readily acknowledged that they could not always be avoided. One could enter into a union with a pure heart and with the best intentions only to be foiled by a deceitful spouse. And while the deceitful spouse went on his (only rarely her) merry way, the innocent spouse remained bound by law to the original union. The element of free choice that was so vital to a contractarian reading of marriage placed an extraordinary burden on a potential female partner. Of course, men too could be deceived, cuckolded, and deserted by a faulty partner, but the consequences were never quite the same. Addressing "The Directory of Love" in the *Royal American,* for example, John Jealous complained that after living for some time in wedded bliss, he found his wife with a gentleman in the most private part of the house. Although "a thousand methods for getting rid of this problem" occurred to him, he wanted to know which option to pursue.[34] As his query suggests, men do not appear in this literature as desperate victims without real options. Women do, in part because of their social subordination to men and in part because marriage was the principal context in which they worked out their destinies.

Justice required a remedy for the wronged spouse, and the remedy was consistently construed as benefiting women as the victims of the double standard. As the author of the *Emigrants* averred in a long aside, "I have no doubt but that the many misfortunes which daily happen in domestic life, and which too often precipitate women of the most virtuous inclinations into the gulf of ruin, proceed from the great difficulty there is in England, of obtaining a divorce." A man, by contrast, had ways of escaping the confines of a miserable marriage. He was free to look "abroad for those amusements which alone can compensate for domestic feuds"; and should he transgress his marriage vows, no one would call him to account. But a woman seeking "some mitigation of sufferings" was destined to be "branded with contempt, and condemned to live in poverty, unnoticed and unpitied."[35]

Queries about how to proceed in untenable marriages flourished in the advice columns of popular periodicals, and although many undoubtedly came from the pens of creative editors, they demonstrate contemporary concern with the problem of failed marriages. "I am one of those unhappy young women," declared A.B., "whom fortune favoured with a husband; but not long after the conjugal rites were ended, he, void to all humanity, left me and went and married a second wife." The balance of the column focused on her right to remarry. She wanted to know: "As my husband married *first,* whether or no I can by law, marry afterwards during his life? . . . Or if it is a felony in the wife, then, was it not a felony in the husband first?"[36]

Court records exhibit no lack of real-life counterparts for A.B., nor is it difficult to understand their readiness to remarry without resorting to the law. Bigamy, like the second marriage of A.B.'s husband, and pseudo-marriage, a union not properly solemnized—like that of our old friend, William Everitt—were portrayed as tools employed by wicked men against innocent women to deceive them and ultimately destroy them. In *Amelia; or, The Faithless Briton,* pseudo-marriage was the source of a hoax perpetrated by a British officer who seduced and impregnated a young American girl by enticing her into a feigned marriage ceremony.[37]

The solution to these outrages lay in sharpening the boundaries around marriage. Blurred boundaries, commentators insisted, nourished the dangerous practice of self-divorce and illicit remarriage because they supported the deceptively simple notion that marriage was a private arrangement to be made and unmade at the will of the two parties. Traditional customs like the reading of the banns were encouraged not only because they buttressed the public character of marriage but also because they embodied the look-before-you-leap approach so popular in advice columns. And although settlements and antenuptial contracts were denounced as European refinements that reduced marriage to a crass business deal, premarital considerations that revolved around character rather than money supported both the affective and reciprocal aspects of the post-Revolutionary marital ideal.[38]

While the political rhetoric of independence helps us understand the inherent radicalism of divorce, post-Revolutionary critiques on blurred boundaries help us tease out its conservative impulses. In this new government of laws, rules providing for exit from the marriage contract were even more important in maintaining social order than those controlling entry. In the wake of revolution, the American legal system did, in fact, move toward both redefining marriage and defining divorce. But the terms on which these parallel movements evolved could not have been more different. Whereas American courts came to recognize a so-called common law marriage, a consummated union to which the parties had agreed, they were not about to recognize a comparable form of divorce. The former put the best face on an existing arrangement, legitimized children from the union, and brought the husband under the obligation of support; the latter menaced the entire institution of marriage.[39]

Supported as it was by the concept of breach of contract, divorce was construed far more strictly than marriage. Contemporaries could not advocate statutory divorce by mutual consent, much less by unilateral decision, because the underlying justification for rescinding an innocent spouse's marriage promise hinged on the assumption that the reciprocal promise already had been broken by the guilty spouse. It is not that eighteenth-century moralists and jurists could not envision a world of no-fault; they could and they did, and it caused them no end of consternation. Fault, so crucial in popular accounts of failed marriages, was no less crucial in creating the rules for their dissolution. It was an integral part of a mental universe that pivoted on causative reasoning. Even the so-called omnibus clauses in early divorce statutes, catchall phrases that provided broad judicial discretion in decreeing divorces, assumed a fault that was too unique or elusive to be defined by statute, but that could be readily apprehended by the judiciary.[40]

This fundamental reliance on causative reasoning not only informed both the legal and moral contours of divorce from the early national period into the nineteenth century; it provided the rationale for legitimating divorce in the first place. As a 1788 pamphlet supporting the right of divorce alleged in ardently anticlerical terms, conscientious attention to causality would permit formal divorce to assume a reasonable middle ground between religious fanaticism on the one hand and runaway anarchy on the other. On the one extreme, argued the anonymous pamphleteer, there was the example of India, where burning the widow alive fulfilled the biblical admonition that what God has joined together should not be put asunder. Here was ample proof that in matters of great importance to the general welfare, a too-literal adherence to Scripture was folly. But at the other extreme, he conceded, there was need to address the danger that "one separation would make way for another like beasts, and their families and kindred would be unknown and unprovided for and their names and distinctions lost." Formal complaints with careful inquiry into the causes and with adequate provisions for children could counter such anarchic possibilities while alleviating individual suffering.[41]

Casual dissolutions were to be avoided at all costs. In the prescriptive literature of the period, statements favoring causeless divorce, as it was called, were likely to come from the lips of a libertine like Major Sanford, a character in Hannah Foster's popular novel *The Coquette*. "As we lived together without love," he reasoned, "we parted without regret." Although his account of a marriage coming apart through no one's fault has a remarkably modern ring, it emanates here from a man who, Foster insists on every other page, was devoid of virtue. Only "a professed Libertine," practiced "in the art of seduction," would treat the boundaries of marriage so cavalierly or entertain its dissolution so casually. A virtuous society, by implication, would mandate strict rules for marriage, strong sanctions against the spouses who broke them, and effective remedies for their innocent victims, including the legal right to remarry.[42]

Anxiety about illicit unions ran as a dour counterpoint to the exuberant theme of the perfect partnership. It made its way into the lyrics of a song titled "The Married Man," which made the case for marital legitimacy with signal clarity:

> The Joys which from lawless connections arise
> Are fugitive—never sincere,
> Oft stolen with haste, and oft snatch'd by surprise
> Interupted [sic] by doubt and by fear;
> But those which in legal attachments we find,
> When the heart is with innocence pure,
> Is from every imbit'ring reflection refin'd
> And while life can taste joy can endure.[43]

The contrast drawn between lawless and lawful connections suggests that divorce was, among other things, part of an effort to differentiate the married from the unmarried. In making such a claim, we need not infer a consensus on either grounds or procedures; but a focus on the problem of marital legitimacy in the post-Revolutionary era helps us account for the widespread legitimation of divorce. Only in retrospect is it evident that it was the decision to accept formal rules for divorce in the first place, not the rules themselves, that constituted the true legal revolution in marriage. Nevertheless, the initial acceptance of divorce proved far less controversial than the subsequent working out of the particularities. On the threshold of the nineteenth century, the notion that divorces could be decreed for gross violations of the marriage contract had already acquired statutory legitimacy, and it had done so with remarkably little opposition.

LEGISLATURES AND LITIGANTS: A FRAGILE CONSENSUS

A half century later, virtually every legal, social, and moral facet of divorce would become the object of intense national scrutiny. The nineteenth-century penchant for dissecting and rejecting the ground rules for divorce stands in striking contrast to the wholesale acceptance of the

divorce process at the end of the eighteenth century. It seems as if in instituting the new rules in spare and simple statutes, eighteenth-century legislators had embraced a solution without fully comprehending the problem. Not only did they neglect to address some thorny substantive and
procedural issues, but they failed to anticipate the sheer numbers of men
and women who would come to rely on the divorce process. Given the
novelty of formal divorce in the early republic, it could hardly have been
otherwise.

Post-Revolutionary legislators were addressing a post-Revolutionary
problem: the persistence of extralegal marital dissolutions. Even as independence provided the intellectual and symbolic resources for accepting
the concept of divorce, concern for marital legitimacy supplied the catalyst for legalizing it. In this context, divorce can be construed as a legal
fiction designed to bring extralegal dissolutions under the aegis of state
government. Couples were ending their unions anyway, and it remained
for legislators to devise new ways to end them legally. In every country
among "the lowest ranks," noted an observer of wife-sale, "men part
with their wives, and wives with their husbands, with as little delay or
remorse as they would move from one boarding house to another." Since
law was "not to be had for nothing" in either England or the United
States, since there was no property in question, and with "the object
being only a wife," wife-sale, he concluded, was not even deemed wor-
thy of formal prosecution. A variant of wife-sale in the marketplace
appeared in the tale of the runaway wife who eloped to Chautauqua,
New York, with her lover, only to be followed by her enraged husband.
When the lover offered the husband fifty dollars to relinquish his wife,
he accepted it and "returned home apparently satisfied, leaving the
happy couple . . . exulting in their triumph."[44]

Since there is little evidence that wife-sale enjoyed as much prominence in North America as it did in England, such stories need to be
taken with a grain of salt. At the same time, the class-based aspects of
extralegal dissolutions illuminate the tensions inherent in providing legal
ones. When Americans of "the lowest ranks" devised their own forms
for divorce, they exhibited very little reverence for fault. As potential litigants, then, they would have a conception of divorce that was far less
stringent than the statutes that provided for it, and in the courts they
would exert enormous pressure on the paradigm of fault. The degree to
which they implicitly challenged the prevailing constructions of the legal
system lends support to a bottom-up model of cultural diffusion.

Fault, the legal bedrock of American divorce, ran contrary to many litigants' best interests. For those spouses who wanted the terms for their marital dissolution to be as easy as possible, mutual consent proved a highly appealing justification not only because it was swift and inexpensive but also because it comported nicely with the pursuit of happiness. And when spouses enlisted the active support of friends and neighbors in ending their unions, they were appealing to the weight customarily accorded to the approval or disapproval of the community. There was a compelling logic to the communal support of divorce by mutual consent, for if a proper marriage hinged on the mutual consent of the couple made public before witnesses, why should not divorce as well?

It was an idea that died hard and perhaps never completely. Well into the nineteenth century, state legislatures were besieged with crude divorce petitions, signed with an X and often accompanied by vague depositions that affirmed the consent of both parties together with broad community approval. In fact, consent often provided the basis for denial of legislative decrees, since it was antithetical to the principle of fault. And yet petitioners evinced an enduring faith that the sheer number of friends and neighbors who supported the dissolution would sway the minds of legislators. Tennessee legislative divorce petitions, for example, could carry up to seventy or eighty signatures. One Pennsylvania community even allowed its members to declare a divorce and arbitrate the division of marital property. Although it is not clear if the members of this informal tribunal were ignorant of the state divorce statute or were reluctant to abide by its relatively liberal terms, their willingness to create easy terms of their own speaks volumes to their belief in the legitimacy of a community-sanctioned dissolution. Moreover, in contrast to wife-sale in the marketplace, a custom that denigrated the wife as an object of property, this form of community approval exhibited a modern juristic dimension by deeming the wife an economic partner.[45]

It is a mistake to read all extralegal resolutions as the stubborn residue of a deeply rooted folk culture; they also represented alternative visions of the sources of post-Revolutionary moral authority. Divorce, in other words, fostered subtle contestation from its very inception. Conflict turned not so much on whether divorce should be legitimated—the Revolution seems to have provided a measure of consensus on that question—as on who should define the terms.[46]

We can discern the terms of "the state" from the language of its statutes. The 1787 New York statute, which enabled the Everitt divorce to take place, carried the message that divorce was to be avoided at all costs and was to be granted only for the most egregious breach of the marriage contract, the sin of adultery. Reading more like a criminal statute on adultery than a civil statute on divorce, its preamble stated that "the laws at present in being within this State respecting adultery are very defective." Yet the law was a good deal more than a statute on adultery. It is likely that extralegal marital dissolutions followed by long-term second unions were occurring just often enough to warrant legislation that rendered both the dissolutions and the subsequent unions more clearly illegal than ever before.[47] To put the proposition another way, to make divorce legitimate was to make all other dissolutions illegitimate. That adultery was to be punished by the prohibition against the remarriage of the guilty spouse exemplifies the punitive thrust of the New York statute. Instead of a scarlet *A*, an adulterous spouse like William Everitt was to carry the burden of an invisible *D*.

The ensuing debate over the 1787 law reveals that what was at stake in these early statutes in New York and other jurisdictions were the terms for closing the gap between formal law, then expressed as divorcelessness, and various customary divorce practices. In the process of balancing the punitive advantages of the New York statute against the undesirable consequences of its restrictiveness, the Council of Revision vetoed it, asserting that unless it were possible to lock up adulterous spouses in a cloister, the prohibition on remarriage was an invitation to immoral and illegal unions. What is more, because a guilty spouse might remarry out of state, or, given the level of record keeping, even within the state, the authorities would face a practical problem of enforcement.

At issue here was nothing less than calculating the long-term, collective influence of divorce law on day-to-day marital behavior. Because legal rules had the power to influence moral choices in an area that had traditionally belonged to the church, even the invisible *D* was not without purpose. As Benjamin Trumbull argued in his assault on easy divorce in Connecticut, statutory failure to provide punishment for the guilty spouse could serve to undermine deeply rooted religious convictions. He warned of dire consequences for the citizens of Connecticut: "The silence and sanction of law in a special manner are such soothing cordials, such effectual opiates, that no flashes or thunder from the divine world would alarm their conscience."[48]

Passing the original statute over the veto of the council, New York legislators presumably wagered that in providing for divorce on highly restrictive terms, they were taking some sort of middle ground between easy divorce and complete divorcelessness; they were discouraging casual legal dissolutions while making some inroads on the extralegal ones. Similar constraints were evident in statutes with broader grounds. The preamble to the Pennsylvania divorce statute of 1785 declared that it was "the design of marriage, and the wish of the parties entering into that state that it should continue during their joint lives."[49]

To see the legitimation of divorce as an effort at social control in which statutory recognition was deemed the lesser of two evils goes a long way toward explaining why it assumed the shapes that it did. The very marginality of our defendant, William Everitt, suggests that he was precisely the sort of person legislators had in mind when they fashioned the New York statute. Nonetheless, a top-down reading of legislative intent obscures the degree to which interest in the stability of marriage cut across both gender and class lines. Given the extensive interdependence of men and women in the political economy of post-Revolutionary marriages, we can understand the willingness of couples to live out their lives in decidedly uncompanionate partnerships despite the possibility of either extralegal or legal dissolutions. Most men and probably most women even more decidedly did not want countless dissolutions and reconstitutions.

What, then, are we to make of the part played by a woman like Sarah Everitt in the statutory recognition of divorce? One important consequence of the legitimation of divorce was the adversarial role it assigned to wives. Furthermore, recent scholarship suggests that in numerous jurisdictions over a variety of time spans women constituted the majority of divorce plaintiffs. Are we to construe their appearances in the courts of the early republic as dutiful and formulaic displays of compliance with legislators' efforts to sharpen the boundaries of marriage, as they sought formal resolutions for marriages that had been ended in fact by long-absent husbands? Or are we to read the suits they initiated against their husbands as acts of personal liberation that embodied the newly ascendant principle of individual autonomy?[50]

If compliance has the edge here, it is because the concept of liberation was so seriously compromised by the socioeconomic disabilities of women as to sap it of practical application. Not only was the principle of individual autonomy just gathering force at the end of the eighteenth century, but it was distinctly masculine in its orientation. Feminist critics of the Enlightenment have marked out the late eighteenth century as a period in which sharp gender differentiation emerged, flourished, and laid the foundations for relegating women to the domestic sphere, where they remained under the authority of husbands and fathers. As economic dependents confronting an all-male legal system that embraced the double standard, women suffered structural disadvantages at the hands of the law that are only too apparent.[51]

Nonetheless, we should not jettison the liberation paradigm entirely. To the extent that suing for divorce was a legal option that depended on the voluntary, active, and even tenacious participation of female plaintiffs, it represented a conceptual reconfiguration of the marriage contract. The old common law fiction that husband and wife were one and the husband was the one could no longer hold quite the same authority once divorce challenged the male-dominated corporatism of marriage.

This brings us at last to Sarah Everitt, whose liberation seems so highly qualified as to create doubts about who was being liberated from whom. We cannot be sure of what lay beneath the simple chancery record, but on its face, it appears that William was the one who liberated himself from Sarah; and, in accord with the compliance paradigm, she legitimated the deed by coming to court. Yet even in Sarah's case, compliance does not tell the whole story. Perhaps there were property considerations, such as earnings or an inheritance, that impelled her to separate her legal identity from that of her husband, or perhaps there was a suitor waiting in the wings. Or perhaps she simply wanted to be free to remarry sometime in the future; presented with an option to put her life in legal order, she pursued it in the courts.

Beyond all these practical considerations, there was surely a powerful symbolic component of the action she took. In a world where the repudiation of a spouse had been a husband's prerogative, we should not dismiss the import of her right as a woman to repudiate her husband in a court of law.[52] One thing is certain: divorce by a woman no longer represented the anarchic breaking of a sacred contract. Since it was William who was defined here as the anarchist who broke the contract, perhaps we should read Sarah's determination to divorce him as a declaration of independence. It was precisely this radical possibility—this slender thread of female autonomy—that would vex and intrigue subsequent generations.

TWO

❖ Refining the Rules, 1800–1850s ❖

When Judge Robert B. Warden addressed the Court of Common Pleas of Hamilton County, Ohio, in 1851, he remarked on the singularity of the divorce before him: "The record will embody a history of two lives, the portraiture of at least two marked and interesting characters, and the story of many important events." The plaintiff was Frances Wright: freethinker, radical feminist, utopian socialist, and onetime champion of the Workingmen's Movement. Her attorney was Timothy Walker: legal reformer, women's rights advocate, and editor of the *Western Law Journal*. Legal fees, set at $800 for the opposing counsels, were no less impressive. Even the certificate confirming Wright's marriage to Phiquepal D'Arusmont, the controversial experimenter in Pestalozzian methods of education, had been witnessed by the marquis de Lafayette, celebrated benefactor of the republic during the darkest days of the Revolution. But the judge moved beyond the cast of characters to depict the case as a text for decoding American divorce. "The bill, the answers, the correspondence," he insisted, "are a volume of moral lessons: the argument would make a book—a valuable book—of equity jurisprudence."[1]

For Warden the meaning of the case lay not so much in the old political engagements of its litigants as in the moral and legal ramifications of their quarrel. The Revolution was long since over, and whereas Wright had been a transitional figure in the 1820s and 1830s, sustaining a militant anticlerical rationalism in an increasingly sentimental and evangelical age, her particular brand of radicalism had run its course by the time of the Ohio suit. When we consider that she had devoted her best years and her formidable skills to warring against what she regarded as the irrational social system of marriage and private property, there was a terrible irony in the suit's turning as it did on a dispute over marital property. This woman whose causes had represented the last bold contests of a restive Enlightenment radicalism was reduced to placing her own bitter contest within the rules of the bourgeois legal order.[2]

Warden's emphasis on the legal complexity of those rules as well as their moral import exemplifies the way divorce was transfigured over the first half of the nineteenth century. Extended grounds and jurisdictional accessibility facilitated the growing use of formal divorce, and the growing use of formal divorce, in turn, subjected statutory rules to rigorous scrutiny. By the time of the D'Arusmont suit, the tacit and largely abstract acceptance of divorce that characterized the post-Revolutionary era had fragmented under the weight of specific and contentious concerns. Divorce was hardly commonplace, but it was being used with enough regularity to destabilize its Enlightenment premises.[3]

Public discourse shifted to encompass the expanding boundaries of the nation and the incessant movement of its population. East to west, country to city, one place to another—the chances to begin life anew became ever more tangible. Turnpikes, canals, and railroads did more than facilitate the disappearance of spouses; increased ease of transportation enabled them to shop for more hospitable jurisdictions. As a result, the divorce statutes of every state assumed a degree of national relevance. At a time when law was emerging as a powerful instrument of social change and, as Christopher Tomlins has put it, "the paradigmatic discourse explaining life in America," the unevenness of divorce law was a source of considerable anxiety. With eyes on the future, both the opponents and proponents of divorce began to imagine its impact on the collective fate of the nation.[4]

THE ANOMALIES OF FEDERALISM
AND THE CRUCIBLE OF EXPERIENCE

As we have seen, at the threshold of the nineteenth century the notion that divorces could be decreed for gross violations of the marriage contract had acquired widespread statutory legitimacy. The broad outlines for a legal script were firmly in place. But while it was understood that an innocent plaintiff might sever her or his conjugal ties to a guilty defendant, the legal prototypes were still spare and lacking texture. There was

often little clarity about precisely what behavior constituted the violations designated by statute, much less what was required as proof or
what was the proper tribunal. The law's fairness to spouses engaged in
the divorce process was assumed rather than defined, and the relation
between the right of divorce and the impact on the society was only
dimly imagined.

Perceptions were refined in the crucible of experience. Jurists and legislators were not the only ones influenced by the flood of information
emanating from the new divorce regimes; laypersons were affected as
well. Extralegal commentary remained sporadic until the middle of the
nineteenth century, but it was colored increasingly by the emerging legal
details. As airy expectations about how the rules would or should work
came to be punctuated with the details of how, in fact, they had worked,
public discourse acquired narrative, quantitative, and comparative
dimensions. Divorce stories flourished.

For a variety of reasons, it was the critics of divorce who dominated
the public dialogue, and each one, it seems, had the perfect tale to
demonstrate the pitfalls of a lax policy. Carried on the tide of the Second
Great Awakening, evocative stories made their way into the sermons of
traditional ministers as well as those affiliated with evangelical denominations. A colorful illustration drawn from the pages of everyday life
could fortify the cause of a clergyman eager to defend the simple truths
of Scripture against the inroads of godless rationalism. Timothy Dwight
employed just such a story to show that liberal grounds were turning
society into "one vast brothel." "Pope Dwight," as Connecticut Repub-
licans called the pious Federalist and former president of Yale, was reit-
erating the antidivorce stance of his predecessor, Benjamin Trumbull. He
did so, however, with all the brio of a backwoods revivalist.[5]

Dwight found just the narrative he needed in the excesses of the
French Revolution. He asked his New Haven parishioners to consider
the profligacy of the French soldier who "lately declared before a judicial tribunal in Paris that he had married eleven wives in eleven years
and boasted of this fact as honourable and meritorious." Buttressing his
anecdote with a barrage of selected statistics, Dwight observed that only
three months after the French National Assembly had sanctioned easy
divorces, the total number of divorces approached the total number of
registered marriages. Connecticut, he warned, was moving in the very
same direction, having granted 400 divorces over the past five years, and
40 in New Haven alone. If the trend were to continue unabated, the
social organization of the whole community would amount to nothing

more than a state of licensed prostitution. Children bereft of homes and fathers would grow up "like the wild men of Poland or Germany," nourished by beasts and left to prowl through life.[6]

Divorce stories like Dwight's, which demonstrated the folly of the legal rules by putting a human face on them, surfaced in satire as well as in sermons. The Indianapolis *Locomotive,* smarting under that city's midcentury reputation as a divorce mill, used the tall tale to shift the spotlight from easy judicial divorces to casual legislative ones. This tale, allegedly told by a New Jersey lobbyist in a Trenton tavern, recounted an incident on the last day of the state's legislative session. After a champagne supper followed by a champagne breakfast, the bleary-eyed lawmakers confused a petition for a divorce with a bill for a turnpike. Instead of freeing the anxious petitioner to jettison his wife and marry an attractive widow, they incorporated him into a turnpike. The turnpike petitioner, for his part, accepted his divorce decree philosophically and promptly left his wife to marry another.[7] Although the locale marks the story as a bit of barroom ribaldry, it was in its own irreverent way another version of the world turned upside down and corrupted.

Recounted at different times and in very different voices, each of the foregoing stories focused on the endemic readiness of men to reject their old unions and enter into new ones. The first, playing on the early-nineteenth-century recoil from the excesses of the French Revolution, linked the social consequences of a liberal divorce policy to the chaos created by a father's absence. The second, drawing on midcentury stereotypes of political venality, underscored the inability of legislators to adjudicate a divorce while it mocked the motives of the petitioners. Both stories, moreover, implicitly constructed women as the passive victims of an omnipresent male licentiousness that was now being unleashed by the state's casual erosion of marital safeguards.[8]

Legal critics, whose discourse was typically gender-neutral, attributed the chaos of the new rules to the amalgam of English precedents and American innovations that rendered procedures random and irregular and challenged professional expertise. It was a point well taken. Because the primary model came from the English ecclesiastical courts, which granted only separations, a significant reconfiguration was necessary. The parliamentary model, which rested on the notion that Parliament functioned as a court of last appeal, was in conflict with the principle of the separation of powers; and in those states where legislative divorce served as a temporary substitute for judicial divorce, petitioners assumed a more immediate access to their legislators than their did English coun-terparts, often inundating the lawmakers with appeals.[9]

As for the Puritan legal model, the dissenting Protestant variant of the ecclesiastical model, it was premised on the moral guidance of a vigilant ministerial elite. The "tide of manners," Timothy Dwight admitted in reviewing the history of divorce in Connecticut, had served as a check on its abuse. But diverse secular communities had little in common with homogeneous Puritan villages and could not be counted on to restrain the moral lapses of their inhabitants. Burgeoning cities, depicted as cen-ters of boundless temptation, intensified fears about the erosion of older forms of social control. Given the changes in nineteenth-century society, the indigenous legal model that had long served New England seemed dangerously lax to many New England moralists.[10]

Each state, moreover, was determined to exercise its sovereignty over the status of its citizens, which meant maintaining its authority over the laws of marriage and divorce. Interstate conflict was inevitable. As Michael Grossberg has noted, the stubborn localism of nineteenth-century family law in the face of jurisdictional conflicts reflected a deeply republican distrust of centralized government in general and centralized control of the family in particular.[11]

Close observers of divorce understood that the multiplicity of legal prototypes embodied a range of moral choices. While the New England states retained the model they knew as a matter of regional custom, they realized that model with important individual differences. Massachu-setts narrowed its grounds in the post-Revolutionary era by excluding desertion, which it did not recognize again until 1838. Cruelty, the early republic's benchmark of a liberal code, was a ground in Massachusetts for separation only, but the state's 1857 statute provided that a formal separation could become a complete divorce after a period of five years. Connecticut, the most visible of the early American divorce jurisdictions by virtue of its numerous decrees, retained its pre-Revolutionary grounds of adultery and desertion. Although in 1815 it recognized con-structive desertion (i.e., desertion brought on by intolerable cruelty), it did not incorporate cruelty alone as a ground until 1843. In 1849, how-ever, it passed an omnibus clause, the most controversial of the available provisions, which gave the judiciary broad discretion in the granting of decrees. Rhode Island, New Hampshire, and Vermont embraced a more liberal model from the start; they all passed statutes in the 1790s recog-nizing, among other grounds, adultery, desertion, and cruelty. Rhode

Island, moreover, was distinguished by including an omnibus clause in its 1798 statute.[12]

Western states, including the area we now call the Midwest, appropriated the Puritan model in its most liberal form as a matter of choice. In the end, it was precisely this liberal (relative to other prototypes) Puritan model that provided the basic framework for American divorce. Overlooking minor variations, such as the uneven acceptance of intemperance, insanity, and incarceration as grounds, and discounting fraud and bigamy (the traditional and uniformly accepted causes for annulment), we can see that the liberal Puritan model would provide final decrees in readily accessible civil courts for three fundamental grounds: adultery, desertion, and cruelty; it was frequently enhanced by an omnibus clause. This model did not prevail without resistance; it was subject to some contraction near the end of the nineteenth century, and it did not make its way into every jurisdiction. Yet it comes closer than any other legal configuration to qualifying as a nineteenth-century American divorce code.

At the same time, in considering public discourse about the rules we need to have a sense of just how varied they could be. Regionalism counted for a good deal as a matter of both custom and choice. Louisiana, in accordance with its French origins, enacted a variation of the Napoleonic Code of 1803, which had significantly modified the lax divorce law of 1792. Nevertheless, the state's version eased access to a decree; by midcentury, critics could denounce Louisiana's divorce code as excessively lax by southern standards. Other states below the Mason-Dixon line, such as Virginia and Maryland, adhered to the English parliamentary model by maintaining legislative jurisdiction over divorce and by issuing decrees on an ad hoc basis. Newer southern states, such as Florida, Arkansas, Tennessee, and Kentucky, appropriated the liberal Puritan model, making the traditional grounds for a formal separation the basis for a complete divorce. Both northern and southern states, including the New England states, retained remnants of legislative jurisdiction over divorce concurrent with their recognition of judicial decrees.[13]

In the South, divorce unfolded in the context of chattel slavery. Though the influence of slavery may not be evident in the lineaments of southern divorce statutes, it would be a mistake to dismiss its impress on southern divorce. To the extent that slavery informed the definition of marriage, it molded attitudes toward formal divorce. Slaves, of course, were prohibited from marrying and were therefore beyond the aegis of divorce. As one antislavery journal put it, every slaveholder is invested with "the Papal prerogative" of "putting asunder those whom God has joined together." The prohibition against slave marriages, however, shaped conjugal boundaries for the free population. When we consider that adultery was the common denominator in all divorce codes, the one ground that even conservative Protestants could accept, we can see how slavery worked against the grain of formal divorce. Not only did it sustain the tacit recognition of sexual relations between male slaveholders and female slaves, thereby undermining adultery as a ground, but it made more acceptable the informal marital dissolutions for poor whites and free blacks, the two groups whose status in the social order was one notch above that of slaves.[14]

To be sure, white southerners divorced, and in some jurisdictions they divorced with considerable ease. Nonetheless, slavery tended to buttress the acceptance of extralegal forms of marital dissolution so long as they did not threaten vital property interests. South Carolina's refusal to legitimate divorce, which presumably reflected the dominance of low country planters, is an extreme manifestation of that pattern. Although formal separations with alimony were available, they were not recognized by statute, and chancellors in the state's equity courts strained to avoid referring to them as divorces from bed and board. It seems the very word *divorce* was an anathema in the local legal culture. Still, the state's extremism was clearly anomalous. In closing off all the formal exits to wedlock, its jurists assumed a stance more conservative than that of the Council of Trent, thereby placing their state in a class by itself in the Anglo-American world.[15]

The rules, then, ran anywhere from South Carolina's decision to make no rules to Iowa's decision via an omnibus clause to abide by whatever rules the judiciary deemed appropriate. Because every statute was measured against the extremities of the legal spectrum, they were disproportionately significant. By the time Joel Prentice Bishop's 1852 treatise on marriage and divorce appeared, the breadth of that spectrum was controversial. As Bishop put it, at one extreme, there was the view that marriage was indissoluble for any cause by any earthly tribunal; it was favored in modern times as "a religious refinement unknown to the primitive church." At the other extreme, there was the view that marriage was a temporary partnership to be dissolved at the will of the two partners; it was held not only "by savage people but some of the polished and refined."[16]

Bishop is alluding here to a cyclical view of civilization in which the early stages are barbaric, the later stages are refined, and the ideal occupies the moderate center. In linking the statutory extremes of divorce to the far ends of an imagined cycle of historical development, he exemplifies how the rules for divorce were becoming compass points for locating the moral course of the nation. That Bishop, a positivist and an empiricist who believed in the capacity of human beings to shape the law to sustain their own progress, could connect divorce to so deterministic a vision attests to the volatility of the divorce question.[17] It suggests that for many of his contemporaries, the rules for divorce reflected the present and foretold the future as no other body of rules could, save perhaps the laws affecting slavery and freedom.

The readiness of midcentury Americans to invest divorce with a weight far in excess of what the number of decrees would seem to warrant derived from a handful of closely related notions. First was the idea that because the rules controlled the relative ease or difficulty of securing a decree, and therefore affected the total number of decrees, they determined the collective consequences of divorce as a social policy. The emphasis here was quantitative. It mattered in an empirical way if grounds were tough or lax and if access to the process was narrow or broad.

Second was the conviction that the rules established moral and ethical boundaries, defined in nineteenth-century terms quite literally as the lines separating good from evil and right from wrong. This characterization is meant not to impugn the conviction as simplistic but rather to pinpoint the particularly Victorian dilemma of setting sharp moral edges on complex legal problems. Grounds imposed an uneasy moral calculus on divorce as a legal institution while procedures served as an index to the justness of the process.

Third, and closely related to the first two ideas, was the notion that law in general and divorce law in particular had the capacity to shape both the behavior and beliefs of individuals. This last belief went to the heart of the controversy, for to judge the influence of divorce on relations between the sexes it was necessary to estimate the impact of divorce on the social construction of gender itself. We turn now to the interplay of these ideas in the first half of the nineteenth century.

THE JUSTNESS OF THE PROCESS

Probably no legal facet of divorce was as instrumental in shaping how women and men ended their marriages as jurisdiction, a term embracing the right of a tribunal to assert its authority over an area of law or a particular case. *Where* one pursued a divorce could determine *if* one secured a decree. As conflicts over jurisdiction flared between states and between the legislature and the judiciary within a state, they engendered different questions. Interstate conflict exposed a substantive gulf in the nation's moral standards; intrastate conflict dramatized the problem of providing equitable access to the process. The former area of conflict could be said to center on the question of what was a morally appropriate plot for divorce; the latter, on who would be included in the cast of characters. We begin with intrastate conflict, for legislative divorce was the earliest target of controversy.

Resting on the assumption that divorces would be rare and therefore amenable to occasional legislative intervention, the exclusive legislative administration of divorce severely restricted the total number of decrees. Like the parliamentary model it copied, it embodied a political process that tended to place decrees beyond the reach of the lower classes and to discourage petitions from women. Of the forty-seven divorce petitions submitted to the Pennsylvania legislature in 1847, thirty-one came from men. Nonetheless, in most states, as was the case in Pennsylvania, the legislature had concurrent jurisdiction with the judiciary and therefore competed with the judiciary in the granting of decrees. When a potential litigant had access to a judicial forum but faced obstacles there, a petition placed in the hands of the right legislator could result in a quick and easy resolution. This puts an entirely different slant on the stubborn practice of legislative decrees. Far from serving as a restriction, in most states it provided an alternative forum, especially for influential, well-to-do men.[18]

But the random, ad hoc nature of parliamentary divorce that had satisfied the needs of a deferential society ran counter to the prevailing conception of justice in the age of democratic politics. Critics persistently deplored its inherent arbitrariness and its potential for corruption. Since legislators were "seldom familiar with the laws and still less frequently habituated to apply them," permitting them to issue decrees bore the familiar earmarks of "arbitrary government." Behind the curtain of committee reports and legislative votes, they argued, raw power prevailed. Those who petitioned for this special legislative favor exerted "the influence of their wealth and their family connections," while "the poor and those who are without friends" were largely ignored. As a delegate to the Pennsylvania Constitutional Convention of 1838 saw it: "The man who has charge of a divorce bill makes it his own—his chicken;—he makes it a personal matter; he solicits the votes of members for it, and the success of this bill becomes connected with that of other bills on very different subjects." The deployment of improper influence could take many forms, but there was little doubt that legislators involved in granting divorces, as Auguste Carlier observed, could be "affected by considerations of the lowest kind."[19]

Legislative divorce was not without a juristic rationale: it was deemed a legitimate alternative for situations that did not fit the statutory slots—in effect, a legislative substitute for an omnibus clause. According to this line of reasoning, the narrower the statutory grounds, the broader a petitioner's access to the legislature ought to be. Nor did such bills fall outside legislators' normal practice; the statute books of any state make clear that legislators were accustomed to passing numerous private bills ranging from charters of incorporation to various acts for individual relief. Arguing at the Indiana Constitutional Convention of 1851 that in all cases where there is a general law, no special law should be passed, Robert Dale Owen reckoned that at least two-thirds of all the legislation since statehood fell into the category of private bills.[20]

As Owen's remarks indicate, on the one hand legislators often issued decrees for existing statutory grounds, thereby competing improperly with the functions of the judiciary; on the other hand, they issued decrees for grounds they refused to write into statutes, which did not sit well with legal critics either. And yet despite mounting criticism, retaining legislative authority over divorce continued to hold considerable appeal for both legislators and their constituents. Legislators relinquished their quasi-judicial role reluctantly, and petitioners continued to appeal to them as judges, even in the face of state constitutional provisions to the contrary.

State legislative records show, paradoxically, that the poor and the legally unsophisticated also tried this route, albeit with less success. Still, they persistently appealed to the legislature both as a court of last resort and as the only court they could afford. Their presence as divorce petitioners in state legislative records requires us to modify the conventional wisdom that divorce appealed only to those concerned with considerations of property. From the regularity with which petitioners cited their poverty, it seems that any economic consequences had more to do with their hopes and expectations than with the disposition of current assets. Their appeals also intimate that divorce could represent a good deal more than the economic reordering of a failed marriage; it fell to legislators to define how much more by determining who would have access to a decree. If formal divorce provided uniform solutions with costs that could not be borne uniformly, it undermined the nation's commitment to an open-ended social mobility. Legislators feared that placing divorce beyond the reach of the women and men who could not afford to mount a suit was tantamount to declaring their marital arrangements beyond the aegis of the law.

From the perspective of needy petitioners, we can see that formal divorce represented the way to sustain their marital legitimacy in the eyes of the law by freeing them to remarry; it also served as a measure of their status in the social order. To be cut out of the divorce process, once it was made available, could force them into conjugal arrangements that were illegal; worse, it made those arrangements inconsequential. Thus the litigants who were too poor to afford the costs of a suit but were respectable enough to pursue a formal decree confronted the legal system with a troubling question. Would the proverbial common man and, no less important, the common woman be able to secure a decree?

States specifically addressed this question in the 1820s and 1830s, when the canons of Jacksonian democracy made it more pressing. With an eye toward reducing the number of legislative petitions citing poverty, the New Jersey divorce statute of 1824 made provisions for those who were unable to afford a suit. By 1830, however, the governor noted that the number of divorce petitions was increasing anyway because of the relative ease of using the legislature. Although it "was formerly supposed that the expense of prosecuting a bid in equity to obtain a divorce prevented an easy access to that court," and although the expense of the suit was reduced and provision was made so that "in cases of extreme poverty" there would be no costs whatsoever, it was clear to him now that the source of the applications had not been the expense at all, but the legislature's lack of standards.[21]

In New York the Revised Statutes of 1829 made provisions for all types of civil suits by poor persons, stipulating that any applicant "not worth twenty dollars, excepting the wearing apparel of himself and his family, and excepting the subject matter of the action," could petition to sue without fees and "to have counsel and attorney assigned to conduct the suit." It is not clear if this option was available to women or how frequently it was used by men, two issues that merit further research. What is clear in this nineteenth-century precursor to legal aid is that the court both acquiesced in and arranged for the cost-free pursuit of a civil suit and then called upon local attorneys to serve in a pro bono capacity. In light of these provisions, it is not surprising that when Levi Longwood petitioned the legislature in 1833, alleging that his wife was guilty of adultery and that he was "a poor man, and unable, owing to his poverty, to seek proper legal redress," his appeal fell on deaf ears. Yet since all that was required in many state legislatures was a petition and minimal documentation, there were good reasons why a litigant like Levi Longwood might try that route.[22]

Debate over full access to the divorce process tended to construct the typical petitioner as male, although the cost of a suit imposed particular burdens on females. Though precedents and statutes stipulated that the husband of an innocent female plaintiff was to foot his wife's legal costs, mounting a suit remained a problem when the husband was no longer in the jurisdiction and was unavailable to post bond. Tennessee addressed the problem directly. Its divorce statute of 1831 made it possible for women in such circumstances to sue without costs. It also altered its procedure for presumptive service, the requirement of publicizing a suit for several weeks in a local newspaper. Women needed only to file a petition and place a subpoena for the defendant in the hands of the local sheriff.[23]

Not all states responded positively to the problem of costs. In 1825, when the House Judiciary Committee of the Pennsylvania legislature was directed to examine the high cost of divorce for poor persons, it concluded that the burdens were no greater than those in other suits and advised against creating "invidious distinctions."[24] Nevertheless, the legislators' initial concern with the poverty of litigants indicates that some of them believed divorce suits warranted special consideration. As for the petitioners, there can be no mistaking their populist thrust. The notion that divorce was different from other suits, that it went beyond the arcane technicalities of the legal system, and that it was a remedy, if not in fact a right, that warranted heroic legislative intervention persisted well into the century. It assumed its most eloquent expression in all the prayers for relief that were pressed on legislators year after year.

Consider the moving appeal of the "fifty sundry citizens" of Warren County, Ohio, who petitioned the legislature in 1835 for the divorce of Richard M'Donald from his wife Jane. Although Jane had extended "every mark of confidence to Richard" over the two years of their courtship, she was all the time "secretly encouraging the address of another." Had Richard only been aware of her true feelings, he never would have persisted in his courtship. Because of parental pressure, Jane went on to marry him but she deserted him almost immediately, "assigning nothing else as a reason for leaving than settled dislike." Here was a tale of deception and coercion whose plot lines did not measure up to the concept of breach of contract or the legal requirement of fault. If there was a fault, it lay not so much with Jane as with the despotism of her parents, who insisted on designating a mate for her instead of leaving her free to choose for herself. The consequences were disastrous for Jane as well as for Richard, avowed the concerned citizens. Therefore both parties to the marriage wanted the divorce and would not reconcile. The judiciary committee ignored their open admission of collusion and gently advised that the petition did not come from the right party. It was Richard who should pray for the divorce, they insisted, and not his numerous friends and neighbors.[25]

What are we to make of such an appeal, which was far from the only one of its kind? Sharp distinctions between traditional and modern mores will not serve us well. The petition appealed to the moral authority of the community while it simultaneously recognized the ultimate authority of the state. Richard, after all, did not place a halter round Jane's neck and sell her in the marketplace. Even the technical error of citing the willingness of both Jane and Richard to dissolve the marriage was just that, for legislators understood that a proper petition drafted by an experienced attorney could represent the very same set of circumstances in crisply adversarial terms that masked the element of collusion.[26] Even worse, they understood that a professional petition could attribute the fault to an innocent defendant and deprive him or her of the right to a hearing.

Nineteenth-century concern with the hypocrisy of the rules and their potential injustice was directed initially at legislative decrees. Legal professionals found the ability of legislators to determine the validity of a petition seriously wanting in comparison to that of judges. At issue were both the neutrality of the law and the struggle for ascendancy between the judiciary and the legislature. One law journal kept a steady watch on the number of legislative decrees in several states while mounting a campaign for their extinction. If law was to be king in America, jurists warned, it should not be random or arbitrary in addressing society's most fundamental compact. A divorce decree should not turn on the discretion of special committees whose members had neither the time nor the expertise to evaluate the evidence and sometimes voted on the basis of no evidence at all. As the governor of New Jersey put it in 1830: "The mode of proceeding in these cases is not favourable to the investigation of truth; and there is reason to fear that in some instances parties connive with each other, and make false acknowledgments and declarations for the purpose of furnishing evidence to effect their improper designs, and if so, it is natural they should turn to that tribunal, which hazard of detection would be the smallest."[27]

Another bone of contention was the dubious constitutionality of leg-islative divorces, since they disregarded both the separation of powers and the obligation of contracts. Marriage was a contract, and its dissolu-tion stipulated that one spouse by violating its terms forfeited all benefit under it; divorce, then, was a distinctly judicial issue. The occasional decree that demonstrated the untold legal mischief created by legislative intervention was bound to be broadly reported in law journals.[28]

Putting an end to legislative divorces, however, was more difficult than one might expect. In both statutes and constitutional clauses, pro-hibitions of the practice were often ambiguous. After concurrent juris-diction with the courts was negated, there remained an indeterminate space in which legislators were free to address nonstatutory grounds. Statutory prohibitions, moreover, were unable to bind the will of future legislatures. Although Maine prohibited legislative divorce in 1838, the house of representatives voted favorably on a joint petition in the fol-lowing year, only to be overruled in the state senate. As petitions con-tinued to pour in, an 1844 Joint Judiciary Committee argued that even if the legislature had the power to grant decrees—and it was a big if—it was "inexpedient" to exercise it because it violated the separation of powers. The committee characterized the logic of providing legislative decrees for nonstatutory grounds as exceedingly twisted, since it was the legislature's obligation to determine proper grounds in the first place.[29]

Some legislators tried to shore up their quasi-judicial authority by acquiescing to modest reforms. The Ohio House Judiciary Committee of 1828 met the rising wave of criticism by advocating stricter and more uniform procedures, including the requirement of advance notice to an out-of-state defendant. As these attempts at reform suggest, internal resistance to giving up the granting of decrees was tenacious.[30] Gover-nors frequently inaugurated legislative sessions by denouncing the prac-tice of legislative divorces only to be stopped in their tracks by deter-mined judiciary committees.

The Pennsylvania legislature's running battle with successive gover-nors exemplifies this pattern of confrontation. In 1829 Governor John Andrew Shulze chided legislators on the procedural irregularities in their divorce decrees and on the time devoted to private matters. Lamenting that in many cases, notice to the defendant was absent, he suggested that if the current statutory grounds were somehow wanting, it would be preferable to broaden them instead of trying to fill the gap with hap-hazard private bills. Though the House Judiciary Committee conceded there was a problem, it translated his remarks into an opportunity to enhance its own power. First its members designated a discretionary or so-called omnibus clause as the only way to empower the judiciary adequately; then they rejected such a clause as "a power that would be dangerous from being indefinite." The power, it seems, belonged in the capable hands of the committee members. The evil in legislative divorce, they reasoned, came from "the legislature itself having given too ready an ear to petitions." The solution was to funnel all petitions through their own committee, which would then ascertain if they were appropriate for legislative consideration or should be sent to the courts.[31]

Their vigilance in screening petitions was evidently wanting, since the state constitution of 1838 specifically stripped the legislature of concurrent jurisdiction with the courts. The determined legislators tried to circumvent the prohibition with an 1842 decree that cited no grounds at all but was vetoed by the governor. Still the decrees continued, putting legislators on a collision course with Governor Francis Rawn Shunk, who vetoed eleven in 1847 alone.[32] In a speech delivered at the start of the 1847 session, Shunk denounced the legislature's divorce record as patently unconstitutional, legally inept, profoundly immoral, and shockingly anti-Christian. For Shunk, who peppered his vetoes with sharp critiques of the legislators' legal mistakes, their failing was as much moral as it was legal. Citing the preamble of the 1815 divorce statute, which reiterated the "precepts of the Christian religion" spelled out in the state's first divorce statute, Shunk reminded the recalcitrant legislators that the casual disregard of marriage vows was the signpost of a society's "degeneracy."[33]

Legislative decrees would ebb under the weight of mounting criticism and constitutional prohibitions. In addition, the move toward judicial control of divorce was part of a larger national trend that was investing the courts with policy-making powers. When California entered the union at midcentury with a constitution prohibiting legislative divorce, legislative jurisdiction was already fading as a focal point of public controversy.[34] Nonetheless, this practice, which drew the first rounds of fire, exposed the difficulty of applying the rules fairly and suggested that declaring one spouse guilty of a specific fault did not necessarily make it so.

THE MORAL IMPLICATIONS OF DIVERSE GROUNDS

Because grounds provided the key to ordering the particular details of a failed marriage into a formal legal narrative, they constructed a morally appropriate plot for a divorce suit. Their definition and elaboration were central to refining the rules. If they were too narrow, warned liberals who took a contractual approach to the story line, they would deprive the victim of a serious breach in the marriage contract of a viable legal remedy and blunt the contractual essence of marriage; but if they were too broad, alleged conservatives who conceptualized the issue theologically, they would violate the teachings of Christ, put asunder those whom God had joined together, and transform exceptions to the principle of marital indissolubility into the norm. The difficulty of defining irrevocably transgressive marital behavior was borne out in the provisions in state statutes, which diverged broadly. The vexing problem of disparate statutory rules exposed American divorce as an incoherent amalgam of inconsistent moral precepts based on competing ideological foundations. And yet jurists and legislators battling to stabilize the meaning of divorce amid all these uncertainties managed to paper over its deepest contradictions. In the end, Victorian divorce, as Lawrence Friedman has astutely observed, was a highly tenuous compromise that sustained a strict official moral code while tolerating a lax unofficial one.[35] We turn now to the fundamental instability of that compromise.

What was a morally acceptable plot? What breach in the behavior of a spouse was so contrary to the purposes of the marriage contract as to render it null and void? Joel Bishop named adultery, desertion, extreme cruelty, imprisonment, and habitual drunkenness. These were tangible departures from acceptable conjugal behavior: they had physical manifestations and were amenable to a measure of corroboration. More shadowy, in his view, were the emerging "mental causes" like "smothered hatred and love turned to the reverse," which he feared were too indefinite for the rational assessment of human tribunals. But while proof was a critical element in establishing the fault, Bishop fully understood and welcomed the discursive play between the letter of the law and its finely tuned adjudication. In a bid for permitting a standard of proof more lax than that in other areas, he urged that the grounds he deemed acceptable be construed broadly. Divorce was remedial, he admonished the advocates of strict construction, and judges should do all they could to give full effect to the remedy.[36]

A comprehensive, midcentury national survey drawn up by New York legislators struggling to liberalize their own rules suggests that although Bishop's statutory standards were recognized in many states, there was no overarching conformity on either grounds or procedures. Despite his distaste for legal indeterminacy, many states included an omnibus clause that could encompass whatever the judiciary chose to define as marital misbehavior, including the vaguest of "mental causes." Conversely, not all states accepted drunkenness or imprisonment as grounds, in part because they were not considered irrevocable conditions. Even worse, in some states divorce was still administered solely by the legislature. Vociferous resistance to Bishop's grounds, moreover, was emerging at precisely the time he voiced his support for them. In 1855, when New York legislators tried to incorporate desertion and habitual drunkenness into a statute, they rightly anticipated that their proposal would "come into conflict . . . with the firmly established prejudices in education, and in some few cases with religious scruples."[37]

Such uncertainties in identifying appropriate grounds were exacerbated by the phenomenon of migratory divorce, which demonstrated the audacious ease with which litigants manipulated the rules. More important, it exposed divergent standards for a morally acceptable divorce plot. No legal aspect of the rules better revealed their moral ambiguity than the readiness of some "unhappy wretches" to travel "to the end of the continent" in search of an easy tribunal. This problem, which emerged early in the century, only intensified as transportation improved. If the statutes of one state were strict, observed an 1813 essayist, "some kind sister state less rigid in its ideas of the matrimonial compact might always extend to the applicant its accommodating powers." Tensions ran especially high at first over the discrepancies between neighboring states. The determination of New York and Massachusetts courts, for example, to invalidate Vermont decrees was spelled out in the doctrine that Vermont decrees, for persons not amenable to the sovereignty of Vermont, "were not to be justified by any principles of comity."[38]

Since Scotland had served as a haven of sorts for some English spouses, American jurists were not without English precedents; they appropriated the 1812 *Case of Lolly* as a model. It provided the example of a man who had married in England, divorced in Scotland, and then returned to England to marry a second time, only to be indicted for bigamy. His plight demonstrated the principle of lex loci, or law of place, and the dire consequences that would ensue from violating it. But in America, where the structural potential for conflict of law existed on an unprecedented scale, and where out-of-state courts rarely exhibited the same restraint in issuing decrees as did the consistory courts of Scotland, there were simply too many Lollys. As a consequence, the divorce standards of strict jurisdictions were perpetually endangered by the laxity of liberal neighbors.[39]

No state was as vulnerable in this regard as South Carolina, whose renowned chancellor, Henry De Saussure, invoked the Lolly doctrine to no avail. He lamented that the indissolubility of marriage, which he was convinced helped to hold South Carolina marriages together in fact as well as in form, was being undermined not only by the liberal provisions of Tennessee but also by Rhode Island's freewheeling omnibus clause. If Tennessee and Rhode Island could dissolve a South Carolina marriage, he predicted, we shall see "our own unhappy matches untied and new ones formed with almost as much dispatch as the same process is effected in some of our sister states." The solution to the pernicious influence of "foreign" divorces was simple. Since they were fraudulent with regard to domicile and violated the rule of lex loci, out-of-state dissolutions of South Carolina marriages would not be recognized within the borders of South Carolina.[40]

But the solution, of course, was not simple. Though the Lolly doctrine was embraced in strict jurisdictions with an eye toward restraining migratory divorces, it was disregarded in the liberal jurisdictions that were granting the decrees; thus some couples were viewed simultaneously as married by one state and divorced by another. The principle was further eroded by waves of westward migration. New arrivals were often the very persons who wanted a divorce regardless of where they had contracted their marriages. For some the desire to end a marriage was subtly intertwined with other motives for moving; for others divorce was the single goal and the move was a total fabrication. This last group, portrayed ultimately in William Dean Howells's *Modern Instance*, embodied the nightmare of a society fraught with deserting spouses in search of fraudulent decrees. By the 1850s, attention was riveted on Indiana as the jurisdiction that would satisfy their needs. Once railroad lines were united in one central Indianapolis depot, the clerk of the Marion County Court estimated that he received on average a letter a day inquiring if a disappearing spouse had applied for a divorce in his jurisdiction.[41] It was precisely these footloose American Lollys who became emblems of the hypocrisy of the divorce process and of the underlying immorality of the rules.

THE OPACITY OF GENDER

Allusions to the Lolly doctrine constructed the itinerant petitioner as either male or genderless and thus avoided confronting gender directly. The paucity of explicit references to gender in legislative debates is especially striking, given the presence of women in the courts as plaintiffs and the remedial nature of divorce. Women, after all, figured one way or another in every decree. Theoretically, at least, the legitimation of specific grounds redefined marriage in ways that freed women from the bonds of an oppressive union. Physical cruelty was a ground that renegotiated the terms on which women contracted marriage; and even the right to sue for a husband's adultery, the one ground on which there was broad consensus, enhanced a wife's status by placing her husband's sexual transgression on a par with her own. Giving wives the right to remarry, moreover, provided women no less than men with the chance to begin life anew.

Gender was clearly central to every facet of the new rules, which redrew the borders of licit sexuality and reallocated marital power. To the extent that the marriage contract was one of the pillars of the modern state and the principal institution through which men dominated women, giving women even a limited right to end the contract worked against marital domination. In providing for divorce, as Joan Scott noted of Revolutionary France, male legislators made women "both objects of legislative concern and subjects with civil rights." It is difficult to conceive of any body of law that intersected what Carole Pateman calls the sexual contract more directly or reconfigured it more provocatively than that giving women the right of divorce.[42] Therein perhaps lies the key to the uncanny reticence about gender in legislative debates.

Because divorce addressed domestic relations in the contractarian terms of the marketplace, focusing on women too directly would collapse the vaunted boundaries between separate spheres and blur the lines of sexual difference. Frank debate would have revealed the degree to which construing wives as subjects with civil rights destabilized the sexual contract. Male legislators, then, could afford to broach the inequalities of class as they considered providing for low-cost suits, but to probe the asymmetries of gender would have threatened the Victorian compromise. Indeed, when we focus on the gendered nature of divorce, including its obfuscation in legislative discourse, we can see that the compromise entailed more than adhering to a strict official code while tolerating a lax unofficial one: it invested wives with a measure of legal independence and then rhetorically obscured it or degraded it. To look at divorce in this way is to see, in a specific historical context, how this liberal legal option at once undermined and sustained gender hierarchy. These competing impulses constitute one of modern divorce's most enduring legacies.

Migratory divorce is an instance of how the rules might construct women as independent, rights-bearing individuals who could negotiate the law to their own advantage no less than rights-bearing men. Despite the reluctance of legislators and jurists to confront such an alternative directly, popular journals were prepared to admit that some Lollys were female and to exploit the implications. An Indianapolis newspaper labeled the women who came to town for divorces "grass widows," a term originally used to describe unwed mothers or abandoned mistresses. Its connotations of illegitimacy lingered in this context, attached not only to the dissembling that was part of migratory divorce but also to the independence of the plaintiffs. The solution to the threat posed by the legally independent wife was the degradation of the autonomous female plaintiff. These were literally loose women—that is, women uncoupled from their husbands—whose legal aggressiveness was translated into unregulated sexuality. Every hotel or tavern had "one or more of those bewitching vixens domiciled with them for ten days, which makes them *citizens* and *residents* of the State of Indiana, and with a little hard swearing, natives, too."[43]

If divorce was a form of moral theater, insisted another critic, it mattered that its courtroom audience included women. Notice, he told his readers, "what an interest they take in the whole proceeding, and you will then understand how much of the mischievous virus has passed from diseased homes into the community." Yet the directness with which this legal writer linked the pollution of divorce to women was unusual before midcentury. The pollution of ancient Rome or Revolutionary France was typically invoked as a warning against lowering the safeguards around marriage, but the notion was rarely deployed in such gender-specific terms before the emergence of the woman's rights movement. Until that time, divorce figured as a general threat to the harmony of the family, whose purpose according to conservatives was to school its members in the precepts of authority and obedience. Questions about where the authority lay and who did the obeying disappeared under universalist appeals to social responsibility. Law puts high barriers around the conjugal relation, a divorce critic avowed in antiseptically gender-neutral terms, so as to enforce "the performance of social duties."[44]

The gendered nature of marital power was both perpetuated and concealed (not, I would argue, in a conscious way) by constructing discourses around less menacing oppositions, such as the needs of the undifferentiated individual versus the collective interests of the state. Both opponents and proponents of divorce shifted their debate on the issues away from focusing on an adversarial contest between husbands and wives, which is how the law framed marital dissolutions, to stressing the wants of the ungendered self versus the welfare of the whole society. Conservatives argued that because the "easy relaxation of the marriage tie" was "calculated to demoralize society, and loosen one of the chief foundations of the social order," it was preferable to permit divorce only rarely despite individual suffering. By employing lifelong monogamy as a trope for law and order, they rendered divorce subversive. A lax divorce policy would invite "the overthrow of parental authority, the decay of filial duty," and "the absence of veneration." Individual hardship in marriage, then, was inevitable. A New York legislator could concede that matrimony "produces many partial evils and much individual suffering" while insisting that "the peace and order of society" mandated tolerating a measure of individual pain.[45] The ever-popular law-and-order argument tied the marriage contract securely to the social contract without revealing the gendered nature of the connections.

Probably as a matter of both strategy and conviction, the proponents of divorce did not counter appeals to law and order by invoking individual rights; instead, they focused on individual wrongs. As Thomas Laqueur has suggested, the humanitarian narrative, with its characteristic understanding of cause and effect, was an important model of social reform. Fault divorce, as we might expect, fit comfortably into its plot lines. Drawing on the compassionate rather than materialistic implications of contractual thinking, the proponents of easy divorce underscored the need to redress personal suffering with legal action. They embedded the prodivorce argument in an emotive narrative, a tale of sorrow and anguish, that nevertheless could be remedied by attending to the causality underpinning fault. The proponents of divorce appealed also to greater transparency in the legal system and greater moral purity in marriage—all for the sake of the children, who were likely to be tainted for life by their parents' discordant unions. Because the interest of the state in marriage pivoted on "legitimate increase," public policy concurred with private right when unions inimical to the welfare of children were dissolved.[46] Here, then, was the rationale supporting the wronged spouse, whose interest in securing a divorce was beneficial to children and in perfect accord with the best interests of society. He/she was the genderless protagonist of the liberal divorce scenario in which there was no conflict whatsoever between individuals and the state or between women and men.

A second opposition displacing that of women versus men was church versus state. On the one hand, divorce owed its institutional origins to the canons of the Catholic Church and the exceptions carved out by the English ecclesiastical courts. On the other hand, it had acquired life within the secular law of a society committed to insulating its legal institutions from the formal reach of established religion. In the context of the nineteenth century, no clear resolution of church-state tensions over divorce was possible. While Henry De Saussure could insist that marriage was a contract so sacred "the act of God alone can dissolve it," Tapping Reeve could avow that there was "nothing in the nature of a marriage contract that is more sacred than that of other contracts." A group of Massachusetts legislators opposed broadening the grounds for divorce by arguing that "the command of our Savior is explicit in this matter," while a group of New York legislators protested that it was not a legislator's "province to solve scriptural rules." Theology would play an even greater role in the antidivorce coalitions of the post–Civil War era, but already at midcentury it commonly appeared in the most secular of settings. What better way to demonstrate the growing divergence between law and morals than to invoke Scripture? Although "laws cannot enforce all that religion commands," insisted a southern divorce critic, they "ought not to encourage what religion condemns."[47]

A third area of contention that obfuscated gender centered on estimates, which diverged widely, regarding the effect of the law on collective behavior. Neither liberals nor conservatives were prepared to address openly the consequences of permitting wives to assert their claims against their husbands or to speculate, as members of the Revolutionary generation had, on how divorce might influence the asymmetry of marriage. The battle of competing prophecies turned on the institutional status of marriage in the next century and beyond, instead of on gender-specific consequences.

But on this uncertain terrain of the future, the opponents of broad-ranging grounds had an edge; they pursued a clear and consistent line of reasoning in which they predicted that the closer a divorce code came to treating marriage as an ordinary contract, the more deleterious the consequences. Relying on a slippery-slope argument, conservatives predicted that one dubious ground would lead to another and still another until grounds themselves would become hollow fictions and fade into oblivion. Indeed, when they looked into the future, they saw nothing less than the emergence of no-fault divorce, which they equated with the end of marriage as they knew it.

Liberals responded defensively, asserting that the social consequences of broad grounds were negligible and predicting that save for a few hapless legal unions that had ceased to function as unions in fact, marriage would remain unchanged. Far from overthrowing deeply rooted values, divorce, they insisted, presented a set of modern legal conventions that

would uphold those very values by taking violations of the marriage contract seriously. Since law was a purely derivative phenomenon, it was no
better or worse than the society it mirrored; the key to the divorce rate,
then, resided in the mores and morals of the society.[48]

One thing is clear: mounting a compelling argument against divorce
was easier than devising one to support it. The legislative record indicates that antidivorce sentiment was coherent, sustained, and spreading.
Inasmuch as divorce was a complicated remedy in an uneven and diverse
legal order, one could not defend it in quite the same impassioned way
that one could defend indissoluble marriage. And whereas supporters of
easier divorce rules were placed in the difficult position of advocating
those rules as a way of supporting and strengthening marriage, their
opponents were inspired by a righteous flame that burned ever brighter
with each expansion in statutory grounds. In the face of mounting legal
defeats, the critics of divorce were fashioning a rhetorically powerful
opposition. It was their terms that pitted the selfish, this-worldly contractualism of divorce against the transcendent communitarianism of
God's law. And it was their images—their mental maps—that set the
stage for more militant contestations.

THE CALIFORNIA CONFLICT

The difficulties that California legislators experienced in passing the
state's first divorce statute in 1851 exemplify the rising tensions associated with divorce rules. In anticipation of passing a statute that placed
responsibility for decrees in the hands of the judiciary, the state's first
constitution prohibited legislative divorces. Debate erupted in the state
senate when a majority of the Select Committee on Divorce reported neg-
atively on the proposed divorce bill. The report began by arguing that
given the express prohibition against divorce as a legislative power, the
legislature could not grant to the judiciary of the state a power it did not
itself possess.

Moving beyond this neat constitutional catch-22, Elcan Heydenfeldt,
the chairman of the committee and author of the report, advanced to
familiar antidivorce terrain. He deplored the contemporary inclination
to view the marriage contract as "merely conventional" as opposed to
"deriving its origin from the law of God or nature." Marriage, he
insisted, must retain its position "as the bond which holds society
together, and the safeguard of civilization and advancement." Remind-
ing fellow legislators that "all legislation must look to the greatest good

for the greatest number," the Heydenfeldt report concluded that the bill before it was both unconstitutional and inexpedient.[49]

The report, however, which touched all the obligatory antidivorce bases, broke new ground by linking "the woman question" to "the divorce question." If marriage was as conventional as other contracts, Heydenfeldt reasoned, then "so is the chastity of woman; so is her modesty, her delicacy, her refinement; and if we desire that these qualities should remain unimpaired, it behooves us to look well" to the effect the bill will have in supporting "opinions which are dangerous to society, or in relaxing those rules which have fixed a high standard of female excellence."[50] At this midcentury juncture in a new western state, the chastity of women (and their potential pollution) became an object of legislative concern. Here also was the implicit suggestion that divorce would alter gender relations irreparably by altering the terms of marriage.

The minority report, drafted by George Tingley, mounted a typical prodivorce defense. It avoided "the woman question" and focused instead on the suffering of innocent children at the hands of a guilty-but-genderless spouse. Most couples, Tingley insisted, evoking harmonious republican imagery, proffered a benign and affectionate example to their children. But those who presented their children with a negative model through the misbehavior of one of the partners became "a festering curse upon the community" and set the stage for humanitarian intervention.[51]

The bumpy road of the state's first divorce bill attests to the bitter feelings it generated. An acrimonious personal battle ensued when it was revealed that Heydenfeldt had written to a local minister, requesting him to deliver an antidivorce sermon while the bill was pending before the senate. That the senate censured him with a resolution stating he exceeded his powers as chairman of the committee seems extreme even for the raw politics of a new state. Heydenfeldt countered by challenging Tingley's eligibility to serve in his district, in a vain effort to unseat him. The senate, in an end run around Heydenfeldt, dismissed the Select Committee on Divorce from considering its bill further and went about the business of its passage. The bill, which recognized impotence, adultery, extreme cruelty, willful desertion or neglect, intemperance, fraud, and conviction of a felony as grounds, squeaked through the assembly, passed the senate, and was signed into law. Hostilities flared once again when antidivorce legislators drafted a repeal that passed the assembly, but it subsequently stalled, leaving Californians, at last, with a liberal divorce statute.[52]

The California conflict, standing as it does in dramatic contrast to the easy legitimation of divorce in the post-Revolutionary era, is instructive. It encapsulates two striking and closely related midcentury trends: one was the widespread acceptance of broad grounds; the other was the increasing vehemence of antidivorce sentiment. It also points us toward the future by suggesting that while the opponents of divorce were losing the legal battle, they were holding their own in the culture wars. And as the language of the Heydenfeldt report illustrates, after decades in which women went unmentioned, "the divorce question" and "the woman question" were beginning to converge.

THREE

❖ Contesting the Rules, 1850s–1870 ❖

When Elizabeth Cady Stanton addressed a rally in 1870 to protest Daniel McFarland's acquittal for the murder of his wife's lover, she characterized the verdict as an indictment against American womanhood. Abby Sage McFarland's Indiana divorce lay at the heart of Daniel McFarland's defense. When she pursued a decree there so that she might marry the writer Albert Richardson, he responded by shooting Richardson at his *New York Tribune* office. In a melodramatic finale to the affair, Abby was married to the dying Albert by Henry Ward Beecher, silver-tongued advocate of a relaxed and liberal Calvinism, who was aided by O. B. Frothingham, pastor of the Unitarian church that Richardson attended.[1]

Public interest in the affair went beyond fascination with the crime of passion to encompass Abby's divorce. The ocean of ink expended on the trial spotlighted a host of controversial issues: the validity of Abby's Indiana decree, her role in New York City "high life," divergent definitions of marital cruelty, disputed arrangements for child custody, and the willingness of two prominent clergymen to administer Christian marriage vows to a woman who, according to both the teachings of the New Testament and the laws of the State of New York, was still married. Abby, moreover, was a female Lolly, a woman who traveled on her own to an out-of-state jurisdiction to reject one husband so as to be legally free to take another.

As Stanton's interest in the case suggests, feminism was now in play in the debate over divorce. The trial, as she saw it, was nothing less than a contest pitting Daniel's traditional common law right to own and control Abby's person against Abby's moral right to leave him and remarry. As the ranking radical in the recently divided "woman movement," Stanton offered her own bold reading of a well-developed critique of marriage that had been worked out in the campaigns for married women's property rights. Invoking the movement's antebellum conflation of the bonds of matrimony with the bondage of slavery, she argued that the falsehood on which the McFarland verdict rested was the common law principle of "the Husband's right of property in the wife." In the heyday of Reconstruction, she drew on the motifs of abolitionism, comparing Abby McFarland's fate to that of Anthony Burns, the fugitive slave who had barely "tasted the sweets of liberty" when a Massachusetts court returned him to slavery. The injustices in the trial, she insisted, mirrored the injustices of slavery; the court declared Abby's divorce illegal so as to exclude her testimony because wives, like slaves, could not testify against their masters. As Elizabeth Clark has observed, for a liberal of Stanton's stamp, viewing marriage as a form of slavery led to equating divorce with emancipation.[2]

Although Stanton's critique of marriage fell within the ideological grooves of antebellum feminism, her legal solution did not. "I think divorce at the will of the parties is not only right," she averred, "but that it is a sin against nature, the family, [and] the state for man or woman to live together in the marriage relation in continual antagonism, indifference, [and] disgust."[3] Her support for easy divorce was unequivocal. Not only did she sweep away fault as a requirement for ending a marriage but she imbued divorce with strongly positive connotations by projecting it as a tool for forging truer unions and by substituting honor for the opprobrium attached to divorced women.

Few of Stanton's colleagues, however, supported an end to statutory fault, and it was by no means clear to them that Abby McFarland Richardson was a suitable test case for prodivorce arguments. When Isabel Beecher Hooker addressed the McFarland-Richardson affair in the pages of the *Revolution*, she defended her brother Henry's decision to marry Abby and Albert but could not align herself with Stanton. In a letter to a friend, she confessed uneasiness with Stanton's characterization of "easy divorce as a blessing and a necessity." Hooker's renowned sibling Harriet Beecher Stowe was much less tentative. She was aghast that women could be so self-destructive as to support easy divorce, a legal innovation she denounced as "a liberty which, once granted, would always tell against the weaker sex."[4]

Despite their divisions over divorce, feminists changed the terms of public discourse with their critiques of marriage. Whether they relied on difference or equality in making their claims, they unveiled the challenge posed when wives acted as adversaries against their husbands. Embedded in invocations of women's moral purity—a typical appeal to difference—were elements of an autonomy that could transfigure marriage in ways legislators had refused to imagine. What would happen if wives applied themselves as morally independent decision makers to the indignities and liabilities of marriage? Or, to pose the question in the rational framework of equality that feminists also invoked, what would happen if they assumed the role of subjects with civil rights rather than remaining objects of legislative concern?[5] Because the McFarland trial embraced precisely these kinds of questions, the conduct of Abby McFarland provided a litmus test for the consequences of investing wives with an individualist ethos.

The warning Daniel McFarland's counsel issued against diverting wives from their self-sacrificing roles is especially telling. Responding to assertions that Daniel had been guilty of a misconduct that provided the basis for Abby's Indiana divorce (she sued on the ground of cruelty), his counsel protested that it was not so. But in an impassioned appeal to the propriety of the double standard, he also insisted that even if there were some misconduct on the part of his client, it would not have excused Abby from her responsibility for the success of the marriage. "Woman never better fulfills her office as a guardian angel than when she is watching over an erring and failing husband," he declared, citing the principle of womanly sacrifice. It is at the moment when her husband first begins to fail that her influence must be exerted "and her arms be wound round him in a tighter and more affectionate embrace to win him back."[6]

What had influenced Abby to reject the role of a loving wife and assume the role of an erring husband? The defense counsel attributed her fall to the influence of an increasingly selfish, libidinous, and irreligious society whose divergent laws for divorce legitimated adultery. In his version of the story, the unraveling of her marriage began when Daniel sent her to summer in the White Mountains, where she met the dissolute people who would contribute to her ruin. "In an evil hour she fell into the society of these Fourierites, agrarians, Mormons, spiritualists, free-lovers, amidst whom every Jack has some other person to gill." Before long she met Albert Richardson, and adultery followed. All that remained to ratify their transgression was a clandestine divorce "in that paradise of adulterers, Indiana."[7]

It is through the voice of Daniel McFarland's defense counsel that we can appreciate how the threat posed by utopian socialism and heterodox religious sects intersected the dialogue on divorce. He linked Abby's moral corruption to communitarian experiments based on Fourierism and anti-Calvinist developments like Spiritualism, both of which subverted traditional gender norms. In the picture he drew to rouse the jurors' sympathy, not only was capitalism at risk but also marriage was under siege by unorthodox religious sects. As the pervasive postbellum anxiety about Mormonism illustrates, deviation from Protestant marriage norms by unorthodox denominations loomed as a terrible threat to the stability of the social order. Post-1850 conflict over divorce, then, did not divide neatly between enlightened rationalists and religious zealots. Nonetheless, the opponents of divorce, sensing that it represented the treacherous seductions of secularism and modernity, equated its proliferation with a crisis in faith. Small wonder that Scripture began to play an ever greater role in the opposition to divorce.

Henry Ward Beecher, who would himself face charges of adultery with a parishioner, provides additional clues to the new tenor of the debate. He was forced to defend himself against the accusation that by marrying Abby McFarland to Albert Richardson, he was "leading lust to her triumph over Religion." He believed, he insisted in a retreat to the terms of the New Testament, that she was justified in divorcing a physically abusive husband who "had also furnished that one extreme ground of divorce which justifies it in the eyes of all Christendom." He did not, in other words, defend the dissolution on the basis of cruelty alone. For the sake of her children, he claimed, she had refrained from naming adultery in her petition.[8]

A number of inferences can be drawn from the vilification of Beecher in the press for performing the ceremony. It suggests first that the shock waves of divorce reached far beyond the doctrinal concerns of institutionalized Christianity to grip the attention of the public at large; second, that the growing recognition of the gendered dimensions of each and every divorce suit raised the debate to an entirely new register; and third, that despite the long-completed shift in social authority from religion to law, a quasi-fundamentalist Christianity animated the opposition to divorce. We turn now to the new emphasis on gender, the revitalized reliance on Scripture, and the omnipresent interplay between family and polity. These were the common threads in the great divorce debate of the 1850s and 1860s.

MARRIAGE, DIVORCE,
AND THE "SEXUAL CONTRACT"

We begin with the "woman movement" of the 1850s and 1860s in order
to probe its exposure of the gendered dimensions of divorce and to map
out the diverse positions it developed regarding divorce. Contemporaries
tended to depict the movement as adding a single voice to public discourse; but despite the essentialist term "woman" that its participants
employed, it was anything but monolithic. Probably no reform divided
the movement as sharply as that of making divorce easier. Although inci-
sive critiques of marriage had shaped the legal agenda of the movement
from its very inception, they were focused initially on married women's
property rights, a goal with widespread legislative and public support.
In assailing the legal disabilities of women under coverture, antebellum
feminists were appropriating and reconfiguring an impulse toward legal
reform that was already under way.

   After the war, the agenda of the movement shifted, in part, to woman
suffrage, a goal routinely defended on the basis of a woman's need to
protect familial interests. It is not hard to understand why many
woman's rights advocates gravitated to suffrage more readily than to
divorce reform. Marriage was not only the principal foundation for the
cultivation of family sentiment and the wellspring of Victorian sensibilities; it was an agency of capital formation that organized the responsibilities of husbands and wives. The American Woman Suffrage Association spoke definitively for the promarriage, profamily wing of
suffragism when it passed a resolution stipulating that "the ballot for
woman means stability for the marriage relations, stability for the home,
and stability for our republican form of government." Liberal divorce,
by contrast, which was already written into numerous statute books but
was ripe for feminist intervention, was far more problematic. Nonetheless, once feminists began their debate over divorce they bared the fric-
tions of gender that legislators avoided and obscured. Regardless of
where they stood on "the divorce question," feminists addressed the way
it intersected "the woman question" by balancing the indignities and liabilities of women's marital subordination against the sanctity and security of lifelong monogamy.[9]

   Members of the movement never failed to address those indignities and
liabilities. As Françoise Basch has noted, their persistent attack on the
husband's right of property in his wife's body struck at the core of patriarchal ideology. To borrow Carole Pateman's compelling term, it pivoted

on the subjection of women in the sexual contract, which both masked and sustained their exclusion from the political privileges of the social contract. The connections between the two contracts were exposed and exploited in the movement's earliest pamphlet literature. Antebellum feminists argued that giving husbands property rights in their wives' bodies and reproductive capacities made marriage the key institution through which men established their authority over women.[10]

But the broad consensus for the proposition that marital subjection lay at the root of women's political exclusion did not extend to a solution for the problems posed by marriage. Whereas Stanton's attack on the McFarland verdict countered a man's sex-right over his wife with her concomitant right to disavow the marriage, most women were reluctant to undermine the institution that sustained and defined them. Moreover, because support for easy divorce left them open to the label of "free loveism," an epithet deployed by critics to evoke "the dominion of lecherous appetite," it constituted dangerous terrain.[11]

When a group of feminist men declared divorce extraneous to the movement's legal agenda because most divorce statutes were gender-neutral, the stigma of free love was also on their minds. With the wariness that typically accompanied discussions of divorce, Wendell Phillips warned that the permanence of marriage is "a question which admits of so many theories, physiological and religious, and what is technically called 'free love,' that it is large enough for a movement of its own." He urged the members of the women's movement to stay focused by keeping their law-oriented, egalitarian goals separate from dangerously open-ended issues like divorce.[12]

But neither Elizabeth Cady Stanton nor Susan B. Anthony was content to stay within the tidy discursive boundaries of legal egalitarianism as Phillips defined them. Rather, they were determined to use tangible inequities—like those that resulted from dividing marital property and providing for child custody—as vehicles for discussing the untidy problem of male power. Anthony responded to Phillips's efforts to close off the divorce debate by arguing that marriage in all its manifestations was central to any woman's rights platform precisely because women had never had a say in its lopsided terms. She designated marriage as a "compact" drafted by men in which "tyrant law and lust reign supreme" and "ready obedience alone befit[s]" women. By evoking the collective male roots of "the compact," Anthony shifted the conceptualization of marriage, transforming it from a contract entered into voluntarily by a man and a woman into a covenant constructed by men to disempower

women. Women had only two options: "accept marriage as man prof-
fers it, or not at all."[13]

Prodivorce feminists argued that because the vast majority of women
accepted marriage "as man proffered it" and marriage determined the
shape of their lives, the terms on which it could be dissolved mattered
more to women than to men. Marriage was the touchstone of a woman's
identity, argued Stanton, but not of a man's, for he was caught up in
worldly concerns through his participation in business and politics. "But
to a woman, marriage is all and everything; her sole object in life—that
for which she is educated—the subject of all her sleeping and her wak-
ing dreams." Stanton, however, had inadvertently put her finger on the
difficulty of incorporating divorce into a woman's rights agenda. It is
precisely because marriage served many woman's rights women as an
emblem of gender identity that they were sorely divided over its dissolution. That emblematic role accounts for their readiness to denounce
marriage as it was in the harshest possible terms while simultaneously
idealizing its most extravagant possibilities.[14]

Both the underlying ambivalence of women toward marriage and
their profound anxiety regarding its dissolution were embodied in the
much-publicized stand taken by Elizabeth Packard, a Spiritualist wife
incarcerated in an Illinois insane asylum at the behest of her husband, a
Presbyterian minister. Her countercultural theology drove him to a modern, institutional solution that was available, it seems, to other husbands
whose wives had demonstrated their emotional instability through acts
of marital insubordination. Though putting a wife in an asylum was not
precisely the same as putting a wife asunder, it smacked of the unilateral
marital power invested in husbands by Mosaic law. According to the
Banner of Light, the leading Spiritualist organ of the day, the Reverend
Theophilus Packard institutionalized his wife because she had refused to
recant religious views that he deemed detrimental to both his children
and his church. Once released, however, Elizabeth Packard embarked on
a new and independent life in which she managed to make a living and
provide a home for her children; she went on to publish several narratives about her experience, to lecture extensively in public, and to lobby
successfully for a statute protecting mental patients against involuntary
confinements. But she refused to divorce the husband who had devised
so Kafkaesque a solution for her acts of insubordination.[15]

Elizabeth Packard's rejection of divorce as a viable remedy for an
already-broken marriage only begins to suggest the deep antipathy of
women toward eroding matrimonial boundaries. In contrast to most

Spiritualists, who viewed divorce in a positive light, she had reservations in part on religious grounds. Divorce, she insisted, in a familiar endorsement of a wife's moral responsibility for the marriage, "violates the conscience of a conscientious Christian wife." A second objection was civic in nature. In an allusion that surely resonated with Americans after the Civil War, she compared divorce to a "secession principle" that undermines our union "and saps the very foundation of our social and civil obligations." But the third objection was for her the strongest: though she openly professed that she needed legal protection from the husband designated by law to protect her, she opposed divorce because of the prestige and respectability she attached to being married. "What we want," she insisted, giving voice to the centrality of marriage in a middle-class woman's identity, "is protection in the union, not . . . a divorce from it."[16]

Packard was sending a decidedly mixed message: protection still encoded both financial support and social status, even as the character of her protector was savagely denounced. But there could be no mistaking the naturalness she attributed to a woman's dependence, which she construed as fixed and naturally opposed to the independence of men. This woman who had battled her minister-husband over the meaning of Scripture in his own Bible classes, who had contravened his instructions on child-rearing—who had contested every vestige of his marital authority—continued to frame marriage in terms that naturalized coverture; man, she avowed, was ideally a woman's "natural protector."[17]

Packard was not alone in advocating lifelong monogamy for those facing a de facto separation. Women who favored improved legal protection in marriage as opposed to easy divorce were prepared to support the principle of celibate separation. If the parties cannot live together in peace, urged Antoinette Brown, "let them not be divorced, but let them each be content to live alone for the good of society." Feminist opposition to remarriage, a powerful marker of sexual impurity, could be adamant. As Elizabeth Oakes Smith wrote in a letter to the *New York Tribune,* "Society should not suffer itself to be outraged by the sight of vagrant husbands and wives going about in search of new partners." A woman, she insisted in a broadly disseminated woman's rights tract pointedly titled *The Sanctity of Marriage,* should say yes to marriage only after very careful consideration; having done so, she should ever after hold her peace.[18]

In these arguments against divorce, the pragmatic benefits of sexual purity were never far from the surface. Fearing that women would be disadvantaged by the opportunity to remarry, antidivorce feminists like

Smith emphasized the capacity of lifelong monogamy both to constrain the sexual urges of men and to protect women as they aged and lost their physical attractiveness. Why empower men further in their relations with women? It was a question raised by a dissident reader of the *Lily*, the temperance and woman's rights journal that lobbied regularly for intemperance as a ground; easy divorce, she warned, would result in women being sought out in the prime of their youth, "dallied with, and then cast off."[19]

Such anxieties were shaped by the same sexual double standard that Victorian feminists were committed to eradicating. Yet they could not evade the discursive power of its terms, much less the palpable effects of its authority. Rather than criticizing them for casting their fears about divorce into the self-defeating patterns of classic melodrama—pitting an immutable feminine vulnerability against the raw power of masculine sexuality—we should remember the hard economic basis of that plot line. When we consider the celebration of female domesticity that attended the growth and diffusion of a market economy, together with the ow wages and uncertainty of employment confronting mid-nineteenth-century women, it is not hard to understand their fears.[20] Marriage, the best available prospect for a decent and secure family life, was an anchor in the crosscurrents of social change.

Given the dubious consequences attributed to divorce, the stoicism with which women endured marital separations was invested with heroic dimensions. Representing Caroline Norton as a courageous English sister who persevered in the absence of a formal remedy, *Godey's Lady's Book* celebrated "the fortitude with which she has borne her cruel fate." If a woman's marital suffering was to be elevated to feminine heroism, it could not be rewarded with an opportunity to take a new partner. In the religious universe of antidivorce sentiment, remarriage was a far greater sin than the act of divorce. As one essayist put it, though a wife surely has the right "to withdraw from the man who imbrutes her," not even a legal divorce justified her remarriage.[21]

While antidivorce feminists like Antoinette Brown and Elizabeth Oakes Smith aimed to shore up marriage so as to control the behavior of men, prodivorce feminists like Elizabeth Cady Stanton and Ernestine Rose envisioned divorce as a tool for liberating women. Stanton, who was convinced that the maxim of marital indissolubility could not work to restrain men, because it was the mechanism through which they established their authority over women, denounced separations for forcing women "into celibate isolation."[22] It is worth underscoring, however, that divergent feminist views on divorce emanated from a common vision of the masculine origins of marital problems. Those problems were rooted, according to one prong of the analysis these feminists shared, in the unjust provisions of an androcentric legal system, and they were played out, according to a second prong of that analysis, in the sexual transgressions of men. Significantly, both pro- and antidivorce sides attributed the failings of marriage as a social institution to the lust of inadequately controlled men, which was fueled by their legal and economic power as husbands.

Male behavior, then, was all-important. A woman who had a good husband might "glide easily along under his protection"; but thanks to the law, a woman with a bad husband could find herself "totally destitute, condemned to hopeless poverty and servitude, with an ungrateful tyrant for a master." While part of the solution lay in reforming the law, the balance lay in reforming men, a project close to the hearts of antidivorce feminists. The drive to make men better husbands was spelled out at the Woman's Rights Convention at Albany in 1854 in the following resolve: "That the family by men as well as women should be held more sacred than all other institutions; that it may not, without sin, be abandoned or neglected by fathers any more than by mothers for the sake of any of the institutions devised by men."[23]

Prodivorce feminists focused instead on expanding the legal rights of divorcing women. They used the economic inequality of women as contracting marital partners to campaign for nondiscretionary alimony statutes and exploited the exalted status of women as mothers to demand women's custody rights. Yet not only were their drives for statutory reforms sporadic and unsuccessful, but they could not agree among themselves on appropriate grounds. Even intemperance, a popular emblem of male depravity, was contested by those adhering to Jesus' words. Since Christ did not teach that "the mere civil contract" cannot be dissolved, Amelia Bloomer alleged in a desperate effort to get past the shoals of Scripture, "we can institute this just cause for divorce without violating the teaching of Christ." Clarina Howard Nichols, however, herself divorced, favored a simple law prohibiting the consumption of alcohol as the way to restrain "man's carnal and wicked appetites."[24]

The influence of temperance on the discourse of divorce was double-edged. It was embodied in the pervasive iconography of the drunkard's wife, a figure who endowed the woman-as-victim theme with a new level of pathos. The persistence with which temperance stories assumed the naturalness of female dependence, a crucial component in the melodramatic narrative, suggests the degree to which they subverted a rights-oriented agenda. But the drive to make intemperance a legal ground also ignited a controversy over a wife's responsibility for her alcoholic spouse, which produced a whole spectrum of responses. Thus a popular Methodist journal counseled that it was better for the wife to bear with the drunkard just as if he were a badly deformed person, remaining secure in the knowledge that her true rewards would come in the next world. Faithful women "love on and hope on, to the end, and when God puts his seal on their foreheads, we know what heroism their lives contained."[25] Prodivorce feminists, however, debunked the redemptive qualities of the alcoholic's wife, thereby undercutting the guardian-angel image of wifehood.

Prodivorce temperance advocates provided a powerful antidote for the self-sacrificing sentiments of domestic ideology by placing the drunkard beyond wifely redemption. Every day, alleged the *Lily,* "bruised and lacerated wives" refuse to prosecute their brutal husbands out of an entirely false sense of love and duty. Stanton, ever the advocate of women's enlightened self-interest, believed that the deep sense of obligation engendered by a dangerously sentimental culture and a relentlessly sexist theology contributed mightily to women's self-destructiveness. "Alas," she lamented, "how many excellent women have dragged out a weary existence in such a partnership, from mistaken ideas of duty— from a false sense of religious obligation?" It was a theme that rose to a crescendo after the Civil War in the Stanton-Anthony wing of the movement, and made its way into the *Revolution.* Recounting ten years of life as a drunkard's wife, Eleanor Kirk asserted that no man as lowly as her husband could ever be redeemed by the love of a good wife.[26]

But although women like Kirk rejected moral suasion in favor of utilitarian legal reforms, their legal agenda was both radicalized and undermined by their deep ambivalence toward law. An unqualified voluntarism in the way they approached the marriage contract, a deep-seated antinomianism regarding the formalism of the legal system, and a profound suspicion of its masculinist orientation brought them ever closer to the free-love position. Because the law of men lay at the heart of what they were assaulting in marriage, legal resolutions were suspect. Marriage laws, according to the *Una,* were simply the bureaucratic components of "a system of organized selfishness controlled by force."[27] Marriage as it was smacked of coercion and depravity; marriage as it might be, as it should be, not only endowed erotic desire with a redemptive spiritual significance but also situated love beyond the aegis of the state.

For those who espoused the position that a love found to be false should not be sustained in a formal union, fault-based grounds were entirely inadequate. At the same time, their assertions that the state through its rigid divorce laws should not impose its weak and warped morality on the sacred union of a man and a woman were only a step away from the position that a truly sacred union required no legal sanctions of any kind.

No less radical was the familiar evangelical insistence on women's moral agency when it was used to deconstruct the male corporatism of marriage. The idea of becoming a vehicle of God's will did not necessarily translate into contesting a husband's will; yet feminists deployed their conceptualizations of a distinctly female moral self both to differentiate a woman's legal and civil identity from that of her husband and to legitimate her moral rejection of virtually any facet of his behavior. An ad for the *Revolution* trumpeted its resistance to the idea that woman "was made for man—his toy, drudge, subject, or even mere companion," while it proclaimed "the higher truth, that like man, she was created by God for INDIVIDUAL MORAL RESPONSIBILITY." No laws or Bibles or edicts, proclaimed Stanton, always underscoring difference as she evoked equality, "can make a noble virtuous woman regard man as her head so long as he is governed by animal appetite rather than moral principle." Even if a woman's "highest and holiest mission was that of wife and mother," asserted Esther Haines, her individual moral agency meant that it did not bind her for life to a hollow and unloving union.[28]

Clearly, nineteenth-century responses to divorce were diverse. Despite their shared concerns about marriage, feminists took stances that ran the gamut from upholding its indissolubility to placing it beyond the aegis of the state. When we sift and weigh the full spectrum of responses, we can see that the spacious sense of female autonomy that nourished support for divorce was offset by the daunting vulnerability women felt at the prospect of eroding its safeguards. Viewed in the context of this ambiguous feminist legacy, Stanton's championship of Abby McFarland's sexual autonomy (which she framed as moral autonomy) against the traditional sex-right of Daniel McFarland moved the discourse to a new plane. Whatever the legal basis of the McFarlands' respective guilt or innocence, the unilateral decision of Abby McFarland to end an unsatisfactory union and marry a man who fulfilled her definition of true love was enough to win Stanton's support. Her refusal to judge Abby McFarland's marital autonomy as an impudent transgression of gender boundaries was a prelude to her support of Victoria Woodhull. While many suffragists viewed Stanton's position with discomfort and even apprehension, the opponents of divorce read it as proof of the "Free-Love tendencies and sympathies of the Woman-Suffrage party" and thus as a symptom of national crisis.[29]

INFIDELS AND CHRISTIANS

In the wake of the Civil War, women and men devoted themselves to renewing the bonds of family that began with conjugal affection. The rising tide of divorce, generated in part by the war itself, compromised the postwar effort to shore up family ties. Moral tensions that had been temporarily overshadowed by the war came once again to public attention, and the prominence of lurid divorce stories dramatized the fragility of family cohesion. As whole systems of belief—indeed, competing worldviews—were appended to the divorce question, the broadening compass of the argument made verbal accommodation difficult. Divorce was being condemned now with a messianic fervor that flowed from the church leadership of a cosmopolitan northeastern elite and spread nationwide. The polarizing effects of this highly visible antidivorce campaign were immediately apparent. Postbellum moralists flattened any discursive nuances left over from the prewar debate into an out-and-out war for the soul of the nation. We turn now to this war, which left its imprint all over the Victorian landscape.

In 1866, Connecticut clergyman Henry Loomis evoked precisely this sense of moral and political combat when he characterized the divorce debate as a contest between worldviews. The "infidel or socialist" view, he claimed in a strikingly reductive description of his opponents, grounded the continuance of a marriage on the pure pleasure of the parties and therefore supported divorce without restraints. The Christian view, in contrast, assessed marriage as a divine institution that provided the foundation for civil society. There could be no denying, then, that opposition to divorce was the logical corollary of an authentically Christian viewpoint. And because marriage and government were inextricably intertwined, divorce was, for the true Christian, akin to a revolution. Evidence that the nation's separation from England had nourished infidel impulses, he noted, was borne out by the radical climate of the Revolutionary era. Now responsible Christians of the nineteenth century were reversing dangerous Enlightenment impulses, and the "infidel theory of the state" that was so popular at the time of the Revolution was at last giving way to a respect for "divine authority."[30]

The conflict between personal autonomy and the authority of God—
or between infidels and Christians, as Loomis would have it—was a leit-
motif in the great divorce debate. The infidels Loomis denounced
belonged to a long and meandering stream of Anglo-American radicalism that ran from the Enlightenment anticlericalism of a Tom Paine
through the utopian socialism of a Robert Owen to the self-styled anar-
chism of a Josiah Warren. In conflating his infidels with socialists,
Loomis was acknowledging the extent to which nineteenth-century radicals incorporated marital reform into their plans for the reorganization
of society. Owen, for example, who viewed the selfishness of the nuclear
family as the bane of civilization, had devoted his experiment at New
Harmony to making the family "productive of individual felicity and
public benefit." For utopian socialists, the evils of men owning women
were not so much a symptom of male depravity as an immediate consequence of the evils of private property.[31] Loomis, accordingly, read the
war over divorce as a battle between socialism and capitalism.

Although his remarks faithfully reflect the growing sense among
mainstream Protestant clergymen (Congregationalists, Methodists, Bap-
tists, Presbyterians, and Episcopalians) that the contest over divorce was
a holy war, he was overly optimistic regarding a resurgent belief in divine
authority. Growing ministerial emphasis on social reforms had thrust
religion into the maelstrom of secular politics at the expense of its most
transcendent concerns. The worldly and instrumental moralism of Victorian Protestantism, which was in fact exemplified by men like Loomis,
ate away at the notion of God's awesome omnipotence. The Arminian
rejection of predestination, which made its way into various Protestant
denominations, opposed Calvinism's most powerful tenet. The effects
were gradual but irreversible. As the prospect of eternal damnation
dimmed, in the minds of evangelicals the battle for the nation's political
future began to assume precedence over the problem of the individual's
eternal fate.[32] Furthermore, Transcendentalism's spacious embrace of
nature and Spiritualism's soaring confidence in progress suggest the
degree to which unorthodox Christians were rejecting divine authority,
the very concept that gave credence to scriptural constraints on divorce.
The infidel theory Loomis condemned received its most ardent expression in the voices of nontraditional Christians.

Few voices were more ardent than that of Andrew Jackson Davis, the
leading philosopher of Spiritualism, which rejected the existence of hell
altogether. Spiritualism was the kind of movement against which Loomis

was assembling his forces. Although it is properly identified by its devotion to spirit communication, it was a significant and highly accessible offshoot of Transcendentalism, drawing many of its adherents from already liberalized Christian sects. Unitarians and Quakers were attracted to Spiritualism, and Universalists, who started from the position that all people will be saved, constituted the primary core of its earliest adherents. A loosely organized movement without official doctrine or centralized leadership, it was congenial to the concept of liberal divorce and even free love because it valorized individualism and was sanguine about human nature. Though Davis did not speak for all Spiritualists with regard to marriage and divorce, he represented the temperament of a movement that had rejected divine authority.[33]

Like Loomis, Davis also formulated the divorce question as a battle of competing ideologies whose outcome would reshape both the moral and political contours of the nation. A war, he declared, although bloodless, was about to be fought. But whereas Loomis foregrounded the role of marriage in anchoring the stability of the state, Davis used the state in its revolutionary form to justify marital dissolutions. In the course of privileging radical politics over biblical injunctions, he insisted that what he called "the covenant of 1777 . . . is sacred still as the testament of a new-born savior." Davis transposed the terms of the opposition from infidels versus Christians to liberators versus tyrants. As a result of the Revolution, America was uniquely positioned to show the world how to eradicate tyranny not only in government but also in relations between the sexes. As for Scripture, it was fruitless to ponder its "orphic ambiguity." Fornication, the single cause of divorce that Jesus sanctioned when he was questioned by the Pharisees, was "too circumscribed to cover the needs of this century" and "too superficial . . . to touch the foundations of human liberty."[34]

Davis, who described true conjugality as "ties of the highest and holiest affections," anticipated that his Harmonial Philosophy would ultimately overcome the barbarism engendered by men owning women and replace it with an egalitarian union of "soul with soul for ever." His doctrine of affinities, one sardonic critic noted, was a precept he eagerly put into practice by finding his own affinity for a woman who was already married and providing the catalyst for her divorce. Davis, however, viewed divorce as a remedy to be employed only until society reached the harmonial plane, at which point enlightened conjugal unions would last from this world into the next. Until that time, no-fault divorce rules should prevail so long as they made adequate provision for children, a

problem that he believed could be alleviated by a Fourierist social organization. Coloring liberal divorce in vividly bright hues that matched the
boundless optimism of his worldview, he depicted it as a temporary stage
in human progress whose upward course was determined by the inherent goodness of both men and women. Divorces were simply "good steps
to better things."[35]

Davis's open-ended, optimistic, no-fault approach flew in the face of
the prevailing divorce paradigm, which had long linked fault to sin.
Although sin had given way to a more contractual conception of fault,
fault still imposed discrete limits on marital dissolutions and supplied
causal explanations for them. But Davis acknowledged that at the center of his no-fault formulation was the highly contested issue of setting
the legitimate limits of personal desire. "How far," he asked, shifting the
site of authority from God to the state, "is the individual entitled to his
personal liberty without the inference [sic] of the state?" For Davis, the
answer, in accord with the principle of individual sovereignty, was as far
as possible.[36]

Because Davis sanctioned experimentation in the search for the perfect partner, a theme that echoed Tom Paine's defense of divorce in the
Revolutionary era, his was a controversial solution. It suggests how a
movement like Spiritualism, with its libertarian credo of individual sovereignty and its devotion to equality between the sexes, contributed to
the vexed and complex nature of the divorce debate. It also suggests how
the divorce debate, in turn, became something of a Pandora's box.
Because ultraists of diverse stripes construed marriage as a prototype for
other hierarchical relationships, the far-ranging consequences of easy
divorce loomed large. Posing questions about marital boundaries invited
questions about other boundaries, thus destabilizing broadly held
assumptions about the nature of power in the social order. At bottom,
it was the intensifying focus on gender that ignited the wider discourse.
It was the prospect of restructuring the "natural" relationships between
women and men that rendered divorce so profoundly controversial.

Proposals from the advocates of liberal divorce and free love for
restructuring marriage exposed the "unnatural" character of marital
indissolubility and provided polarizing reference points for the great
divorce debate. Liberal divorce, of course, was not synonymous with free
love; for that matter, the mid-nineteenth-century "free lovers" themselves
hardly were the adherents of sexual promiscuity painted by conservatives. What separated free-love advocates from divorce reformers was
their disdain for law. As Ann Braude has noted, the men and women who

identified themselves as free-love advocates supported noncoercive unions based on mutual desire with or without legal sanctions. They viewed excessive sex in general as a hazard to health and longevity, and they denounced coercive sex in marriage in particular as the cruel consequence of a despotic legal system. In the process of critiquing legal marriage, however, they significantly modified the standards for chastity. Chastity was to be measured by the wholehearted affection and genuine volition of the parties as opposed to their formal legal status: formal law, as they saw it, was the essence of the problem. Indeed, the conviction that unjust laws had turned marriage into "a huge Bastille of spiritual tyranny" constituted the very foundation of free-love ideology.[37]

Although the proponents of liberal divorce and free love developed remarkably similar arguments, they pursued them to sharply divergent conclusions. Whereas free-love advocates renounced the authority of law over relations between the sexes, divorce reformers evinced a great esteem for the formalities of marriage, as evidenced by their concern with legitimating remarriage. Although the differences in their respective idioms were not always razor-sharp, they were politically significant. Free love, according to its critics, was the archetypal Victorian radicalism, the essence of erotic desire loosed from the controls of both church and state.[38] And yet because a deep reverence for marriage was the line conservatives used to mark off respectable moderates from wild-eyed radicals, they were eager to draw it as unambiguously as possible. Better to lump the advocates of liberal divorce and their no-fault agenda together with ultraist free lovers than to muddy the field with distinctions and particularities. Better to represent the issues as a battle between fixed and antithetical ideologies than as a broad spectrum of shifting positions.

For conservatives, then, the divorce question boiled down to a contest between Christians (those favoring the single ground of adultery, or perhaps adultery and desertion) and infidels (feminists, Fourierites, Mormons, Spiritualists, Perfectionists, socialists, anarchists, free lovers, liberal divorce reformers, and various other foes of the Christian position). That these moral conservatives were themselves a loose and changing coalition riddled with ambiguities is best demonstrated by the antidivorce stance of Horace Greeley—who, although he dabbled from time to time in ultraist reforms, denounced divorce as individualism run amok.

The reductiveness with which Greeley waged his war against divorce in the columns of his *New York Tribune* exemplifies the contemporary penchant for collapsing distinct divorce positions. The hostilities began in 1852 when Henry James, Sr., supported liberal divorce and opposed free love in a *Tribune* review of a free-love tract. Greeley then printed a series of James's responses to the *New York Observer*, a Presbyterian organ that critiqued James's liberal prodivorce stand, along with letters from Stephen Pearl Andrews, an anarchist proponent of free love. The second round of hostilities was played out almost a decade later in a heated exchange between Greeley and Robert Dale Owen, onetime collaborator of Frances Wright and son of Robert Owen. The point here is that although James, Andrews, and Owen each represented different positions, they provided a monolithic foil for Greeley's support of indissoluble marriage. When Greeley stopped printing Andrews's letters, which he regarded as "offensive to public decency," he devoted the full force of his opposition to James. Yet since he saw divorce as the slippery slope to free love, he was still responding implicitly to Andrews.[39]

Andrews's stance was in many ways a mirror image of Greeley's. He was similarly unwilling to acknowledge any intermediate positions. As far as he was concerned, there was no middle ground "upon which a man of sense can permanently stand, between Absolutism, Blind Faith, and Implicit Obedience to authority, on the one hand, and on the other, 'the Sovereignty of the Individual.'" He too cast the debate as a mortal struggle: but from his perspective, it was between the despotic forces of authoritarianism as represented by the state and the liberating impulses of individualism operating in a cooperative social order. Andrews, moreover, directed his conception of the sovereign self to the "emancipation and self-ownership" of women. Human beings, he insisted, if given a cooperative social environment, do not need to be taken care of, a proposition he believed applied to women equally with men. In the present organization of society, however, marriage was "the slaughter-house of the female sex."[40]

Gender was as prominent on the other side of the debate. To provide an antidote for such stinging allegations, the proponents of traditional marriage turned to melancholy narratives about sexual danger. Anecdotal evidence, a flexible tool for all participants in the discourse, could bring a flesh-and-blood dimension to timeworn pleas for the sanctity of Christian marriage. Thus Horace Greeley reprinted a newspaper account of a young female millworker who, after her lover reneged on his promise to marry her, gave birth to an out-of-wedlock child. The child died soon after, leaving its mother in solitary despair. Bereft of both child and lover and unable to face the barbs of public opinion, the young woman wasted away, becoming in the end "a raving maniac." The story functioned on a variety of levels. From the perspective of class, it pointed up the unregulated sexuality that flourished when women left home to become wage workers and fathers and husbands failed to protect them. From the perspective of gender, it was a cautionary tale about sexual difference aimed at alerting women to the pitfalls of blurring marital boundaries. If such boundaries mattered, they mattered doubly to women, and to impair them was to impair the protection that Christianity afforded women. Woman "has risen with Christian marriage," intoned John Ellis in a similar vein. "It has been her strongest defense, her greatest safeguard."[41]

Divorce critics often directed their overwrought stories to an explicitly female audience. In a stunning reversal of late-eighteenth-century admonitions against the snares of reading fiction, a Congregationalist minister went so far as to suggest that women should shape their lives to conform to successful fiction. If life was to have a happy ending, it should follow the narrative lines of a satisfying novel; hero and heroine must be united for life. No one would read the first chapter if they knew the last ended with a divorce. External influences that deterred women from dedicating themselves to marriage, such as the emergent job opportunities of the post–Civil War economy, threatened the happy ending. Theodore Woolsey, president of Yale and founder of the New England movement to restrict divorce, denounced the woman who reacted to her husband's objections to her nightly outings by moving out and securing a job in another town.[42]

Antidivorce anecdotes collectively illustrate how the universalist terms of an earlier discourse were giving way to specific references to both class and gender. The free-floating anxiety that had attended the prospect of increasing numbers of divorces was targeted now at particular social groups. Tales of marital transgressions by middle-class wives, whose chastity was the benchmark of the society's moral well-being, were offered up as proof of the divorce crisis. These seemingly decent wives, the great moral bulwark between "the wicked fashionable and the wicked poor," averred George Ellington, were succumbing to a sensualism in the culture unleashed by artifacts like Hiram Powers's nude statue, *The Greek Slave*, and by the insidious spread of photography.[43] When the wives of clerks, storekeepers, mechanics, and young professionals no longer counted marriage as sacred, the whole society was imperiled.

Class antagonism almost rivaled sexual antagonism in the postbellum assault on divorce. The gravest social threat posed by easy divorce, according to Theodore Woolsey, came from its impact on the unchurched working classes, who were rejecting the admonitions of concerned clergymen as invidious attempts at social coercion. Woolsey's worries about the inefficacy of traditional forms of Protestant uplift in the face of working-class recalcitrance illuminate the class-based concerns of the antidivorce movement. Changes in American society from the time of the Revolution, he believed, had affected the divorce process, which in turn was weakening the moral fabric of society despite the best efforts of ministers and their church communities.

Woolsey's critique of divorce was a jeremiad lamenting the fall of lifelong monogamy, which he celebrated as the bedrock of Christian morality. He attributed the slow national declension to the diminished sway of an eastern elite. Burgeoning cities, "with their peculiar vices and their low population," a westward migration that had yielded eastern land "to an inferior class of society," and the presence of foreigners "trained up under the loose laws of divorce" were great transformations that all militated against the old communal constraints. The real culprit, however, in his narrative of deterioration was the law itself, which he was convinced was undermining even the most aggressive efforts at religious reformation. Unable to mediate between the strict rules of the New Testament and the loose laws of divorce, the working classes, he asserted, would always gravitate toward the law for their "sensual gratification." How could they know or care about self-control, given the laxity of divorce? "Free rum, free Sundays, free suffrage, free divorce, and the like are their watchwords." But if law was the culprit here, it was the remedy as well. Stricter grounds could work to reform that group which is "most demoralized and corrupted by the fatal facility of existing laws." Otherwise, he observed dryly, "people will begin to wish that the lower classes, among whom now divorce principally prevails, could come under Catholic influence."[44]

That law was the focal point of this battle between Christians and infidels is not without some irony. Not only do Woolsey's remarks grudgingly concede the doctrinal coherence of Catholicism, but they openly acknowledge the superior weight of the law over the influence of Protestant moralism. Although he painted working-class litigants as barbarians at the gate, he believed in the capacity of the law to turn them back. The possibility of significantly reversing divorce, then, was not lost to conservative clergymen, but they were compelled to address the law on its own terms. Grounds needed to be narrowed and omnibus clauses obliterated in order to return the concept of fault to its punitive roots.

As one might expect, migratory divorce served as the primary target for Christian moralists' critiques of divorce. The constant effort on the part of litigants to take refuge under the legislation of another state, Woolsey noted, was facilitated by "dishonest lawyers . . . ready enough to aid their clients in very questionable ways." These included trumping up charges, acting in interstate divorce networks, and even creating fraudulent decrees. As a result, the divorce process was subverting the moral framework it was supposed to support. Truth was falling by the wayside, and the concept of fault was being emptied of its moral connotations. Divorce, as Henry Loomis pointed out, did not originate as "a release from virtuous restraint, but [as] an exemplary punishment of a conjugal crime." But with the fantasies that passed for truth nowadays, there was neither crime nor punishment, and the rhetoric of blame was rendered moot by greedy and dishonest attorneys.[45]

The endemic American hostility toward lawyers was focused here on the excesses of divorce lawyers. One needed only to look at their sumptuous offices to see "how these vultures prosper in their illegal traffic." In New York, according to George Ellington, lawyers employed detectives to discover marital infidelities whether or not they existed. In Ohio, another critic observed, there is a class of divorce lawyers "who live absolutely by perjury and fraud." Even the Catholic clergy, who boasted erroneously that their parishioners were immune to the corruptions of divorce law, exhorted lawyers to do something to wipe out the stigma that shoddy divorce practices brought on the legal profession.[46]

At the heart of the Christian assault on divorce was the conviction that as the divorce process became looser and securing a decree became easier, the attendant shame would evaporate. Critics railed against the vulgar influence of divorce stories, which they believed encouraged spouses to end their marriages for the pettiest of offenses. With newspapers recounting the lurid details of failed marriages, and with men repeating those details in taverns and women taking them up at their sociables, each divorce sowed the seeds for others and blunted the impress of shame. In some ways, conflicting attitudes toward shame reveal as much about the fault lines in the divorce debate as any other facet of the argument. Whereas "infidels" like Stanton endeavored to take shame out of divorce, "Christians" like Woolsey dedicated themselves to putting it back in.[47]

But the agenda of these righteous postbellum Christians went beyond suffusing divorce with shame; their attacks evolved into an organized legal crusade to roll back liberal statutes. It gathered its first adherents in a drive by Yale theologians to eradicate Connecticut's omnibus clause, subsequently addressed divorce in other New England states, and went on as the New England Divorce Reform League to become the leading edge of a national movement championing a uniform national divorce code. Theodore Woolsey, who took his cues from Henry Loomis, became the president of the League. Its executive secretary, the Congregationalist minister Samuel Dike, took the League to national prominence by mixing clergymen, lawyers, and social scientists together on the executive board. Dike then convinced Congress to fund a national survey on marriage and divorce, which was compiled by a similarly concerned reformer, Carroll D. Wright.[48]

Scripture, however, continued to animate the efforts of antidivorce crusaders. Dike was a Congregationalist minister who lost his church when he refused to remarry a divorced parishioner. That the loss of his congregation provided the inspiration for his reform activities exemplifies the theological underpinnings of the movement. The most glaring problem was improper grounds, but as denominational conferences focused increasingly on the issue of remarriage, it became apparent that officiating at the remarriage of the guilty spouse posed a second and no-less-knotty problem. The gulf between Scripture and civil law was dramatized in the dilemma neo-orthodox ministers like Dike faced on being asked to remarry a congregant whose grounds for divorce did not align with their theology.[49]

The debate over remarriage also served to expose the theological weaknesses in the antidivorce crusade. Catholic clergy, who forged a loose coalition with Protestant crusaders, were quick to point out that the remarriage problem was rooted in the historic willingness of Protestants to desacramentalize marriage and place it under the aegis of the civil law. Protestants, therefore, had no basis for declaring marriage a divine institution that could not be altered by the sweep of popular opinion. Unless they were willing to return to the Catholic fold, which was the true repository of indissoluble marriage, they could hope only to slow down the advance of the false principle they had admitted into their theology in the first place. Protestants, of course, were hardly prepared to return to indissoluble marriage as defined by the Council of Trent, the principal agency of the Counter-Reformation, much less heed the advice of Catholic clergymen. Most would probably agree with the Congregationalist minister who declared that there "is Scylla on one hand, and Charybdis on the other; and the Savior put his finger on just the meridian line that guides us between them."[50]

Casting the principal players as infidels versus Christians may have provided the opponents of divorce with icons that resonated more powerfully than the prodivorce icons of liberators versus tyrants. But institutional Protestantism, by its own admission, did not have the spiritual resources to rebuff the infidels at the gate. Its most formidable obstacle was neither the sexual antagonism of suffragist women nor the uncontrollable libidos of working-class men: it was the corrosive power of the law itself. This power was so irresistible, as clergymen conceded, that it had succeeded in pressuring the church's own ministers to relax their ban on the remarriage of improperly divorced persons. Instead of the church reforming the law, the law was contaminating the church.

To be sure, the religious right of the postbellum era was hardly without moral influence, and it deployed its narrowly scriptural conception of Christian marriage to invest divorce with shame well into the twentieth century. It made inroads on the law as well: in some states omnibus clauses were wiped out while in others residency requirements were tightened. But given organized Protestantism's diluted spirituality and watered-down sense of its own authority, religion could not provide an effective counterforce either to the compelling power of the law or to the sheer determination of the litigants. Indeed, if we construe Christian marriage as strictly as these dedicated opponents of divorce did, we have to conclude that the Catholic press was prescient when it characterized the rush of Protestant antidivorce activity as a mere "breakwater in the way of the current . . . sweeping away the Christian institution of marriage."[51]

NEW YORK AND INDIANA

We turn now from the trope of Christians versus infidels, with its allusions to Scripture, to that of New York versus Indiana, with its appeals to law. We are, in fact, addressing the same debate from a new perspective by using its most evocative jurisdictional symbols.

When Heinrich Schliemann, the renowned European businessman-archaeologist, divorced his Russian wife, Catherine, in 1860, he did so in the thriving railroad town of Indianapolis. An occasional resident of New York, he opted for a jurisdiction where his New York counsel anticipated he would encounter the fewest obstacles. Though an Indiana decree was not the only path a resourceful, divorce-seeking New Yorker might have chosen, it was by far the most visible one. Yet according to the notes in Schliemann's diary, a New York City attorney named Peter Cook could have provided him with a decree in a matter of weeks.

Not only did Schliemann seek out a more respectable legal route than the one Cook proffered, which probably would have entailed accusing his wife of adultery and then paying witnesses to perjure themselves, but he wanted a decree that could withstand a transatlantic challenge from Catherine.[52]

In Indiana, a jurisdiction that was notoriously casual in requiring proof of residency, he went to greater lengths than most migratory plaintiffs. He purchased a house that he had no intention of living in and put down a $350 deposit toward a $12,000 share in a starch factory that he had no intention of purchasing. Two obliging witnesses came to court and attested to his determination to live and do business in the state. Schliemann, moreover, lobbied state legislators to present amendments to a pending divorce bill that might have blocked his own suit entirely. These amendments, he confessed, "were offered by 24 democrats whom I had succeeded to get on my side through second hand."[53] As it turned out, the amendments he sought were unnecessary. With his decree in hand, he went abroad to remarry, an option he apparently was contemplating when he initiated the divorce, and went on to excavate ancient Troy, a dig that secured his reputation for posterity. Although he forfeited his deposit on the starch factory, since he made no further payments, the contract was declared null and void. Once Catherine Schliemann's transatlantic counterclaims regarding his "bigamy" were put to rest, he sold his Indiana house.[54]

Heinrich Schliemann, who could afford to try out one of the first sleeping cars as he traveled west, was part of a procession of litigants whose quest to end a marriage began with boarding a train in an eastern depot and ended with dissembling in a "western" courtroom. Abby McFarland was another. That migration, which left its mark on the American imagination, is a vital piece of the story of American divorce. William Dean Howells would seize on the westward trek for a divorce as a way of juxtaposing the raw depravity of the West against the stuffy decadence of the East. Once railroad lines linked eastern cities to what is now the Midwest, New York and Indiana became perfect emblems of a strict and loose jurisdiction, respectively.[55]

In the spring of 1860, the contrast between the two jurisdictions was played out in the pages of Horace Greeley's *Tribune*. Responding to a New York legislative effort to liberalize grounds, Greeley attacked the easy divorce laws of Indiana, reducing them to a simple foil for the strict standards of New York. In the process of using Indiana's moral depravity to construct New York's legal righteousness, Greeley casually attributed the loose divorce laws in that "paradise of free-lovers" to Robert Dale Owen, the Indiana politician and jurist whose statutory revisions, he insisted, permitted "men or women to get unmarried nearly at pleasure."[56] Greeley sensed that the rapid evolution of divorce—from a dissolution granted for a conjugal sin through the concept of breach of contract to the emergence of virtually no-fault rules—had culminated in the divorce process of Indiana, where an omnibus clause permitted divorce at the discretion of the judiciary and residence requirements were ignored.

Robert Dale Owen, who described himself in 1860 as retired from public life, could not let Greeley's allegations pass. He was stung by the way Greeley attached the free-love epithet to Indiana and hastened to add that he was responsible only for adding habitual drunkenness to Indiana's already liberal grounds. Creating a wholesome counterimage to Greeley's portrait of depravity, he celebrated Indiana divorce law for serving the needs of "plain, hardy, industrious farmers" who cared about the well-being of their wives and worried about the chastity of their daughters. It was only in a strict jurisdiction like New York, he observed, that free love prevailed, because of the difficulty of securing a decree.[57]

In subsequent issues of the *Tribune,* Greeley and Owen delineated the terms of their disagreement. With regard to Scripture, Greeley, of course, was on solid ground. Embracing a literal reading of Christ's words in the New Testament, he could boast that the state of New York conformed perfectly to the teachings of Christ by permitting the single ground of adultery. Owen's reading of the New Testament was unavoidably tendentious. He responded to the challenge of Scripture by relying on a historical Jesus whose efforts to reform Mosaic law represented an early stage in the evolution of divorce. Views of divorce, he reasoned, evolved over time, and just as the divorce law of the Jews was unsatisfactory for Jesus' time, so too was the divorce law of Jesus unsatisfactory for modern times.[58]

But the essence of the rift between Greeley and Owen turned on their diverging views of marriage: nowhere was the ideological gulf between enforcing self-control and marital obligations on the one hand and embracing romantic love and personal gratification on the other more evident. We can discern echoes from their argument in the acrimonious divorce debates of our own time. Greeley, who saw the primary purpose of marriage as procreation, underscored the necessity for spouses to repress their egotism for the needs and wants of their children. He translated divorce into an act of consummate selfishness. Owen, while acknowledging the importance of parenting, emphasized the benefits and pleasures of an affectionate union. Love, ventured the old utopian socialist in response to the charge of egotism, "crushes man's innate selfishness, and teaches him the great lesson that the best happiness is to be found in care for another."[59]

The Greeley-Owen exchanges also provide us with a striking example of the deep interplay between the familial and the political. Divorce always carried political freight. The confrontation in the *Tribune* exemplifies how the act of marital dissolution could encode tensions in the political community by telescoping them into opposing positions on divorce. Turning to the ever-popular example of Rome in his denunciation of Indiana, Greeley connected its geopolitical decline to its lax divorce code; and he blithely attributed the economic supremacy of Europe over Asia to its adherence to Christian marriage. Greeley's message was clear. Easy divorce generated political and economic decline; lifelong monogamy provided the foundations for capitalist enterprise and augured both a prosperous and orderly America. In keeping with his radical past, Owen looked to the Revolution. He responded by appealing to the historic right of Americans to dissolve the bonds of a tyrannical union as affirmed in the Declaration of Independence. That he evoked the script for national independence suggests its continued resonance in a transformed landscape. His words were familiar. He conceded that "no light or transient cause" should provide the basis for ending a marriage; but "when a long train of abuses and immoralities" renders a marriage "destructive of its holy ends," it was a right and even a duty "to dissolve the bands which connect the ill-mated members together."[60] Owen's message was no less clear. The right of divorce, like the brief for independence, was a sacred national legacy.

PART TWO

❖ Mediations ❖

Divorce evolved as a legal institution in the county courts of the nineteenth century, where litigants and their attorneys framed their complaints to fit the statutory guidelines. In these local courts of original jurisdiction, the steady press of petitioners with their woeful tales of betrayal opened up spaces between the letter of the law and its adjudication. Thanks to the ready acquiescence of hard-pressed judges, day-to-day proceedings in the courts looked quite different from the abstract model of fault divorce. That is not to say that the notion of fault was jettisoned. Yet the vast majority of cases were ex parte proceedings in which the defendant failed to appear, a circumstance that contributed to a liberal construction of the statutes. The widespread acceptance of casual and even dubious evidence of "the fault," moreover, seems light years away from the acrimonious debates over appropriate grounds.

As this observation suggests, county court records reveal a stunning dissonance between public discourse and local practice, thereby illustrating the advantage we gain by changing perspectives. What follows is dramatically different in both tone and substance from the preceding section. Once we turn to the county courts, we are no longer in the realm of Christians and infidels: we are in the midst of ordinary women and men.

In this section, titled "Mediations," I purposely revisit New York and Indiana to look at them now not as emblems of ideological conflict but as two legally divergent jurisdictions whose county courts were *compelled to adjudicate similar kinds of marital problems. My primary goal in exchanging the wide-angle lens I used in "Rules" for the close-up lens I employ here is less to track law at the ground level, although that figures in my account, than to see law through the eyes of the women and men who came to court for a remedy. Inasmuch as statutory grounds forced the account of a failed marriage into a formal legal narrative, this is no easy task. Useful as my camera metaphor is, with its emphasis on changing lenses, it implies a simple transparency that is not at all the case. Yet court documents not only contain concrete evidence about the remedial dimensions of divorce but also—with some cautious reading between the lines—provide extraordinary glimpses into the intimate details of a failed marriage. So vivid are the details in some suits that placing myself in the presence of the duped husbands and abandoned wives who poured out their rage against their duplicitous partners makes me feel more voyeur than scholar.*

Despite the striking gulf between "Rules" and "Mediations" that emanates from my reliance on very different kinds of sources, my under-lying concerns remain the same. The problem of female autonomy underpins both sections and, indeed, this entire book; so too does the gendered nature of divorce. I begin here with the very same question that initiated my discussion of the rules: what did it mean to invest women with the right to end a marriage? I ask also what it meant to invest men with that right. In the ensuing two chapters, then, I pursue the gendered nature of divorce by viewing it alternately as a woman's remedy and a man's remedy. Some benefits in the divorce process, including the right to tell one's story, accrued to women and men alike. But while women as a group confronted the uneven economic consequences of ending an economically unequal partnership, men struggled against the weakening of their authority in the face of novel forms of subversion.

One thing is clear: home emerges in these suits as a highly unstable site in which both husbands and wives assumed the sway of masculine authority but battled over its limits. The persistence of that assumption in a society that celebrated companionate marriage may be the other face of women's economic dependency. Nonetheless, the evidence from these suits of the widespread recognition by women as well as men of male marital authority riddles the concept of companionate marriage with a host of qualifications. The reader will also do well to keep the problem-atic nature of romantic love and the romantic self in mind, not only because it surfaces in litigants' depictions of their marriages but also because it will reappear in "Representations."

❖ When Women Go to Court ❖

When Thomas Jefferson assessed the pros and cons of legalizing divorce prior to the American Revolution, he came out firmly on the side of divorce. Among the misgivings he had, however, was the problem of dividing marital assets; and while he was convinced that a man could get a wife at any age, he was concerned that a woman beyond a certain age would be unable to find a new partner. Yet he envisioned divorce as a woman's remedy. A husband, he noted, had "many ways of rendering his domestic affairs agreeable, by Command or desertion," whereas a wife was "confined & subject." That he assessed divorce as a woman's remedy while representing a client intent on blocking a wife's separate maintenance is not without some irony. Still, in a world where the repudiation of a spouse had been a husband's prerogative, he believed that the freedom to divorce would restore "to women their natural right of equality."[1]

The tensions implicit in Jefferson's remarks provide a fitting introduction for considering divorce as a woman's remedy. As we have seen, almost a century after Jefferson imagined the benefits of divorce for women, woman's rights advocates were divided over its impact. Since one way to evaluate the impact of divorce on women's lives lies in women's legal experiences as plaintiffs, we turn now to the courts.[2]

Historians have long been intrigued by the social ramifications of divorce. Beginning with Nancy Cott's pathbreaking studies of eighteenth-century Massachusetts, their research has tended to connect the presence of female divorce plaintiffs to women's enhanced status and rising expectations in the context of a more companionate model of marriage. Historical views of companionate marriage, in turn, have developed from a broader body of scholarship that has mapped out the antipatriarchal dimensions of a new emphasis on the reciprocal affection of the marital partners. To be sure, historians in general and historians of women in particular have underscored the continuing asymmetry of marriage, and some scholars have argued that the perpetuation of patriarchy was updated and masked by modern legal devices like divorce.[3] Nonetheless, it is from historians' compelling reconstructions of a more affective marital ideal, especially for the middle classes, that divorce has emerged as a focal point of gender realignment.

Despite the proliferation of scholarship, there has been little work on the implementation of divorce in the county courts during the formative stages of its legal development. Because we know very little about divorce in this period at the level where it touched the most lives, we know very little about it as a woman's remedy. This chapter seeks to begin to fill the void by exploring "the relief in the premises" that divorce afforded women in the county courts of New York and Indiana. That simple phrase, used regularly in equity petitions to denote the full redress or benefit available to the petitioner at the hands of the court, sums up the primary focus here. But although our principal concern is with tangible results like alimony and property settlements that can be traced through court records, we shall also wrestle with what the legal experiences of female plaintiffs reveal about the intersections of divorce and gender.

NEW YORK AND INDIANA REVISITED

As with other areas of nineteenth-century law, the choice of an appropriate jurisdiction in which to explore divorce constitutes a vexing problem. Why turn, then, to New York and Indiana, the ultrastrict and ultraliberal objects of midcentury controversy? For one thing, the emblematic role of the two states as it was played out in the pages of Horace Greeley's *Tribune* and in the imagery of the great divorce debate presents an irresistible invitation to take a closer look. Furthermore, since there is no representative state, much less a representative county, any patterns shared by two highly disparate jurisdictions were likely to be repeated elsewhere. Taking up divorces in Indiana and New York for the years between 1815 and 1870, we focus on rural and urban counties, respectively, within those states. Monroe County, Indiana, was settled in the long course of westward migration and remained a farming community through 1870 and after. It is a jurisdiction that provides us with glimpses of the problems of farm labor and introduces us to contests over agricultural property. New York County, which encompasses Manhattan and derived much of its burgeoning population from successive waves of immigration, is the quintessential urban jurisdiction. Synonymous with phenomenal growth, it had already begun to manifest a thriving manufacturing and service economy as early as the 1820s. The goal here is not so much to contrast these socially distinctive and legally disparate jurisdictions as to explore what they had in common—a possibility, of course, that Horace Greeley and Robert Dale Owen refused to address.

The Monroe County evidence consists of 112 divorce actions, all those documented in the county from its inception in 1818 through 1870. They are recorded in Civil Order Books and Final Records, which sometimes overlap chronologically and cover the same cases. Evidence ranges from several densely detailed accounts of marital conflict to concise descriptions of the complaint and decree. Court papers were inaccessible. Yet these records invariably include both alimony claims and awards and have the advantage of covering other legal actions by divorce litigants. They also record unsuccessful and suspended divorce actions. They are supplemented with a small sampling of post-1850 divorces from Marion County, Indiana, which encompasses Indianapolis.[4]

The New York County evidence consists of judgment rolls from 230 matrimonial actions (189 divorces, 21 separations, 17 annulments, and 3 actions related to former matrimonials) adjudicated between 1787 and 1870 in the Supreme Court of New York County, the jurisdictional equivalent of the Monroe County Circuit Court. Judgment rolls include original complaints, answers, proofs of service, depositions, examinations of witnesses, reports of the master in chancery or supreme court referee, decrees, exhibits of letters, financial statements, and even some daguerreotypes, all of which are literally rolled together and tied with red ribbons, faded now almost to a dull brown. Some of these rolls are extraordinarily rich in detail, a veritable compendium of the idiosyncrasies and particularities of marital hopes and disappointments, but they, too, are uneven. One can never be certain from the rolls alone about subsequent alimony awards, but when used in conjunction with "An Index to Matrimonials," where subsequent awards should appear, they become more reliable. New York records do not include unsuccessful divorce actions; these were sealed and remain unindexed.[5]

The importance of women as plaintiffs, however, is graphically illustrated by the change in New York City complaints. As midcentury divorce plaintiffs began to rely increasingly on printed forms, the forms invariably identified the plaintiff as "she" and obliged the attorney to cross out the s for a male plaintiff. The new forms were an accurate reflection of the preponderance of women seeking to dissolve their unions. Of the 189 complete divorces surveyed in New York County, 116 of the complainants were women. The single ground of adultery may have encouraged women to serve as complainants in those divorces that were collusive; when both partners agreed to put an end to their union, it was surely less onerous for the husband to be found guilty of adultery than the wife. But jurisdictions with broader grounds had a preponderance of female complainants as well. Quantitative assessments of the percentage of female plaintiffs nationwide tell us that by the time of the Gilded Age, divorce was very much a woman's remedy, at least in a formal legal sense.[6] Through a close reading of the divorce documents from two states, we will consider qualitatively what it was that divorce remedied and what kind of remedy it was.

THE RECOVERY OF PROPERTY

In December of 1849, Mary Warren, an Indiana farmwife, appeared before the Circuit Court of Monroe County to petition for a divorce from her husband Eli. Her petition alleged that Eli "has for a long time treated your petitioner with great cruelty and inhumanity by beating her frequently so as to render it unsafe and improper for her to live with him," that he was often intoxicated, and that he persistently expressed his intention to abandon her and finally did so, leaving her with two minor children and no means of support. Having established two statutory grounds for divorce—cruelty and willful desertion—and having compounded them with an allegation of intemperance, the petition went on to outline her contributions to the marriage. The couple's first homestead, a small North Carolina farm they worked together, was a wedding present from her father, and they subsequently sold it and used the proceeds to purchase eighty acres in Indiana. During their marriage her brother gave her $500 "for her own use" and $50 each to their two children and Eli, which Eli then used to purchase another 160 acres in Monroe County. The balance of Mary Warren's long and finely detailed petition spelled out Eli's maneuvers in anticipation of her claim to alimony. It documented his sale of the bulk of their Indiana property, including some thirty acres of standing corn, seven large hogs, six head of cattle, and twenty sheep, all of which were conveyed without Mary's permission to a Robert Cowden for the sum of $600. Cowden, meanwhile, was gathering up the corn, seizing the livestock, and had begun ejectment proceedings against Mary.[7]

As a document in social history, Mary Warren's petition exemplifies the tantalizing elusiveness of divorce sources, often obscuring as much as it reveals. Its opening allegations were formulaic, casting Mary in the role of the innocent and pathetic victim with Eli as the cruel and intemperate villain. In a state renowned for its liberality in granting divorces, other petitioners cited the same grounds in almost the very same words. Legal rules and conventions converted all the complexities in a disintegrating marriage into a simple little tale; and uncontested as most divorces were, it tended to be a lopsided tale. As Lawrence Stone has put it, given the persistence of both collusion and deception, divorce is like "a fig leaf covering the very different reality of human behavior."[8]

Perhaps we cannot trust Mary Warren and her attorney as tellers of the tale, but we can rely on the tale itself to illuminate the legal process. Although documents in the Warren divorce reduce the intimate travails of their marriage to the spare, impersonal terms of statutory fault, they tell us a great deal about the formal dissolution of a marriage. In particular, they provide a solid starting point for exploring both the extent and limits of divorce as a woman's remedy. Moreover, embedded in the meticulous compilation of bequests, conveyances, and transactions that distinguish this divorce there are traces of the gritty resilience with which Mary Warren played out her role as plaintiff.

Mary Warren pressed her claims in two distinct actions. On her first round in court, she won a divorce, custody of her children, a temporary injunction restraining Cowden from removing the corn, and $300 still owed to Eli, a lump-sum settlement construed by the court as her alimony. She returned to court at planting time in the following spring. After the injunction against Cowden dissolved and he rejected her offer to farm the acreage jointly, she sued for her dower in the land. Cowden had ejected her from thirteen acres she had laboriously plowed and was proceeding to plant it himself. The court appointed three commissioners to set out one-third of the land by metes and bounds as her dower, as if her husband were dead. By combining her suit for divorce with a suit for dower, Mary Warren succeeded in getting the court to award her a portion of the family farm. To be sure, Eli Warren walked away from the marriage with at least $300, but the divorce provided Mary with the remaining assets.[9] The speed with which she moved, her knowledge and resourcefulness, the skill of her attorney, the liberality of Indiana grounds, and the acquiescence of the court were all factors in her ability to get some relief, which was surely better than no relief at all.

The scope of her relief, however, merits closer consideration. The divorce itself did not free her from the abuses of an intemperate husband, if indeed she had been suffering such abuses; rather Eli provided her with that remedy by deserting her, at which point she came to court. By dissolving the marriage and providing Mary with the status of a single woman along with whatever Eli had left behind, the decree brought legal and economic order to the chaos created by Eli's desertion. The pattern of his desertion—one more move in a life of moves—was multiplied many times over in nineteenth-century divorce records. Like countless other families, the Warrens migrated westward into states carved out of the Northwest Territory; their North Carolina origins reflected the steady flow of southerners into southern Indiana and beyond. We have no way of knowing if the move contributed to the strains in their marriage, but geographic mobility was a common motif in nineteenth-century divorces if only because it touched so much of the population. At the time of the Warren divorce in 1850, innumerable husbands were mysteriously disappearing in a quest for gold in California.[10] Divorce, then, was bound to have profound economic consequences for a woman deserted by her husband and removed from her family of origin.

Mary was fortunate to have been the recipient of gifts from her family and to have had some assets remaining in the marriage. While her financial remedy hinged on Eli's unilateral sale of their acreage and, of course, the court's ready acceptance of his guilt and her innocence, it also relied on her contribution to their intermingled assets, which her petition had attempted to clothe with the legitimacy of a married woman's separate estate. Still, in Mary's case, in which the farm was a small family venture, the desertion of her husband deprived her of the only adult male worker in the enterprise, leaving her with a workforce made up of herself, her fourteen-year-old daughter, and her eight-year-old son. Her labor problem helps explain both her attempt to enlist Cowden in a partnership and the intensity with which she pursued the acreage plowed with her own labor. In the rural West (now the Midwest) of the antebellum era, where farming depended on the labor of both husband and wife, plowing and other types of heavy fieldwork were considered male tasks. Thus Eli's desertion not only doubled Mary's workload but also relegated her to doing a man's work.[11]

Mary Hermann, a German immigrant who petitioned for a divorce in the Supreme Court of New York County in 1857, can serve as Mary Warren's wage-earning urban counterpart. A participant in the great transatlantic migrations of the nineteenth century, she too relied on the divorce process as a remedy for desertion. New York, of course, was a very different sort of jurisdiction. It offered the single ground of adultery, which rendered a divorce more difficult; by midcentury its court calendars were choked with cases; and the legal costs of a divorce suit were high. Nonetheless, litigants and their attorneys managed to thread their way through statutory obstacles with considerable ingenuity. Just as the Indiana judiciary accepted casual evidence of desertion—Eli Warren had not been absent for more than a few weeks, and Mary's attorney was the only witness to attest to his willful desertion—so too did the New York judiciary accept dubious if not fraudulent evidence of adultery, especially through its reliance either on prostitutes or on what one editorial referred to as "hotel evidence."[12] Hotel evidence, however, was often unnecessary. By the time a divorce reached the courts, the defendant was often living with a paramour in a long-term relationship and raising a second family, a practice suggesting the tenacity of customary forms of self-divorce and pseudo-remarriage.

Mary Hermann's petition alleged that in July of 1854, she returned from shopping to discover that her husband Nicholas had deserted her, taking with him all their articles of value, including $1,681 she brought to her marriage. Inasmuch as she was a domestic in service, and in view of the exactness with which the sum was listed, there is a good chance that it represented her life savings rather than a dowry furnished by her family (as a round number might have suggested). The couple lived in an apartment owned by her employer, whose son, Frederick Geisenhower, served as her attorney and translated the court proceedings from English into German for her. Her petition identified Nicholas Hermann as a wine and liquor dealer "doing a good business," and it requested alimony for Mary.[13]

Not only was a request for alimony uncommon in both Indiana and New York petitions, but Nicholas Hermann was among the few defendants to be served with a summons in person, file an answer, and make an appearance in court. Nicholas had not gone far. Geisenhower, who located him in the city several months after his disappearance, found him living with a Maria Steinbinger in a relationship where they "passed as man and wife." By the time the divorce reached the court, there were two children from the second union. Although Maria Steinbinger admitted on cross-examination that she was aware Nicholas had "a wife living," she asserted she was his "second wife." In view of her own tenuous position, her assertion was undoubtedly self-serving, an effort to legitimate her two children and her union with Nicholas; but even the complaint delineating the union as an adulterous one identified her as Maria or Mary Hermann, thereby subtly acknowledging her status and ironically confusing her identity with that of the plaintiff.[14]

Nicholas's answer acknowledged his second family and at least technically his adultery, but it averred that his "first wife" was perfectly capable of supporting herself while he earned just enough to support himself comfortably. More important, it provided a justification for his replacing the first Mary with the second by alleging that his first wife "was physically incompetent to enter into and consumate [sic] the marriage contract," and it carried a threat to force Mary to subject herself to a medical examination if she persisted in the suit.[15] In the end Geisenhower agreed to drop the request for alimony in return for the withdrawal of the assertion that the marriage was not consummated. That Nicholas failed to pursue an annulment does not necessarily controvert his allegation that the marriage was unconsummated but could reflect any or all of the following: his disinclination to use the legal process, his reluctance to pay its costs, and his determination to keep Mary's money.

Mary Hermann won a divorce, her court costs, and her $1,681. In accordance with the New York statute, Nicholas, as the adulterous spouse, was prohibited from remarrying so long as Mary was alive. Mary's remedy, then, consisted in the return of her legal status as a single woman, the control over her own earnings, the recovery of what must have been the most valuable part of her personal property (the $1,681), and perhaps some satisfaction from the punitive prohibition against the remarriage of her guilty spouse. Yet the prohibition, which held serious legal consequences for the partners in the second union, probably had little immediate impact on their lives. They apparently considered themselves very much married; and should they have desired to formalize their union, it would not have been difficult to accomplish.[16]

Although we cannot ascertain the validity of Nicholas's counterclaim, which may have been nothing more than an adept legal ploy to defeat Mary's claim to alimony, we can surely imagine the psychic costs of the suit to Mary. Her inability to speak English and her legal and economic reliance on her employer highlight the insularity of her world. She lived in a German-speaking community that could rival any eighteenth-century New England village for its lack of privacy and penchant for gossip. In immigrant communities in particular and in the urban setting in general, everyone seemed to know and care about everyone else's business. Consider Mary Hermann's humiliation as the focal point of a proceeding that not only discussed her physical capacity to engage in sexual intercourse but even alluded to her bad breath, reputed to be so unpleasant "that no man could live with her."[17]

The Warren and Hermann divorces illustrate the ambiguities in assessing the relief afforded by a decree. When we examine who was being freed from whom, it seems more appropriate to link the two cases to a new independence for men from the bonds of matrimony than to a new autonomy for women. From the perspective of the plaintiffs, moreover, divorce seems to represent declining standards in marriage more than rising expectations, at least with respect to the husband's obligation of support. As for the concept of companionate marriage, it may provide a way of accounting for the actions of the two defendants or even for doctrinal innovations in divorce law, but it obscures the role played by the two women as plaintiffs. Their husbands were long gone. Although the role played by female plaintiffs may reflect collusion in some cases, there is considerable evidence to indicate that the desertion of women by men was widespread.[18] Indeed, the prevalence of desertion and the growing facility with which it was accomplished as the century unfolded suggest that it became ever easier for *men* to find new companions and start all over again. Thus as men created de facto divorces, women sought out legal ones.

The economic configurations in the two cases demonstrate one of three broad remedial patterns available to female plaintiffs. On a spectrum of possible legal results ranging from provisions for alimony through the wife's right to recoup her property and earnings to a simple decree dissolving the marriage, they fall squarely in the middle. Although divorce left the two women with more financial security than most female plaintiffs, it was a security based on their own efforts and contributions rather than on legally enforced provisions from their husbands. It was, nonetheless, an important form of legal relief.

The foregoing pattern is an important one. The women who fared best in the divorce process were those who already enjoyed some financial independence outside of marriage. We can speculate that such women comprised a disproportionately large percentage of plaintiffs out of the entire number of women in failed marriages precisely because they had the most to gain from the legal process and the most to lose from inertia. Female plaintiffs with their own trades, businesses, and property used the courts to good advantage to assert their financial autonomy by reacquiring single status. Martha Codd's divorce decree, for instance, ruled that the destitute Matthew Codd was to deliver over to her all her deeds, patents, agreements, and leases. Such a remedy encompassed any property an innocent wife brought to or acquired during her marriage, even though, as in both the Warren and Hermann divorces, it was not set apart in a trust or antenuptial agreement and was intermingled with the husband's assets.[19]

The concept of separate marital property was firmly entrenched in the Anglo-American legal tradition, far more so than that of a community of goods; and despite the constraints of coverture, the notion that the gifts or dowry a wife brought to the marriage should return to her with its dissolution enjoyed broad currency even in advance of the married women's property acts. The concept extended, moreover, to the simplest household utensils. In their petitions wives consistently catalogued the specific items they contributed to the marriage, such as a single article of furniture, a family Bible, a bedstead and bedding, or small amounts of cash.

Though a husband was entitled by law to reduce his wife's personal property to his possession, nevertheless if he lost it in an unsuccessful venture—or worse, squandered it in dissipation or absconded with it— petitioners cited the loss not only in calculating assets but also as a moral indictment. Lavinia Moore contended that her husband sold off fifty dollars' worth of personal property she brought to the marriage in order to pay his whiskey bill, and the remaining property in her possession, "the result of her own labour," did not exceed fifty dollars in value. Male plaintiffs were no less attentive in documenting the absence of a wife's property. In an 1822 petition in Monroe County, Samuel Caring claimed that "he never received any property with his said wife," and the circuit court ascertained that Harriet Caring had no property except for the apparel she took with her when she abandoned Samuel.[20]

The concept of separate marital property was particularly influential when second marriages were dissolved. In an Indianapolis case in which a widow brought property to a second marriage, her new husband's efforts to bring it under his control after he had failed to provide her with "necessaries" was viewed with suspicion by the court. Sixty-year-old Sarah McConnell accused her second husband, Joseph, of failing to provide for her at a time when she became "infirm." The heart of her complaint, however, was not about Joseph's lack of support; it turned on her allegation that Joseph had tried to seize assets that had been hers while she was "sole and unmarried" and had independently filed suits for money that was due her. The defendant, her complaint insisted, who is "irresponsible and insolvent," was trying to vest her property and choses in action (in this case, the debts owed to her) in his own name. Joseph McConnell contested the divorce, arguing that it was her intent to place such notes beyond his control and "smuggle her own property" into the hands of her son John by assigning him her notes. By law, he noted, her personal property and choses in action were his; and since he had been a faithful and dutiful husband, they should come under his control. Nonetheless, Sarah was successful in enjoining him against collecting her debt judgments. The divorce was granted, all claims and notes were vested absolutely in Sarah, and Joseph was restrained from receiving, assigning, selling "or in any way meddling with said claims."[21]

ALIMONY

Alimony, which was rooted in settlements for separations made by the English ecclesiastical courts, rested on the husband's obligation to support and quite literally to nourish the wife with a stipend out of his own property; it was indistinguishable in these cases from child support. Alimony evolved in nineteenth-century American law to include a percentage of a husband's yearly wages and even lump-sum settlements. In 1852 Indiana limited alimony to a onetime, lump-sum settlement to be paid out at most over a few years. Such settlements were rarely as ample as New York alimony provisions, which at their best approximated dower. As the master in chancery put it in an early New York divorce: "I have considered it as the general rule of the Court, allowing a sum for a separate maintenance, to make it by analogy to the Right of Dower of the Wife and to her interest under the Statute of Distribution if her husband was dead intestate, subject however to alteration in the discretion of the Court according to the Circumstances of the case."[22]

Alimony, however, never enjoyed the same fundamental legitimacy as either dower or the wife's separate estate, or even the separate maintenance provisions in legal separations. It was subject always to considerations of the wife's behavior and to judicial assessments of her needs. When separation agreements gave way to divorce proceedings, wives rarely fared as well financially as they had when they were only separated. Once the marriage was officially over, the customary obligation of support lost much of its force and was further eroded by the practical difficulty of compelling support from an errant ex-husband.

In New York legal separation (a divorce from bed and board) was an alternative to divorce, and it tended to provide women with far more favorable financial terms than a complete divorce. Separated spouses often came to court following a breakdown in their own private agreements, another important way to end a marriage informally and one that was employed by well-to-do families.[23] New York women also relied on legal separations to win guarantees preventing their husbands from interfering in the management and profits of their tenements, shops, boardinghouses, schools, and wage labor.

This was true for Sabrina Anderson, an ambitious music teacher whose husband had taken off first for Ohio and then Illinois; she used the formal separation process to legitimate her right to both her own earnings and the custody of her nine-year-old daughter. Her husband Thomas, she claimed, had reappeared periodically to siphon off her earnings, but he had promised her at their last meeting in Buffalo that "he was on his way to the West" and would not trouble her again. Sabrina, according to one of her witnesses, was the "highly esteemed" soprano singer at St. Paul's Methodist Episcopal Church and was fully capable of supporting herself and her daughter from the salary the trustees paid her, together with the money she earned giving lessons. All that she needed was the assurance that there would be no interference from her wayward husband.[24]

Self-supporting women showed considerable pride in their economic independence when they came to court for formal protection against the depredations of their legal protectors. Clementine Durchsprung spelled out her ability to support herself and her six-year-old daughter in no uncertain terms. "I work for a living," she attested, "such as sewing, washing, ironing etc. I am 29," she continued, "and healthy and strong, and make a good living for myself and [my] child. In case I was taken sick, the child would be well provided for, as I have sufficient laid up for any such emergency."[25]

The formal continuation of a marriage in the midst of a de facto separation could also serve to reinforce the husband's traditional obligation of support. Emma Barron's suit demonstrates the financial possibilities for women in legal separations. She used the New York courts to secure continued support from her husband John with the stipulation that he "may not meddle" in her millinery business. At issue was a $500 loan made to Emma and secured by her allotment from John's salary as a second assistant engineer in the navy during the Civil War, an event that figured prominently in post-1860 divorces. After John cut off her allotment, her attorney located him aboard a ship blockading the North Carolina coast. Representing him as a patriot "endeavoring to suppress the rebellion against the said government," John's attorney portrayed his client as harassed and undermined in that important endeavor by the machinations of his extravagant wife. Emma, he alleged, announced to John that "she would rather be hanged" than live with him in Baltimore, and if he were truly serious about wanting to live with her, it would have to be in New York. She entered the millinery business, he argued, without John's permission, was known to the public by a name other than her husband's, and illegally claimed New York as her domicile.[26]

The referee, an official whose report virtually determined the outcomes in New York matrimonial actions, saw it otherwise. Emma and John began married life as professional actors, and he depicted the couple as perpetually on the move, barely eking out a living, and returning from time to time to live with Emma's parents in New York. In Richmond, Virginia, where Emma and John took rooms near the theater, Emma did all the housework, supplemented their income by taking in boarders, and then appeared on stage in the evening. Their only child lived less than a month. Emma successfully demonstrated that she had been the principal means of their support, and although she had already paid off $300 of the controversial loan, she needed the allotment to sustain her business, which she characterized "as yet a mere experiment." The referee estimated the stock and furniture in her store to be worth $2,000, four times her purchase price; yet he awarded Emma $400 yearly of John's $1,000 salary, noting that her health was precarious due to excessively hard work. One year later Emma was still listed under milliners in *Trow's New York City Directory* as "Mme Barronne, Modes de Paris," specializing in "French Dress Making" and offering a "Choice Assortment of Mourning Goods."[27]

Emma Barron was precisely the sort of litigant who used matrimonial litigation to good advantage, although there were obvious limits to her remedy. She could not remarry legally, and given John's history of nonsupport, it is unlikely his allotments continued for long. Nonetheless, she did indeed free herself from the constraints of a bad marriage bargain. Her motives in the action and her feelings toward her husband were summed up in a letter cited by John's attorney. She allegedly wrote to John, "Let me have your allotment, and you can go where you like, only leave me alone."[28] The circumstances of her marriage and the evidence of her dogged enterprise give us little reason to doubt the validity of the letter.

Most women, however, were not in comparable circumstances: they had neither independent sources of income nor access to a husband's wages or assets. Because financial remediation was often contingent on a timely injunction restraining the husband from selling off his assets, a husband might mask his intention to leave while he did just that. The duplicity with which husbands functioned in anticipation of divorce is a striking pattern in these records, with often devastating consequences for the wives of shopkeepers and petty tradesmen. For Lydia Catlin, whose husband owned a dry goods store in New York City, it was just such a strategy that deprived her of a financial remedy. Charles Catlin went to Boston on a Thursday and telegraphed Lydia he would be back on Tuesday. Meanwhile he instructed an employee to sell all his inventory and deposit the funds to cover a draft he had written. Lydia won a divorce, custody of their only child, and the right to apply for alimony at some future time should Charles ever reappear.[29]

Yet an injunction against the alienation of a husband's property could prove highly effective. Consider the case of Timothy Dandy, a successful Irish cordwainer who skillfully bypassed the formal divorce process for a time. After separating from his wife in New York City in 1818, he "married" Catherine Schenck in the same city in 1820. Dandy's assets included four city houses and lots as well as a thriving shoe shop, and but for his failure to support his first wife in accordance with their private separation agreement, he might have continued to live undisturbed with his second. Sophia Dandy, who had married him in Ireland when she was thirteen years old and was instrumental in the success of his shoe shop, claimed that she "was induced to agree to a final separation." A few days after the divorce complaint was filed and an injunction was issued against the alienation of his property, Timothy fled the city. When he gave Thomas Brooks, his friend and leather dealer, power of attorney, he told him he would be gone for a few years.[30] In this case his first wife had a remedy in the assets he was compelled to leave behind; the second was not so fortunate.

Whatever its limitations, alimony was enough of a threat to motivate the secret liquidation of a husband's assets. Alimony, then, could provide wives anticipating divorce with some leverage. Peter Bolenbacher responded to his wife Amelia's impending suit and demand for alimony in Maryland by placing $500 worth of real estate in trust for her use. She, in return, released her dower right in his Maryland realty and withdrew the suit. Yet the balance of the Bolenbacher case reflects the customary advantages men enjoyed in battles over alimony. Peter was not only economically independent but also willing and able to travel to secure a divorce on his own terms. He sold off the rest of his Maryland holdings and divorced Amelia in Indiana, charging her with "lewd conduct with Negroes" in Maryland. If, as his petition asserted, Amelia's Maryland suit was designed "to frighten him" into taking her back, it was not frightening enough.[31]

As the Bolenbacher case indicates, attorneys developed and streamlined strategies for divorce. Extraneous information was progressively winnowed out of the process. Complaints detailed the place, date, duration, and intensity of the wrong committed and juxtaposed the plaintiff's pathetic innocence against the defendant's callous guilt in terms satisfying the requirements of the statute. The clearer the delineation of guilt and innocence, the better the chance of success. Contesting the complaint or filing a counterclaim could endanger the entire outcome and thus could serve as a bargaining chip in financial arrangements.

The development of sophisticated divorce strategies tended to encourage negotiation in advance of litigation, but it also tended to discourage requests for alimony in those divorces that were truly adversarial. Even when ample assets were available and the husband remained within the jurisdiction of the court, a request for alimony could be hazardous. It contributed to the likelihood the divorce would be delayed, contested, or even denied. Aside from the problem of conflicting estimates of the husband's total worth, there was always the risk of retaliation that would undermine the wife's assertion of her innocence and her husband's guilt: and guilt and innocence were the legal bedrock on which fault divorce rested.

Awards of alimony might be adjusted accordingly. Matilda Langdon petitioned for divorce in Indiana and requested custody of her only child, her court costs, and alimony. She estimated her husband Samuel's assets to be worth $10,000, "most in cash," presumably because he was "running his funds out of the state." When Samuel appealed the circuit court's award of temporary alimony of $100 to be paid out in thirds at ninety-day intervals, the supreme court upheld the award. However, in a response to a separate application for permanent alimony, Samuel filed a bill of exceptions and counterclaimed Matilda's adultery. Matilda won her divorce, nonetheless, with custody of their only child and $75 yearly to be paid to the county clerk for her support until the sum of $750 was attained.[32] A reduction from the temporary award, it amounted to little more than six dollars per month. If her assessment of Samuel's total worth was accurate, it was but a small fraction of what she might have received as Samuel's widow, the formula used in the most generous New York awards. More important, it was scarcely adequate to sustain her and her child.

Most women, in both jurisdictions, received no financial relief whatsoever. Part of the problem was the poverty of many defendants whose desertion was not always willful in the precise legal sense; rather, what began as a search to earn a living in another place ended in a failure to return. Divorce, then, was often the result of the defendant's inability to support his family in a shifting, unstable economy. The range of male defendants in New York divorces included day laborers, seamen, tailors, grooms, servants, and petty criminals—the poorest and most marginal inhabitants of the city. Indiana records, although less revealing, encompass bankrupt farmers and land speculators and propertyless rural migrants.[33] The absence of formal requests for alimony in the vast majority of divorce petitions suggests there were no assets or earnings from which to allot it.

When Mary Jane Humphrey came to court in Monroe County in 1844, alleging that her husband Silas abandoned her "without any good cause whatever, with the intention of never returning to live with her again," she declared that they "accumulated no property during the time they lived together." She asked for "her bed and bedding that she received from her parents at the time of the intermarriage" and, in the time-honored, all-purpose words of a petition in equity, "such other and further relief in the premises as may comport with integrity and good conscience." The decree awarded her a divorce and her bed and bedding because they represented the available relief in the premises. Her simple petition with its traditional phrases and the court's equally simple decree constitute the most common pattern of divorce for women in both jurisdictions, except that in New York the allegation of desertion would have been compounded with adultery.[34]

OTHER FORMS OF RELIEF

Because everything in these records points to the paucity of financial provisions for women, one would expect the remedial dimensions of matrimonial actions to be found in other forms of relief. In New York cruelty was a ground for legal separation, and liberal statutes like Indiana's carried the promise of freeing the wife entirely from a physically abusive husband. As Robert Griswold has noted, state appellate courts gradually expanded definitions of cruelty to incorporate aspects of mental cruelty. Then too, the ability of women to take legal custody of their children reversed patriarchal common law assumptions. Yet none of these remedies figures prominently in the divorces surveyed. Although cruelty did serve to validate a wife's leaving her husband's domicile and thus provided a defense against his counterclaim of her desertion, as a ground it was scrutinized closely, and it was likely to be combined in petitions with allegations of desertion. Custody was rarely at issue in these divorces, because often couples were childless or their children were old enough to be on their own.[35] Although minor children routinely went to the innocent female plaintiff without a contest, custody battles could easily go the other way.

Henrietta Heine's suit pitting her and two adult children against her husband Solomon exemplifies the ferocity with which such battles were fought, as well as the risks they carried for female plaintiffs. She lost a bid for separation and for the custody of two minor sons whom Solomon had determined to send away to boarding school. Her complaint alleged that although Solomon was living apart from her, he came home from time to time to take meals and to beat her. She claimed that on one occasion he locked her up in the house and told her "he wanted her to die like a dog." Furthermore, both a son-in-law and an adult son testified that Solomon was planning to move to Texas. Solomon's answer contended that Henrietta was ignorant, unable to read or write German or English (her complaint was signed with an X), and unqualified to educate or "manage" the boys. Her physical problems, he asserted, resulted not from his cruelty to her, which he categorically denied, but from "the ordinary monthly disease to which females are ordinarily subject."

More important to this suit, which specifically tested the balance between a wife's freedom of action and her husband's expectations of obedience, was Henrietta's allocation of family assets, including her expenditures on food and clothing. Both Solomon and his adult son owned apothecary shops, and Henrietta had taken tea, herbs, flour, sulphur, and balsam from Solomon's shop and given them to their son. For Solomon the suit hinged on Henrietta's transfer of his property, an action he viewed as a conspiracy against him and contrary to a wife's obligations in the marriage contract. As he noted, he had come to the United States with only enough for a few weeks, he had worked hard, and he had used the strictest economy so that his children would become "respectable and useful members of the community." Now he was being undermined by "a combination and Confederation" of the members of his own family, including his wife, whose unilateral actions he characterized as "contrary to the Express Commands of this defendant." That her complaint was dismissed suggests the reluctance of judges to confer power on wives at the direct expense of their husbands.[36]

Jette Ball, a petitioner who sought the financial support of a legal separation to escape the battering of an authoritarian husband, was similarly unsuccessful. As in the Heine case, her acts of defiance undermined the narrative of victimization that supported allegations of cruelty. Jette Ball described a six-year-long, physically abusive marriage that was plagued by sporadic beatings even during her pregnancy, resulting in two successive stillbirths. But her responses in court did not mesh with the pathos or docility required in contemporary constructions of marital cruelty. On the contrary, her testimony gives us glimpses of the spaces carved out by wives to contest a husband's conjugal authority. In Jette's case her inflammatory words and irreverent actions, the perennial catalysts for the beatings, may have set off doubts about her ability to function as a properly cooperative helpmeet; but they seem to have given her a measure of satisfaction. As a clerk in her husband's New Rochelle tailor shop, she objected when he brought her sewing to do for his niece Paulina. "I told him," she testified, "I had sewing enough of my own to do, and that I could not be a clerk too. Then he jumped and pushed me out of the store, and gave me two slaps in my face. So I went in," she continued, "to take my hat and shawl to go to the City, and he seen that and he locked me up and beat me awful."

Though Jette's testimony bears witness to the readiness of husbands to demand obedience from their wives, it also demonstrates the determination of wives to set limits on their husbands' authority. When she discovered Michael in the basement of their house in a compromising position with niece Paulina, she responded by whacking him with her broom. But because Jette was, by her own admission, no shrinking violet, her case was weaker. A second weakness was her intermittent leaving and returning, because the pattern raised doubts about the severity of the beatings. Michael Ball "was often good to her after he beated her bad," admitted Jette's brother; and in any case, he observed in a telling reference to her economic vulnerability, she could not help but return since "she had no money to live on." Still, it is revealing that the most persistent source of her husband's flare-ups was her defiance of his commands. "So he said to me," she testified as she described complaining to him about her heavy workload, "it was sugar with coffee that he gave me before. Now he said he could . . . do as he pleased, he was the boss over me. He gave me two shillings a day to keep house . . . and said if I don't like it I should leave." In the end, he locked her out of the parlor and best bedroom, a common response on the part of thwarted husbands, until she finally departed, having been closed out of her domestic domain. Michael, a rising merchant-tailor earning $2,500 a year, convincingly argued that Jette left his bed and board without real cause or provocation. Since he demonstrated he had been willing to provide for her at the time she last deserted him, she was entitled to nothing.[37]

A WOMAN'S REMEDY?

The Ball case represents the bleakest scenario in the spectrum of possible legal results. Most women fared better than Jette Ball did, largely because their suits went unchallenged. Yet the principal form of relief that divorce afforded them was single status, and with it, the right to remarry. These were not inconsequential gains, but they need to be balanced against the fact that many women were contending with desertion. In other cases, divorce embodied the disparate consequences of dissolving an unequal partnership in which most husbands assumed, like Michael Ball, that they were the bosses. Divorce could help to restore to women "their natural right of equality," to repeat Jefferson's hopeful assessment, only if they did not need to depend on the partnership financially. Otherwise the overall costs for women could be high.

Furthermore, in a culture that increasing invested middle-class women with a powerful moral influence over their husbands, that valorized the role of women in the domestic sphere, and that indeed imbued women with an idealized autonomy in marriage, to succeed in divorce was tantamount to a more fundamental sort of failure. A true woman was expected to exert her moral influence to prevent her husband from roving—or, at the very least, to do nothing that would encourage him to cast about for a new companion. The emergent ideals of Victorian manhood were no less demanding or incongruous. Earning a living was synonymous with being a real man, and a real man was expected not only to support his wife and children but also to function as a loving companion. Still, in the course of incorporating Victorian gender roles into the legal process, divorce imposed particular burdens on female plaintiffs. A woman subjected the intimate details of her marriage to the scrutiny of an all-male judiciary, and while the text of the divorce focused on her husband's guilt, the subtext revolved around her own innocence. Surely when they balanced the value of the remedy against its psychic and economic costs, countless women opted for simpler, cheaper, extralegal alternatives. Surely they "passed" as spinsters, widows, or wives; or, as the prevalence of bigamy in these records suggests, they remarried without ever coming within the purview of the courts.

The readiness of women to come to court despite daunting emotional and financial costs, however, merits our attention. Consider the anguish of Louisa Haskin, who divorced her second husband, William, for living in open adultery with her eighteen-year-old daughter, and who heard her pregnant daughter's testimony in court. "I am living with him as his wife," the daughter alleged regarding her relationship with her stepfather, but "I am not married to him." Consider the determination of Eleanor Camp, whose husband had divorced her in Indiana, alleging her refusal to live where he chose; she responded by divorcing him in New York and used his second marriage and his new family as evidence of his adultery.[38] Since no alimony was awarded and there are no references to property in the judgment roll, we can speculate that the attribution of desertion carried a stigma with which she refused to live.

The willingness of women to sue for a formal delineation of their marital status is a measure of the value they attached to legal divorce. It reflects a quest for identity, order, and respectability generated by the penetration of state law into areas of family life once regulated by religious and communal norms. Given the option of a legal resolution of their status, women displayed a remarkable propensity to use it. But though we may see women's agency in the courts as a symptom of their independence, it tells us little about their independence in marriage. The most boldly self-assertive impulses by the women in these records—the occasional request to reassume a maiden name or the more common effort to assert clear control over property and wages—were directed toward their expectations outside of marriage.

As for women's expectations within marriage, these divorces suggest that wives, like their husbands, were predisposed to accept the principle of a husband's marital authority, which was often the other face of economic protection and which obscured women's contributions to the family economy. The real bone of contention in legal contests over a husband's authority lay in establishing its proper limits. As A. James Hammerton has argued, conflicting marital expectations on the part of husbands and wives over the limits of a husband's power unleashed a torrent of sexual antagonism.[39] That did not preclude women from valorizing the loving aspects of a companionate marital ideal; but we need to consider how seriously the ideal was compromised by broadly held assumptions about the legitimacy of a husband's marital authority.

Love clearly mattered to both women and men, and it carried egalitarian implications. Over the course of the nineteenth century, divorcing women gave ever more explicit voice to the pain they experienced when love was inverted to hate and intimacy turned into estrangement. A letter included by a husband responding to his wife's 1859 petition documented her abiding hatred of him not only indicates that he anticipated the court's respect for the importance of marital love; it demonstrates that his wife set out to wound him as deeply as possible by declaring she had never loved him. "I will tell you something I never knew," wrote the embittered wife to the husband she accused of adultery. *"I never loved you. . . .* [I] cheated myself into the belief that I loved you. . . . I admit I deceived you, for what could I do? I was tied to you. I resolved to make the best of it. . . . For seven years we never lived a week without a quarrel. Can you deny this. You often told me that I acted at times as though I hated you—you never hit on a greater truth."[40]

Perhaps the nub of the problem in interpreting divorce as a woman's remedy is the conflation of divorce with the end of a marriage. In the narrative imposed by the legal ground rules, wives cast off cruel and adulterous husbands in an adversarial proceeding in court; more often than not, wives who had themselves been cast off by their husbands received a unilateral and essentially sympathetic hearing in court. While women pursued new legal identities in the local courts of the nineteenth century, men found anonymity in the expanding national landscape. It is more than coincidental that one New York witness associated the disappearance of a wayward husband with the festivities celebrating the opening of the Erie Canal.[41] Simply stated, there were more places to go and more ways to get there. In rural hamlets, in mushrooming cities, and on the frontier, life could begin anew. National expansion, improvements in transportation, the volatility of the economy—the whole socioeconomic context in which American divorce law developed—at once informed and transformed the nature of divorce as a legal remedy. Such a context suggests that even as divorce modified the asymmetrical relationship between men and women in marriage by punishing husbands for their faulty behavior and compensating their innocent wives, it implicitly legitimated the behavior it discouraged.

Nonetheless, there were benefits for women too. Despite the failure of nineteenth-century divorce to redress the inequities of marital power, a task jurists neither provided for nor even envisioned, the new access to a divorce was an improvement (albeit a modest one). And although the narrative of fault imposed by a proceeding in equity defined female petitioners as the objects of judicial concern whose husbands had failed to protect them, some petitioners had the wherewithal to see themselves as subjects with rights that they deployed against their husbands. It was precisely this possibility so rarely realized in these suits—that women could use divorce to bend life in their own direction—that animated the prodivorce vision of Elizabeth Cady Stanton.

Evidence of women's capacity to bend life in their own direction, however, can be found more readily in their willingness to abandon men. We should look, then, to female defendants. We should look to Amanda Edwards, who left her husband Charles because "she was unhappy with him" and eloped aboard the steamship *Best Western* with her lover from Barcelona. We should look to Rachel Augusthuys, who deserted her husband to live with a man in California.[42] In contrast to most female plaintiffs, these women created their own divorces with their own remedies. Small wonder that their remedies entailed a dependence on new companions. Other women returned to parental households or were compelled to rely on the aid of relatives and friends.

A final point remains to be made about the connections between the right of divorce and a companionate paradigm for marriage. A more affective, loving, conjugal ideal undoubtedly unleashed some dissatisfaction with marital realities, but the capacity to translate that dissatisfaction into an action to dissolve a marriage, in contrast to reacting to one that had already been dissolved, was bound up with economic assumptions and realities. The breadwinner ethic—the extent to which women continued to rely on the financial support of men and men continued to have an obligation to support them—shaped the way both men and women played out their roles in divorce. Inasmuch as couples in the nineteenth century fused modern notions of love with traditional concepts of protection and support, we should not be surprised to find the interplay of similar elements in divorce. As one defendant warned his wife, "Remember Mary Ann, in how awkward a situation a female places herself when she attempts to live apart from a husband who loves and wishes to be kind to her and to protect her." An heiress with a separate estate, Mary Ann successfully pursued a divorce from her reluctant husband precisely because she was not in so awkward a situation.[43] For all those women who were, his warning alerts us to the limits of divorce as a woman's remedy.

FIVE

❖ When Men Go to Court ❖

Over the course of his life, Isaiah Thomas, Massachusetts Revolutionary War printer and early national philanthropist, married three times. His first marriage was in 1769 to Mary Dill, a young woman from Bermuda who bore him his only two children; the second was in 1779 to Mary Fowle, a war widow whose children had died; the third was in 1819 to Rebecca Armstrong, a cousin, companion, and general housekeeper to his second wife. From all the available accounts, including Thomas's own diary, it was the second union that afforded him the pleasures of a steadfast partnership with a caring spouse. "My truly dear and beloved Consort departed this life," he wrote in the fall of 1818, as he lamented his second wife's death and permitted his grief to surface in the terse phrases with which he recorded his life. Clearly she was sorely missed. Visiting her tomb in the following summer, he expressed his need "to view the spot where rest the ashes of my late departed best friend and wife."[1]

Thomas's other two marriages, however, were distinctly uncompanionate. A grandson memorializing him in 1874 wrote of his union with Mary Dill, "The connection was not a happy one, and he was separated from her a few years afterward." Inasmuch as that marriage was dissolved by a divorce decree, the grandson's reluctance to call it what it was suggests that divorce was embarrassing enough to be bleached out of family reminiscences. Were it not for the legal documents collected in family papers, we would not know that Thomas had divorced his first wife for adultery, a cause to which she eventually confessed. His official complaint claimed that "to his great mortification," she not only had violated the all-important commitment to sexual fidelity at the heart of the marriage contract, but she was "destitute of that affection and regard for him which is necessary to render a State of Matrimony easy and happy."[2]

As that formal language suggests, in the divorce documents of the late eighteenth century, wifely virtues such as affection and regard were inextricably intertwined with chastity and submissiveness. In this case, it was Mary Dill Thomas's obdurate refusal to stay close to hearth and home that set the stage for her adultery. When Isaiah remonstrated with her for "journeying at so unreasonable a time of the Year . . . she swore she would go if it was to her eternal Ruin." "The sequel," his complaint bitterly noted, "discovers her motives": her determination to travel despite his express desire that she remain at home culminated in a series of trysts with a Major Thompson, who held himself out to various innkeepers as her lawful husband.[3]

As for his third marriage, undertaken late in his life, Thomas's new wife proved similarly restless, albeit chaste; she spent her time "riding out" from his Worcester residence and visiting friends instead of providing him with the loyal companionship and personal attention that he considered his due. After living with her for two years, he signed a separation agreement before witnesses in which he agreed to maintain her in a Boston residence while she promised to return specific household items. Although both partners seemed eager to put an end to a vexing relationship, they explicitly sought to conceal the nature of their troubles from the courts and the outside world. In their agreement they pledged "that whatever difficulties or unpleasant things may have taken place between them, or may hereafter take place, with which the world has no concern, that they will not divulge or mention them to any person whatever without mutual consent." Only Thomas's diary offers clues to the emotional cost of this unhappy union. "Had a meeting with Mrs. Thomas and her friends, in a friendly way," he wrote. "Separation thought best and mutually agreed to. Very bad headache and I may add heartache—these have attended me the last 2 years."[4]

The marital history of Isaiah Thomas raises provocative questions about the marital expectations of divorcing men and the circumstances under which they turned to the courts. Thomas's first wife allegedly committed the one conjugal fault written into every divorce statute in the country and recognized as a legitimate ground by the vast majority of

Protestant clergymen; his third wife, by contrast, merely made his life miserable. Although she was enough of a thorn in his side to give him a headache and heartache, she had not breached her marriage contract in a way that was recognized by Massachusetts law. Possibly age was also a factor in their choosing a private resolution as opposed to a formal bed-and-board separation, an option available at the time in the Massachusetts courts. Whereas in his first marriage, Thomas was a young man with minor children and was intent on remarrying and assuming new obligations, the agreement with his third wife described them both "being of advanced age." More important, they indicated their mutual desire for privacy regarding their personal affairs when they declared it was their duty "to do that for ourselves, which we judge will best promote our own happiness without injury to others and with which others have no concern."[5] Yet what emerges from their tidy agreement to live apart is that Isaiah Thomas's conception of a happy marriage diverged sharply from that of his wife. She evidently assumed the complete propriety of continuing her travels and sustaining an independent social life while he viewed her compliance with his wishes and her attention to his daily needs as his rightful prerogative.

Because Isaiah Thomas's notion of marital affection included wifely submission, his responses to his checkered marital history provide a fitting introduction to the concerns of male litigants. As the sexual transgression of his first wife illustrates, a roving wife could be tempted to the ultimate act of insubordination. But added to the "mortification" of being cuckolded was the anguish he revealed at his inability to get his third wife to conform to his expectations, an anguish that reappeared many times over in nineteenth-century divorce complaints. Even with the growing emphasis in these complaints on the role of love in marriage and on the wounded feelings of the male petitioner, the lines between a husband's emotional pain at his wife's disaffection and the anger he experienced at his loss of conjugal control were never very clear.

AFFECTION AND OBEDIENCE

We turn again to mediations in the Indiana and New York courts to consider divorce as a man's remedy. In particular, we will explore men's notions of an unsatisfactory marriage together with the circumstances that propelled them into court. In practical terms, of course, men appeared in court for many of the same reasons women did: to sever their economic ties to a wayward spouse, to determine the custody of their children, to clarify their marital status, and to give themselves the right to remarry legally. Like women, they came also to ameliorate what Isaiah Thomas referred to as "his great mortification" by publicly repudiating their dissolute spouses. But for men, the legal repudiation of a spouse represented a particularly important means of reaffirming their manhood. Husbands, who came not to ask for support but to sever the obligation of support, juxtaposed their own steadfastness and even heroism as providers against their wives' disloyalty, contentiousness, and wantonness. The assertion of male honor, which no longer took the form of dueling or other rituals, especially in the North, was being played out now in civil courts that defined the new marital order.

Men's growing preference for the courts over extralegal resolutions softened the patriarchal edges of marriage. For one thing, a civil suit like divorce presumed the formal legal equality of the spouses; for another, a commitment to the ideal of mutual affection suggested a more symmetrical model of marriage. What is striking, however, is how neatly traditional and companionate values meshed together in the statements of male litigants, who invariably compounded sentimental notions of affection with customary expectations of obedience. Their petitions often linked acts of wifely independence such as going out without notice or visiting too long with friends to more serious breaches of marital behavior. Concerns about adultery and doubts about paternity were never far from the surface of their complaints. The consistency with which men related acts of minor insubordination to serious sexual transgressions suggests the anxiety they experienced in maintaining their conjugal authority as an increasingly affective model of marriage became dominant.

That is not to downplay the role of love as the barometer of a good marriage. On the contrary, men looked to marriage as the wellspring of intimate feelings and the source of mutual solace. Nineteenth-century divorce records emphatically confirm the crucial role of emotions in marriage for men as well as for women. In Indiana, with its broad statutory grounds, the persistence with which male petitioners attributed the failure of their marriages to their wives' lack of affection indicates the readiness of the court at least to consider the emotional components of marriage.

Men, no less than women, gave evidence of suffering unrelenting psychological cruelty. Thomas House, for example, alleged that his wife Betsy "treated him unkindly and cruelly and manifested a great deal of malevolence and disaffection." Disaffection in a relationship spelled chaos if not the functional end of the marriage. James Scoby insisted that his wife left him for no substantive cause, "only alledging [*sic*] that she had no regard for him and that she had manifested for some years . . . before said separation a great deal of displeasure and dislike for him." As one witness explained while testifying on the breakdown of his son's marriage, "a hard feeling existed between him and his wife" soon after they were married. Yet time and again men's petitions implied that hard feelings coupled with a measure of insubordination paved the way for a woman's sexual infidelity. In this last case, the husband was able to prove to the court's satisfaction that the child born to his wife could not have been his, given the dates of their intermittent separations, and that she was therefore guilty of adultery.[6]

Emphasis on the warmly affective aspects of a harmonious union provided a convenient foil for demonstrating the emotional price paid when a life was filled with hatred and acrimony. Zachariah Mann, an Indianapolis petitioner, insisted that he could only have married his wife "during a period of mental imbecility" brought on by disease, and that he lived with her "under circumstances of mutual and deep-seated hatred and aversion" until she finally abandoned him. His wife had then dishonored and slandered him among his friends, he protested, by accusing him of adultery with a niece who was keeping house for him. In a jurisdiction like Indiana where an omnibus clause could bring divorce close to late-twentieth-century no-fault standards, confessions of a deep-seated mutual enmity were sometimes sufficient when delivered with enough brio. Zachariah Mann described his hatred for his wife as "so fixed and confirmed and indelible that nothing but death can subdue it." In fact, "death itself would be a willing release from her if no other can be found." For Zachariah, another release was found. A divorce was decreed, and by agreement of the parties, he gratefully paid his wife's court costs.[7]

From the perspective of male plaintiffs, one way a woman expressed her love was through her abiding loyalty to her husband in public as well as in private life. A wife who turned against her partner and openly berated him disgraced him before the community and humiliated him before his male peers. Aaron Wright protested that his wife Julia had "slandered and abused your complainant to his friends, for the purpose, as she said, of devilling him." He averred that when his old neighbors came to visit him, she withheld all hospitality, "would get out of temper, become sulky and refuse to them the least curtesy [*sic*] or civility," after which they ceased to visit altogether. This was neither the marital behavior he had once known nor that which he had anticipated, and he expressed his dismay openly. A widower when he married the inhospitable Julia, he protested that she "abused and outraged" the memory of his first wife, the love of his youth with whom he had lived so happily. As for Julia, he claimed that he could not live with her "in peace and quiet, or in any manner at all."[8]

A focus on the corrosive effects of unrelenting hatred was only one consequence of the intensifying emphasis on romantic love. When love was constructed as something more erotic and less restrained than gentle affection—when it revolved around the heedless impulses of the romantic self—there was always the possibility of a man's being cuckolded by an impassioned wife who discovered her true love elsewhere. This is precisely what happened to the rising New York businessman Charles Edwards, who supported his wife Amanda handsomely, showered her with gifts, and expressed his deepest devotion to her. Nonetheless, she left for Europe with a man with whom she had "carnal connection" in Edwards's own house while he was out attending to the demands of his business. In this case, Amanda's desire for another man was compounded with her deep disaffection for Charles. A family friend reported that when he remonstrated with her about her intention to desert Charles, she insisted that she was determined to leave him with or without her paramour. Although she conceded that Charles was "a perfect gentleman," a reference perhaps to his attention to duty and his lack of passion, she was nonetheless "unhappy" with him. Yet Charles, it seems, was oblivious to her negative feelings. A witness to the alleged adultery admitted he did not have the nerve to mention it to his good friend Charles, because "in the first place I might have got my hand broke and in the next I would not have been believed." What is clear is that Amanda's elopement dealt a devastating personal blow to the husband who had lavished his affection on her and assumed he was happily married. Describing Charles's response to his wife's defection, the witness claimed that "he cried like a child when he told me of it."[9]

THE PROBLEM OF MARITAL AUTHORITY

Although historians have elaborated on the feminization of the middle-class household, that household emerges in nineteenth-century divorce records as a hotly contested site in which men strove to preserve their authority against novel forms of subversion. An emphasis on feelings may very well have intensified the pleasures of marriage, but it exacerbated conflicts over marital control. For male litigants, the feminization of the household ended where their fundamental authority began. As A. James Hammerton has observed, at both an ideological and experiential level, middle-class ideas about marriage revolved around "the complementary virtues of benevolent manliness and compliant femininity."[10] Yet for a variety of reasons, feminine compliance was wanting. Urban entertainments, new modes of transportation, troublesome in-laws, close female friendships, and even the vaunted separation of male and female spheres—all these could undermine the single-minded devotion of wife to husband that lay at the heart of the Victorian marital ideal.

The problem of exerting marital authority in its newly benevolent form was a paramount concern for the men who came to court. Even those few male defendants who chose not to follow the standard ex parte divorce proceeding and appeared in court tried to justify lapses in their own behavior by documenting challenges to their power as husbands. Encroachment on their authority not only was the avowed focal point of much of their anger and frustration; it also afforded them a legal strategy with which they contested their wives' petitions. Charles Von Cort, an unlicensed Brooklyn physician with an unsavory past, a Prussian prison record, and, it was alleged, a Prussian wife, blamed the suit filed by his wealthy American wife on interfering in-laws. He complained that his wife Eliza was always with her mother, whom he had once treated successfully for "a paralytic affliction" but who subsequently expelled him from the house. In his scenario, the meddlesome mother-in-law was destroying the couple's only chance for a future by exerting her poisonous influence on the opinions of her grown daughter. Noting that Eliza was already thirty-five and he forty-one, he argued, to no avail, that they might have been very happy together but for her mother's intervention.[11]

Implicit in such arguments was the notion that the companionate family was a nuclear family whose claims always took precedence over the claims of kinship. Ironically, in such appeals husbands attempted to assert their traditional authority in the name of a new conjugal intimacy that created formidable barriers against any sort of outside intervention. Demanding siblings could prove as troublesome as overweening parents in breaching a couple's marital privacy. Matthias Brown, a legal defendant who lived apart from his wife, but who stalked her every Sunday when she left for church and threatened to take custody of his children, located the source of his marital difficulties in the interference of his wife's kinfolk. When two of his sisters-in-law moved in, he complained, "scarce a meal could be had without one or both relatives flying into the most violent passions." Small wonder, he argued, that he became intemperate from time to time, for he was driven to that state by the enmity and financial drain of his wife's meddlesome family. By the time he came to plead his cause in court and argue unsuccessfully for the custody of his children, he had already written off his marriage. Nonetheless, he expressed his dismay at what he regarded as the assault on his character and the challenge to his authority in a letter to his estranged wife. "As the Mother of my children, I wish you well," he wrote, "but as the Calumniator of my character I detest you."[12]

Divorce became something of a grievance mechanism through which men filtered their apprehensions about maintaining control over households that were rendered chaotic by their wives' misplaced loyalties. Second marriages were particularly vulnerable in this regard, especially when children were involved. Adult children from a prior marriage might divert a wife's attention from her marital obligations and undermine her commitment to her husband's needs and desires. One Indiana plaintiff alleged that his marital difficulties began only when his wife became unhappy with his attitude toward her children, so that she finally "went to her son's house and to houses of divers other persons" until she ceased to return home. The enraged husband attributed her delinquency to "the bitter and unrelenting enmity of female malevolence."[13]

Outside interference came in many forms, but probably no nineteenth-century development either disrupted marital stability or undermined conjugal authority more dramatically than did the Civil War. To an even greater extent than the gold rush of 1849, the war removed men from the vicinity of home, left women unsure of their return, and encouraged wives to consider taking up with a new partner. Although wives of officers who could afford it often traveled to the front to be close to their spouses, the vast majority of women stayed behind. No matter how much middle-class Americans sentimentalized the experiences of war and the bonds of family, absence did not necessarily make the heart grow fonder; more often than not, it created hardship and doubt. Given the precariousness of wartime conditions, it is not difficult to understand how some wives became unfaithful to their husbands. Anna Bird, for example, could not have any degree of certainty that her husband would return; at the same time, his prolonged absence created an opportunity for her to seek out a new partner. Her punishment was unequivocal. Jacob Bird did in fact return, and as a result of Anna's having had sexual relations with two other men, he divorced her and assumed custody of their three children.[14]

As in the gold rush, in the war a long-delayed return could make a wife's marriage vows fade from view and encourage her to begin married life all over again. Clarissa Cole had lived in New York with her husband Alfred for only three weeks before he went to serve with the Union forces in New Orleans. As he explained in his petition, the blockade precluded a timely reunion with his wife. She, however, managed to sweep their brief marriage under the rug, and when Alfred came home at last, he found her living in Canada with a James Robb to whom she was allegedly married. Cole came to court not only to divorce the wife who had given up on his return but also to have the child she had borne declared illegitimate.[15]

There can be no denying either the war's impact on marital dissolutions or its challenge to conjugal authority. At a time when Victorian men and women looked to feelings to solidify and enhance their marriages, the uncertainties of war provided them with an unprecedented opportunity to redirect their feelings into illicit relationships. Consider the case of Thomas and Marie Egan, a New York couple who lived in a boardinghouse on Fourteenth Street along with Charles Stone, a Canal Street jeweler. Because both men served in the Fortieth New York Volunteers, Charles had an added convenient context in which to become intimate with Marie. At Thomas Egan's request, Charles Stone conducted Marie Egan to the camp near Washington where her husband was stationed. By the time Marie had returned to New York and Charles had resigned his commission, there was, in the words of the landlady who ran the boardinghouse they continued to live in, "more familiarity between" them "than was becoming a married lady." Marie allegedly asked her landlady for the source of the following line of Scripture: "Entreat me not to leave thee or return from following after thee." Marie, it seems, had fallen deeply in love with the man to whom her husband had entrusted her.

Charles Stone and Marie Egan pursued a series of trysts at various sites in the New York area, including a rented house in Yonkers. Thomas Egan, meanwhile, returned to the New York area to recruit for his regiment in Yonkers. Catching wind of the affair, he broke into the house where his beloved wife and stalwart friend were sharing a bed and proceeded to beat Stone about the head. The hack driver who accompanied him claimed that Stone "did not show much fight" and jumped out the window while Marie pleaded with her husband not to kill her lover. But Thomas Egan ultimately affirmed his manhood not through acts of violence but through the mediations of the law. Although the war temporarily interrupted his bid for a divorce decree, he eventually had his day in court. He returned to divorce Marie and take custody of their only son, promising in accord with her plea to bring him "to some respectable hotel or private residence" for a week's visit with his mother in the summer and at Christmas.[16]

War was not the only novel context in which a husband's marital authority was sorely tested. New York records underscore the role played by the city itself as a seedbed for marital discord. Urbanization, according to petitioners, afforded women all too many opportunities to neglect their wifely responsibilities and reject the confinement of their households. Offering transiency and anonymity, the city presented women of both the working and middle classes with a host of enticements and distractions that diverted their attention from their husbands; the new and dangerous urban sociability pulled them ever closer to adultery. Thomas Gilhooley accused his wife of associating with "dissipated women" and "lecherous men" whom she accompanied on sleigh rides and to fire company balls. A female neighbor characterized her as "gay and thoughtless for a married woman," while another disparaged her behavior in a daguerreotype shop where the shop owner had whispered in her ear and disappeared with her into the back room. Although testimony such as this did not constitute proof of adultery, it was used to strengthen the plaintiff's case. More important, it corroborates Victorian assumptions about the ties between women's growing access to public spaces and new opportunities for adultery.[17]

Despite the masculine ideal of benevolent authority in what we might term the new double standard, benevolence could be suspended in cases of extreme intransigence. The boldness with which a woman stepped out, especially in mixed company, could serve to justify a righteous husband's beatings. William Fowler, who was involved in a series of countersuits with his wife over child custody, admitted to two incidents of physical violence that the court declined to define as cruelty, given his wife's subversive behavior. The first incident, the referee determined, was set off "by the undutiful and undecorous conduct of his wife in attending a horse race or ladies Equestrian Exhibition at a race course on Long Island in the company with a Stranger." In the second incident, he explained, William was "trying to separate his wife from a gentleman who was accompanying her in the street against her husband's wishes." Furthermore, her unruly behavior at home, which included throwing dishes and furniture, was characterized as "calculated to provoke him."[18]

Complaints about a wife's insubordination were ineluctably linked to the problem of sexual control. Even the act of stepping out into the seemingly respectable social environs of the church rendered one jealous husband uncertain about his wife's chastity. Thomas Butler insisted that the real reason his wife went to church was to solicit men. Although he was unsuccessful in contesting his wife's divorce petition, his response to her social independence may very well represent a widespread marital anxiety taken to its extreme. The degree to which he equated his authority over his wife's movements with his control over her sexual fidelity was borne out in his wife's testimony. "He threatened that if I went to [a] lecture tha[t] evening . . . he would blow my brains out. I did go," she admitted, exemplifying the robust strain of wifely disobedience that punctuates these records, and because she disobeyed he called her "a God damn whore."[19]

As we have seen, the availability of divorce rationalized the readiness of men to desert women, thereby rendering wives economically vulnerable. But it also rationalized the readiness of women to desert men, albeit in far fewer numbers and with less serious economic ramifications for their deserted partners. The desertion of men by women, moreover, was regarded as an extreme form of social deviance. Still, like their male counterparts, some women took up with a new partner within the same general vicinity while others left the area altogether. Margaret Ellen Goff left John Goff of Manhattan for John Sweeney of Brooklyn, where, according to the complaint, "they continue to live together as man and wife." Susanna Hurst, denounced by her husband as nothing more than "a common prostitute," put more distance between herself and her spouse. She was described as living with her paramour in Buffalo "as his wife." Lena Florence, another New Yorker, went even further. Accused of committing adultery with Jacob Roots of Sullivan County, she was alleged to be living with him in open adultery in Iowa.[20]

The desertion of men by women was often not so much a matter of fleeing an abusive spouse as opting for a more attractive alternative. Though these records indicate that divorce afforded female plaintiffs a limited remedy, the documents depicting runaway wives suggest a measure of real choice. Numerous women made their conscious desire for a new partner as explicit as possible. When Sarah Barnes eloped with Abraham Marchant, a Mormon preacher, for the Utah Territory, she wrote her husband of her decision to stay in Utah and become a Mormon and she urged him to remarry. An English emigrant who had been living in New York while waiting for her English husband, she responded to an inquiry about the probable date of his arrival by stating "that she did not know nor did not care and that she did not want to see him any more." She was determined to accompany Marchant, with whom she was living "as his wife," to Salt Lake City. It is difficult, of course, to assess the reliability of witnesses for male plaintiffs, especially in New York proceedings where their testimony was calculated to corroborate the single ground of adultery. Yet precisely because explicit statements regarding a wife's antipathy to her husband did not constitute legal proof, they have the ring of authenticity. Barnes, according to one witness, arrived in New York shortly after her departure and, as soon as he saved enough money, went after her, hoping to induce her to return.[21]

Among the many narratives underscoring the lewdness of an erring wife, Barnes's story was exceptional in his readiness to take his wife back. Witnesses, both male and female, persistently documented the moral depravity of deserting wives. Ada Coan was described by a male witness as "a woman of loose character" who when he put his hands on her bosom "offered no resistance. . . . My hand," he continued, "was beneath her clothes and on the promised land." Her landlady testified that when she saw Ada "singing, laughing, and carousing" with men, she was satisfied that "she was not a virtuous woman." More revealing was Ada's alleged free-love construction of her own virtue. "The defendant told me," claimed another witness, "that she had no affection for her husband and in consequence that she thought she had a perfect right to do as she pleased in relation to criminal intercourse with any man she pleased."[22] It is unlikely that Ada used the phrase "criminal intercourse" to describe her relations with men, since she saw nothing criminal about impassioned and voluntary sex with a man to whom she was whole-heartedly committed.

Although castigating an erring wife in court may have provided the plaintiff with some satisfaction, deserted husbands did not always turn to the law for redress. Often they permitted their wives to live with their paramours without any legal interference. Divorce was expensive, time-consuming, and disruptive. Yet sometimes a single incident could pro-pel a phlegmatic husband into court, as was the case with Cary Harris. He permitted his wife Mary to live with Peter Bennett, "a seafaring man," for a period of ten years, during which she had two children and passed as Peter's wife. Cary, who had retained custody of their daugh-ter, claimed he had allowed his wife's transgression to pass for the sake of "domestic peace." He was galvanized into action, however, when his wife had the effrontery to join the church where he was a deacon. When he objected to her membership on the ground of her "adulterous marriage," he was overruled.[23] In this case, where Cary Harris staked his honor on the moral standards of his church and his church failed him, he turned to the law for a remedy.

VIRTUE, CUSTODY, AND LEGITIMACY

The Harris divorce emerged from a long-standing accord that broke down thanks to Mary Harris's audacious behavior. The terms of the accord are revealing. That Cary Harris retained custody of their only daughter suggests that both partners shared an understanding about the links between sexual fidelity and the legitimacy and custody of children. At the very least, they acquiesced in supporting the prevailing moral sentiment that a wife's chastity was pivotal to the organization of the family and was therefore the bedrock of the social structure. Unchaste behavior on the part of a wife spelled both personal dishonor and social chaos. As James Atwood put it when he described his "lewd and incontinent" wife, she had become "unmindful of . . . all sense of virtue and honor."[24] Similar phrases appeared in other petitions. Given the concern with the legitimacy of children that underpinned the legal framework for both marriage and divorce, it is not surprising to find a punitive thrust in the divorce process. Some husbands took the fault dimensions of the law very seriously and were determined to use the courts to affirm their own honor by publicly exposing a dishonorable wife.

The punitive component in divorce law, then, could prove more than formulaic when applied to dissolute wives, who sometimes alluded to the disgrace of their exposure. When William Harvey sued his wife Kassandra for adultery in Monroe County, she petitioned the Indiana legislature for a legislative decree so as "to avoid as much as possible the Odium and disgrace of Proof being made in open court." Kassandra readily admitted her guilt. "I freely consent to giving him a divorce," she insisted, "in the cheapest and speediest way it can be obtained." William, however, declined her bid for a legislative decree. Since Kassandra was living in the county in open adultery with her paramour, her odium and disgrace constituted a meaningful part of William's remedy. It is not clear if Kassandra finally appeared in court, but in light of the gossipy nature of a rural community, the legal process was not without shame for her. The court ordered a summons for the illiterate Kassandra's appearance and instructed the county sheriff to read it aloud before her, her paramour, and assembled witnesses.[25]

As their choice of witnesses suggests, for some men finding fault amounted to more than meeting the statutory requirements. In contrast to their female counterparts, male plaintiffs were prepared to draw on their children to corroborate acts of adultery. Their readiness to do so emanated in part from children's day-to-day proximity to their mothers, which provided opportunities to observe sexual lapses. But it also relied on the common understanding that adultery by a married woman so entirely disqualified her as a mother that it was appropriate to resort to a child's testimony. Her infidelity, in other words, stripped her of all legitimacy as a parent. Thus Thomas Collins's twelve-year-old son Edward attested to his mother's adultery during a period when she was awaiting his father's arrival from Dublin. They were living with his maternal grandparents at the time, and Edward alleged that saw Harry Moloney kiss his mother while they were in bed together. Thomas Collins, moreover, was not content to rely on the standard New York statutory prohibition against the remarriage of the guilty spouse, which went into effect automatically when a decree was granted: he wanted to ensure that the censorious and judgmental ethos at the core of the statute was particularized in his decree. His petition specifically requested that the defendant "be restrained and prohibited by the decree . . . from marrying again during the lifetime of the plaintiff."[26]

Similarly, Francis Crussel's son William averred that when his father went to California in 1849, he lived with his mother and a John Everard as they migrated from Buffalo to Cincinnati to St. Louis. Because Crussel continued to send support money, his absence was not construed as a form of abandonment. The son noted that finally in the fall of 1859, "my father came on to St. Louis and my brother and myself were delivered by the Court to the custody of our Father." Francis Crussel received a divorce decree, custody of his two sons, and the satisfaction of the statutory prohibition against the remarriage of Mary Crussel.[27]

Although it is difficult to fathom how Francis Crussel might relate to the sons with whom he had had little or no contact for ten years, a father's demand for custody in the face of a mother's adultery was an important means of reaffirming his familial authority. As we have seen, custody, which was generally uncontested in the case of female plaintiffs, went readily to the allegedly innocent spouse. Likewise when male plaintiffs petitioned for custody, even after a prolonged absence, they were generally successful. As Margaret Hyatt's defense indicates, women's appeals to extenuating circumstances met with little credence in the courts. Responding to Joshua Hyatt's divorce suit, Margaret, who admitted to living with a paramour, argued she had done so because her husband had abandoned her when her daughter was a few months old. How, she asked, could he come back now after so long an absence to rear a six-year-old girl when he "is out of business and living on the charity of his father, who is advanced in years and not possessed of large means"? Yet Joshua successfully invoked the harmful effects of her flagrant immorality, arguing that her life as "a courtesan" was bad for the child. At issue here was the profound gravity of Margaret's adultery, not her fundamental competence as a parent. To be sure, the courts did not always comply with the custody demands of male plaintiffs; but when custody was contested, a woman's sexual fidelity became highly significant. A female defendant from Indianapolis, for example, who was *not* accused of adultery, managed to retain custody of her ten-month-old daughter based on the so-called tender years doctrine by arguing the child was in frail health and in need of her mother.[28]

Some female defendants, however, were depicted as so bereft of the "natural" attributes of motherhood that they had forfeited any chance for custody. James Emmens argued that his wife was so deeply "addicted to habits of gross intoxication" that she was hopelessly unfit to have the custody and control of children. Not only had she committed adultery, he alleged, but she was also rough and abusive to the children and had already served time in the penitentiary at Blackwell's Island for disorderly conduct and intoxication. Similar accusations of female intemperance were not limited to women of the working classes who, like Mary Ann Emmens, might have been arrested on the streets for drunkenness or even prostitution. Malinda Foster, mother of three and the sole and unencumbered owner of two lots and houses in Brooklyn, was described by her husband Henry as regularly intoxicated by midmorning and unable to retain the family's servants. She was a habitual drunkard, he complained, who sometimes fell down the stairs, always needed to be assisted up the stairs, and invariably was put to bed unconscious. Yet she was devious about her drinking, he warned. Even though she was unfit to care for her children, she had schooled them "to screen her own conduct." A New York referee concurred with her husband's assessment. The separation decree declared it "unsafe and improper for him to cohabit" with Malinda and granted him the care and custody of the children.[29]

In a few cases husbands who were officially guilty of adultery won custody of their children with the acquiescence of their wives. Julia Ann Dredger alleged that her husband William was raising her four children with a woman with whom he was living in open adultery. Yet instead of demanding custody, a request that ordinarily would have been granted to her, she merely asked the court to "make such disposition of the said children . . . as in the judgment of this court shall be deemed just and proper." Despite William's open admission of guilt, he appealed to the court to consider the context in which their separation had occurred. His wife, he noted, was frequently intoxicated and unfit to raise the children; and in any case, the children much preferred to live with him. Here the simple calculus of punishment and reward implicit in the single ground of adultery resulted in a paradoxical decree in which the guilty husband, who was forbidden from remarrying, was permitted to raise his children within an illicit relationship.[30] Despite the prohibition against collusion, this case suggests that the parties had worked out a satisfactory way around the narrow constraints of the statute.

William Dredger apparently had no doubt that the children for whom he was caring were his. Men's suits, however, frequently pivoted on the thorny problem of paternity. Unlike the biological relation between mother and child, the biological relation between father and child was impossible to ascertain with any certainty. Indeed, in these divorce records male anxiety about paternity is pervasive. This, of course, partly accounts for the continued double standard in divorce suits, where the sexual transgressions of women were judged more harshly than those of men. "Fatherhood," as Carole Pateman has observed, "never quite escapes from uncertainty." Thus Michael Fotcher, who went to war in 1861 and returned in 1864, insisted that the child his wife bore after she separated from him was illegitimate. He requested custody of two older children but wanted the youngest declared not to be his. After some close calculation of his leaves, the referee awarded custody of all three children to him, declaring that the son born in June of 1865 was the legitimate child of the marriage. Louisa Fotcher was duly served but made no appearance, thereby permitting the custody award to go unchallenged.[31]

Maria Blackwell, in contrast, was a more dogged defendant who tried to turn anxieties about paternity to her own advantage. She attempted to block her husband Jacob from assuming custody of her only child by claiming that the child was not his. A friend of Jacob's testified to her extramarital activities with such gusto that her legal tack, at first glance, appears convincing. The friend claimed he went with Jacob and pried open the shutters of a house to find a man sitting on the bed with Maria and attempting to conceal his legs under a quilt. "At that, Mrs. Black-well tried to cover her breast and her face. I says hallo, just take a look at you," he continued, unable to restrain his enthusiasm at the exposure. Nevertheless, Maria's insistence on the illegitimacy of her child along with her implicit appeal to the biologically superior claim of motherhood proved unsuccessful. Since she and Jacob had been living together when she became pregnant and they had married after the child was born, the court decreed that Jacob was to receive "absolute, and sole control, care, and custody" of the child.[32]

Clarifying legitimacy held important implications for inheritance and the division of property. When Ira Elkins, who was already separated from his wife, discovered that his marriage to her was illegal because her first husband had been alive, he came to court to have his marriage annulled, to legitimize his children, and to assume their custody. It seems that Jane Elkins's first husband had been relegated to a series of insane asylums; but although she claimed that he had died earlier at Bloomingdale, an upstate overseer of the poor dated his death shortly after her second wedding. Jane's act of technical bigamy resulted in her loss of custody. The marriage was annulled, no charge of bigamy was made, Ira received custody of an eleven-year-old son and a seven-year-old daughter, and *both* parties were permitted to remarry. More important from Ira's perspective, the court decreed that "Frank M. Elkins and Aida shall be entitled to succeed in the same manner as legitimate children to the real and personal estate of the plaintiff."[33]

As we have seen, husbands used the divorce process both to wrest custody from a transgressive wife and to reject responsibility for illicit children. Legitimacy was a paramount concern as a practical as well as a moral matter. Not only was a wife's adultery deemed socially reprehensible but husbands were understandably fearful of having to support another man's child. Wives caught in an illicit pregnancy from an extramarital affair made heroic efforts either to conceal the source of the pregnancy or to abort the child. The stakes here were high. Theresa Bayer lost custody of her first child when she became pregnant with a second at a time when her husband William had not had sexual relations with her. Witnesses described her frantic efforts to secure an abortion so as to ward off a divorce that was bound to imperil both her financial support and her custody rights. But those efforts only solidified the case against her. A married couple, a druggist and a midwife, testified that Theresa told them she "was in a family way" and needed an abortifacient even if it cost her her life. The druggist, however, did not permit his wife to abort Theresa Bayer despite her pleas that she needed the abortion at any cost.[34]

Given the importance placed on sexual fidelity in women, it is not surprising that a woman's lack of premarital virtue figured extensively in men's complaints. Men protested they had been duped into thinking they were marrying sexual innocents when they had, in fact, fallen prey to loose women. Abner Duryea's witnesses, for example, claimed that Marietta Duryea was nothing more than a common prostitute both before and after her marriage, which lasted a total of two months. Both the class and gender implications of their testimony were apparent as they spoke on behalf of their deluded young friend. Their proof of Marietta's vulgar status rested on the fact that she frequented the third tier of the Bowery Theater, a favorite haunt of New York prostitutes. Abner married her after a night of carousing, they insisted, when his judgment was impaired by drink. "I do not think he would have married her," explained one witness, "if he had been sober."[35]

Lack of virginity at the time of marriage was not a statutory ground for either divorce or separation; it was, nonetheless, a recurring motif in men's denunciations of their wives. One husband's campaign to punish his wife, which included depriving her of control of the household, flowed from his conviction that she had deceived him regarding her virginity. His marriage, he claimed in response to her request for a separation with alimony, was based on the "misinformation" she had given him when they began married life. A year later, he alleged, she admitted she had lived as "a kept mistress," a confession that from his point of view put an end to their union even though it carried no weight at law. His rage at her premarital affair was borne out in the allegations of cruelty in her complaint. When he locked her up in the kitchen and she escaped into the yard to protest to two policemen, he told her he was sorry he had not killed her. Money was not the sticking point here; he agreed to pay her five dollars a week if she would simply leave. Yet because he considered her a woman of loose morals who had deceived him about her premarital experience and thus deserved his retribution, he wanted her complaint dismissed. Although he was prepared to pay to rid himself of his unchaste wife, justifying himself against her charges of cruelty mattered a great deal. The court denied his appeal, granted his wife a formal separation, and ordered him to pay five dollars and fifty cents per week plus his wife's court costs.[36]

Lack of virginity may have had no standing as a legal ground, but marrying when pregnant with another man's child was a serious fraud that merited an annulment in the New York courts. George Bunte, a Canal Street grocer, described himself as deceived in precisely this way by his wife Minna, who had represented herself as a chaste and virtuous young woman. Minna, however, was pregnant at the time of their marriage, and George had had no prior sexual intercourse with her. The court annulled the marriage on the basis of the fraud to which Minna confessed shortly after the birth of her child.

Unfortunately, we are without any direct testimony from Minna; she had moved to Chicago by the time of the court action. Still, it is not hard to imagine the desperation with which she courted George or to appreciate the extent to which she herself had been duped by her lover, August Rhebock. Rhebock, who said he was not sure if he was himself divorced at the time he first met Minna, characterized her as exceedingly "loose." When asked if he had "carnal connection" with her, he declined to answer, arguing that it might injure his reputation, thus implying that he had. When she came to him with her problem, he told her "it was none of my business. She knew best herself." Although Rhebock disavowed responsibility for Minna's pregnancy by suggesting she had sex with another man, witnesses testified he made promises to her that he had no intention of keeping. When charged by Minna with being the father, he explained, "I told her I had nothing to do with other people's children. I have seen her in a privy at nine or ten at night with a man who works for me named John."[37]

George Bunte told a somewhat different story. Claiming that Minna's father would have killed her had she not married him, he described how Minna came into his store with a friend who aggressively promoted her as a prospective wife. She depicted Minna as a "smart, decent young girl" who "ought to have a husband," and she appealed to George's entrepreneurial instincts by predicting Minna "would learn the business quick." George, for his part, emphasized his complete passivity in the courtship—if, indeed, it could be called a courtship. "I never called to see her at all," he claimed. She, on the other hand, came to see him about seven times before the marriage, promising that she was virtuous, had no lovers, and never went to balls. On the night they married, he insisted, her family got him so drunk that he could not tell whether she was a virgin or not. But the principal figure in the scheme to deceive him, according to George's version of the story, was August Rhebock, who first promised to marry Minna, then claimed he was already married, and finally advised her to get an abortion. Because she was afraid of the abortion, George explained, he convinced her to undertake this trickery, declaring "I was not smart enough to find anything out about her condition."

The Bunte case represents in its most explicit form the degree to which the dilemma of controlling female sexuality informed the concerns of nineteenth-century male litigants. But it also exemplifies the tendency on the part of male litigants to fuse the constraints of traditional marital values with the soaring possibilities of romantic love. George may not have been smart enough to apprehend the condition of his troubled bride, but his aspirations about marriage went well beyond the basic expectations of chastity and mutual support. Speculating on what had gone wrong, he compounded the age-old concern with paternity with sentimental notions of love. This duped Canal Street grocer confessed that he and his wife had never been happy even before he had learned the truth about her; now, at last, he understood why. "That she loved another man better than me," he declared bitterly, "was the cause."[38]

PART THREE

❖ Representations ❖

Divorce made its way into the collective imagination of Americans through newspaper accounts of sensational cases. Enterprising editors collated the best of these cases into pamphlets that were sold widely and over an extended period of time. The stories chronicled in this provocative Victorian genre provide the lens for much of this section, titled "Representations." Although they recount real lawsuits between real women and men—an essential part of their cachet—they depart in important ways from the suits profiled in "Mediations." For one thing, the divorces reported in this way were invariably contested; for another, their adjudication took the form of a jury trial to determine allegations of adultery. Moreover, the litigants, whose lives typically afforded glimpses of extramarital passion, were either rich, famous, or eccentric enough to engage a large and diverse audience.

More important with regard to furnishing a historically distinctive frame for viewing American divorce, the genre of the trial pamphlet literally re-presented the cases it covered. Pamphlets customarily opened with a retrospective summary of a suit's relevant details, editorialized extensively about the entire cast of characters, and commented liberally on what was at stake in the outcome. Because women stood at center stage in these courtroom dramas, an affecting portrait of the embattled wife often graced the pamphlet's cover. Clearly much creativity and strategizing went into the making and marketing of trial pamphlets. My goal in turning to these widely disseminated narratives of divorce, which always delivered two versions of the same story, is to try to get at what they imparted to the public at large. Countless women and men surely made sense of divorce and assimilated it into their lives by reading stories about the flamboyant marital conflicts of the urban gentry.

Collectively, these midcentury stories dramatize the gnawing ambiguities of marital power unleashed by a new social freedom for urban women and the ascendant ethos of romantic love. Despite the lurid and contested nature of the divorces that achieved pamphlet status, in their plot lines we see the same concerns as were felt by the male plaintiffs surveyed in "Mediations." They turned on a confrontation over the social freedom of the wife and the conjugal authority of the husband that was played out in the starkly melodramatic form of an adultery trial. What is remarkable, however, is the extraordinary sympathy extended to these wives by reporters and jurors alike. The scenario of female suffering, which exemplifies the Victorian penchant for voyeurism and lies at the heart of melodrama, overshadowed considerations of the wife's guilt.

But trial pamphlets were also dramas without closure, and in the conflicting stories they told it is evident that the women on whom they focused displayed an astonishing readiness to depart hearth and home for the pleasures of urban life, including socializing with men. Small wonder that both the opponents and proponents of divorce believed that these courtroom dramas took the shame out of divorce. Given the underlying rebelliousness of their leading ladies and the open-endedness of their plots, they were inherently subversive.

Even as trial reports took the shame out of divorce, sentimental novelists worked to put it back in. The sentimental novel, the lens I use to conclude "Representations," stands in an implicitly dialectical relation to the trial pamphlet. Contrasts between the two genres are stunning. Whereas newsmen unveiled and, in fact, spotlighted the erotic underside of romantic love, novelists emptied romantic love of its erotic component. Fictional wives, like the litigants in trials, were victims and even martyrs, but unlike their real-life counterparts, they rarely rebelled; those who did paid a price.

A final alert to the reader is in order here. I want to stress that sentimental novels create a bridge between the artificially disjoined realms of "rules" and "representations." The woman-as-victim theme resonates deeply in the anxieties reflected in sentimental fiction and parallels the *anxieties voiced by antidivorce feminists. And contract, the central organizing principle of nineteenth-century economic and political life, is linked in familiar ways to the marriage contract by novelists working to illustrate the larger significance of indissoluble marriage. Indeed, in their fictions, we are once again in the presence of Christians and infidels.*

MRS. DUNHAM.

" Her appearance was neat and tasteful in point of dress—she being arrayed in a brown silk dress, black mantilla and veil, and a straw bonnet with ribbons of deep colors and flowers to match. Her face is of the Grecian cast, with her dark hair arranged placedly on the cheek."—(Report of the Great Divorce Case, page 22.)

Plate 1. Eliza Dunham, who was countersued for adultery in the Dunham divorce case. Boston, 1842. Courtesy American Antiquarian Society.

Plate 2. Lithograph "The Seven Stages of Matrimony" by Nathaniel Currier. New York, c. 1845.
Courtesy American Antiquarian Society.

Plate 3. Lithograph "The Divorce Suit," showing Edwin Forrest playing Othello with his attorney, John Van Buren, at his side. Philadelphia, 1852. Courtesy American Antiquarian Society.

REPORT OF THE

FORREST DIVORCE CASE,

CONTAINING THE FULL AND UNABRIDGED TESTIMONY OF
ALL THE WITNESSES, THE AFFIDAVITS AND
DEPOSITIONS, TOGETHER WITH THE

CONSUELO AND FORNEY LETTERS.

This Edition is published under the direct supervision of the

LAW REPORTER OF THE NEW YORK HERALD,

and is the only one containing the Suppressed Testimony.

NEW YORK:
ROBERT M. DE WITT, PUBLISHER,
13 FRANKFORT STREET.

Plate 4. Catherine Forrest on the cover of the 1852 *New York Herald* pamphlet detailing her suit against Forrest. Note the reference to the pamphlet's inclusion of suppressed testimony. Courtesy American Antiquarian Society.

THE DALTON DIVORCE CASE.

DOMESTIC DISSENSIONS IN FASHIONABLE LIFE. EXPOSITION OF GALLANTRY,
GAIETY, GOSSIP, GUILT, AND GUTTA-PERCHA.

LEGAL PROCEEDINGS, WITH ALL THE EVIDENCE IN THIS MOST
EXCITING AND REMARKABLE CASE.

FROM A DAGUERREOTYPE BY HORTON.
Published under the Copyright of the " BEE." For sale by all Periodical Dealers.

Plate 5. Helen "Nellie" Dalton on the cover of the 1857 *Boston Bee* pamphlet detailing her trial. Courtesy American Antiquarian Society.

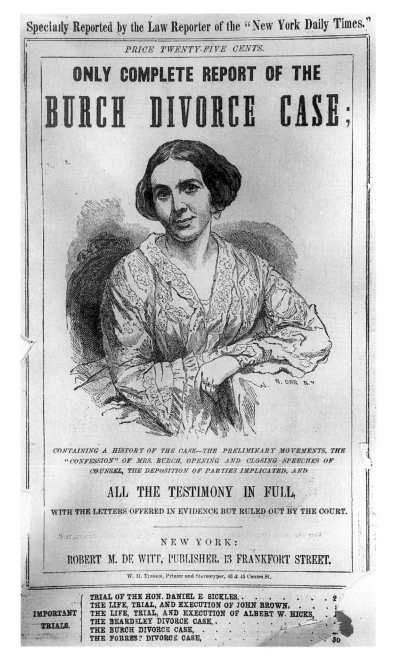

PRICE TWENTY-FIVE CENTS.

ONLY COMPLETE REPORT OF THE

BURCH DIVORCE CASE;

J. N. ORR N.Y.

CONTAINING A HISTORY OF THE CASE—THE PRELIMINARY MOVEMENTS, THE "CONFESSION" OF MRS. BURCH, OPENING AND CLOSING SPEECHES OF COUNSEL, THE DEPOSITION OF PARTIES IMPLICATED, AND

ALL THE TESTIMONY IN FULL,

WITH THE LETTERS OFFERED IN EVIDENCE BUT RULED OUT BY THE COURT.

NEW YORK:

ROBERT M. DE WITT, PUBLISHER, 13 FRANKFORT STREET.

W. H. TINSON, Printer and Stereotyper, 43 & 45 Centre St.

Plate 6.   Mary Burch on the cover of the 1860 *New York Daily Times* pamphlet recounting her Chicago suit. Note the references to other trial pamphlets. Courtesy American Antiquarian Society.

THE HUSBAND.   THE WIFE.

MARRIED LIFE IN NEW YORK.

Plate 7.   "Married Life in New York" from George Ellington's *The Women of New York, or the Under-World of the Great City* (New York, 1869). Courtesy American Antiquarian Society.

Plate 8.   Abby McFarland Richardson on the cover of an 1870 Philadelphia pamphlet detailing her ex-husband's New York City murder trial.
Courtesy American Antiquarian Society.

SIX

❖ Divorce Stories ❖

The room was crowded to its utmost capacity; and the interest of the spectators seemed to have increased as this singularly delicate and most important case approached its termination. The curiosity of the public on such occasions . . . [—]seeking as it does, food in the secret relations of private and domestic life, and gloating over the most indelicate scenes—is susceptible of explanation in the constitution and very frame of the human mind and heart, which will ever take cognizance of things bearing upon the disruption of social ties, and the most cherished feeling and associations of the sanctuary of the domestic circle.[1]

This 1842 account by a Boston newspaper reporter describes the much-publicized Dunham divorce trial on the day spectators pressed into the courtroom to await the final summations. Printed first in a Boston daily and then collated with the paper's other daily reports into a twenty-five-cent pamphlet, it exemplifies how divorce trials were marketed for mass consumption. For those who could not attend the trial, reading about it was the next best thing. Blow-by-blow depictions of each day's events, including the examination of key witnesses, were facilitated by stenographic reports. Although daily coverage was necessarily selective, it was elaborately detailed.

Astute newsmen supplied the vivid touches that transported the reader to the courtroom. The shedding of tears, the trembling of hands, the pallor of a witness, the garb of a litigant, the eloquence of counsel, the response of the crowd—no item of human interest was left to the reader's imagination. Reporters exploited the public fascination with such trials brilliantly, taking careful stock of the emotions they unleashed in the participants and ferreting out secrets about the recesses of domestic life.

Captions conveniently prepared readers for shocking disclosures. "DOMESTIC DISSENSIONS IN FASHIONABLE LIFE," trumpeted one trial report, which promised an "EXPOSITION OF GALLANTRY, GAIETY, GOSSIP, GUILT, AND GUTTA PERCHA."[2] The growing devotion to the ideal of domestic privacy only whetted the public's appetite for the most intimate disclosures. The nagging sense that divorce trials breached domestic privacy to the point of indecency contributed to their burgeoning popularity. It was the so-called indelicate scenes, after all, that sold newspapers. Even as the reporter at the Dunham trial disparaged the "gloating" that accompanied its revelations, he simultaneously appealed to his readers' most voyeuristic impulses.

Although trial reports were hardly a new phenomenon, the growing scope of their circulation heightened their influence. The pamphlet devoted to the Dunham case belonged to a large and lurid body of popular works that began to emerge in the 1830s as publishers learned to capitalize fully on the public thirst for sensationalism. The timing is significant. As Daniel Cohen has persuasively argued in his analysis of antebellum crime literature, in a society deeply conflicted over simultaneous demands for sexual restraint on the one hand and romantic engagement on the other, the seemingly transhistorical fascination with sex and violence assumed historically specific contours. The trial pamphlet, moreover, was an integral part of an information explosion that was marked by the extravagant profusion of print. Dependent at first on the rise of penny newspapers, whose editors were quick to satisfy the public appetite for scandal at a readily affordable price, printed reports of an entire trial presented readers with a similarly attractive bargain. Whereas the average antebellum book ran between seventy-five cents and a dollar and a quarter, trial reports sold at twenty-five cents or less.[3]

When we consider how readily nineteenth-century divorce trials are available in contemporary research libraries and how many editions were printed, it is safe to assume their circulation was large, though it was not geographically uniform. The dissemination of trial pamphlets, which were sold in corner bookstalls, at railroad depots, and by traveling peddlers, was shaped by the growth of the railroad. Yet even before the emergence of a comprehensive railway network, the broad and aggressive way in which these pamphlets were marketed departed dramatically from the traditional approach, which assumed that publishing was a gender-specific enterprise directed toward a discrete and limited readership. On the contrary, the evidence suggests divorce pamphlets were peddled to a large and heterogeneous audience, both female and male.[4]

The divorce stories consumed by this new mass audience were exceptional in every sense. They embraced only the most bitterly contested suits and profiled litigants of great wealth, high social standing, and considerable celebrity. Reporters' allusions to a litigant's affluence or cosmopolitan mores carried a populist thrust, and the genre thrived on exposing the foibles of the rich and the famous. Elaborating on the suit filed by Sarah Jarvis before the Connecticut legislature, a New York editor highlighted "the high standing of the parties—the array of counsel on both sides," and the taste for overseas travel and European art exhibited by the respondent, a minister of "ample fortune" whose house was "more showy than the residence of any private gentleman in Connecticut." Attention to the details of a glittering social life heightened the case's appeal. Nowhere was the frivolousness critics imputed to divorce more evident than in the flamboyant legal contests of the urban gentry, whose marriages seem to have been imperiled by the diverting social life of the city. Alluding to the shoals of an urban lifestyle, an editor for the Beardsley trial extolled his report for the "glimpses it affords of Metropolitan life" and predicted it would "be read eagerly from one end of the country to the other."[5]

Some divorce trials were, in fact, read from one end of the country to the other. Newspapers, with their steady coverage of out-of-state divorces, were instrumental in transforming the status of a newsworthy case from local gossip to a national scandal. A single edition of the *Indiana State Sentinel*, for example, carried news of both a New York and a Kentucky suit. Because such sweeping coverage propelled select cases into a broad and lasting national prominence, it transformed the entire trajectory of divorce stories. Although newspapers and trial pamphlets were ephemeral forms of print, scandalous cases exhibited remarkable staying power. "Scandalous" meant allegations of adultery against the wife that were contested and resulted in a jury trial, an option rarely exercised by midcentury litigants. The Dunham trial, in which Eliza Dunham was accused of committing adultery with her physician while her husband was traveling on business, was recounted decades later in a reputedly international collection of divorce stories; its author boasted that no other Boston divorce had ever attracted so much attention.[6]

As his reference to Boston suggests, most of the American cases chronicled for public consumption were tried in northeastern cities. Nonetheless, by midcentury there was a national divorce lore that was shaped
by the widely available information about sensational trials. The aggressive marketing and creative assembling of these trials by opportunistic
newsmen are a critical element in the story of divorce stories, and one
important by-product was the reduction of litigants to stock characters.
Those who enjoyed reading one racy case were guided by publishers' ads
to others. Even divorces from abroad, like that of the much-admired
Charles Dickens, intrigued American readers, especially since Dickens's
behavior seemed to belie his "sweet and truthful sketches of domestic
life."[7]

What, then, was the cachet of these real-life stories of infidelity and cruelty, and how did readers make sense of them? At one level they constituted a form of voyeurism that managed to titillate without the stigma of
pornography. "I looked through the keyhole," testified Eliza Dunham's
servant, and "saw her lying on the sofa—her clothes above her knees. He
[Dr. Marcellus Bowen] was doing something to his pants—I can't say
what." Printing such testimony in painstaking detail gave the reader an
opportunity to peer through the keyhole along with the witness. At the
same time, divorce stories worked as cautionary tales about the snares of
illicit sex. By presenting an array of occasions for moralizing, they
invested the genre with respectability. Even the mere appearance of
unchaste behavior might be condemned where marital trust was at stake.
"I did not think she was sick enough," observed another of Eliza Dunham's reproachful employees, as to require "a doctor three times a day."[8]

In conflating the didactic with the sensational, publishers created a
striking doubleness in these divorce stories. Quasi-pornographic
accounts of illicit sex, they were nonetheless suffused with appeals to a
morality that would somehow manifest itself to the reader through a
faithful presentation of the facts. Given the elaborate justifications that
prefaced trial reports, this point deserves emphasis. "We are not out to
invade the privacy of the parties," protested a Connecticut reporter in
defense of his paper's coverage of the Jarvis case, or "to gratify merely
the impertinent curiosity of the community." His duty, as he saw it, was
to lay out the truth for his readers by presenting a full and accurate
account, which was in itself an "act of justice."[9]

At once erotic and respectable, irreverent and conformist, sensational
and didactic, emotive and rational, trial reports constituted a strangely

mixed genre that drew freely on the conventions of sentimental culture. Open displays of heartfelt emotion were prized even when they came from men. Trials, it seems, with their stunning revelations of the underside of domestic life, unleashed intense reactions among participants and spectators alike, and attorneys who were instrumental in eliciting the outbursts were praised for their ability. The *New York Times* lauded John Graham, counsel for Daniel McFarland in the McFarland-Richardson trial, for moving "the Court, jury, and spectators to tears": "STRONG MEN WEEP LIKE WOMEN," read the caption for the day's story. Graham himself reportedly was "so fatigued and affected when he concluded that he could not reply to his friends, and sat with the tears rolling down his cheeks." The "manly emotionality" he displayed mirrored the favored acting style in the American popular theater, which celebrated tears as evidence of both an actor's talent and sincerity.[10]

Drama in the courtroom was palpable and exploitable, and it flowed in an easy confluence with the Victorian regard for transparency. As newsmen were fond of pointing out, trial pamphlets provided their readers with all the familiar elements of popular theater. Employing such phrases as "the curtain opened," "the dramatis personae," and "the domestic drama," reporters persistently framed the trials they were covering in a theatrical idiom. Readers were typically invited to scrutinize the carriage and countenance of the leading lady, who always garnered more newsprint than the leading man. The portrayal of Eliza Dunham, who was allotted a full-page drawing in the Dunham trial pamphlet, included a detailed description of her brown silk dress, her black mantilla, her beribboned bonnet, and her delicate beauty. "[O]ur ears," claimed the reporter, "were constantly saluted with such expressions as 'beautiful,' 'what a form,' 'what a foot and ancle [*sic*],' 'such a spiritual face,' 'how majestic and like a Juno in her form.'"[11]

But trials also diverged sharply from nineteenth-century dramas by virtue of their indeterminacy, and it is their indeterminacy that constitutes their most subversive characteristic. Who could be certain about how "spiritual" Eliza Dunham really was, and how did readers respond to that inescapable uncertainty? Reports suggest they thrived on it. According to one Boston daily, the enigma of Eliza Dunham's chastity accounted for the case's unprecedented popularity. Public interest in the case, it declared, ran high thanks to "the conflicting character of the evidence"—which was well suited, it seems, to the divergent sensibilities of a mass readership. As Daniel Cohen has suggested, nineteenth-century trial reports relied on a modern epistemology that substituted complex and fragmented images of life for a simple, didactic view of the truth.[12]

The fact remains that no matter how engaged readers were by these rival narratives of marital conflict, they were dramas without closure. Was Eliza Dunham an innocent victim of a jealous and vindictive spouse who had distorted her desperate need for a doctor into a lurid affair? Or was she a devious and unchaste wife who had seized on her hardworking husband's temporary absence to satisfy her illicit desires? Which of these dramas was the reader to believe? Or was there a more nuanced and less adversarial version that readers constructed on their own as they read between and around the conflicting lines of the plot?

One useful way to approach the interplay between these fragmented, multivalent stories and their amorphous mass audience is to concentrate on the questions they raised instead of which versions triumphed. As trial reports pushed the conceptualization of divorce away from the confines of biblical and juridical exegesis and into the chaos of human behavior, they must have provoked uncertainty about the adequacy of statutory categories. What was the relationship between the implacably fault-based and originally sin-based foundation for divorce and the tangled circumstances of litigants, who often appeared to have contributed mutually to the breakdown of their marriages? How did society measure the gravity of marital infidelity, and to what extent was it defined by the double standard? What behavior constituted marital cruelty? Was it limited to acts of physical violence, and was physical violence by a husband against his wife ever justified? What were the proper limits of women's activities outside the proverbial sanctity of the domestic circle, and what right, if any, did their husbands have to control them?

The gendered tensions at the heart of these contests were never more evident than in the ambiguities of marital power. All the women who stood at center stage in these fiercely contested suits had sorely tested the limits of their husbands' authority, thereby raising the specter of female autonomy. Given the destabilizing elements in these richly detailed divorce stories, when we calculate their impact it appears that subversion outweighs multivalency. Surely as they concretized and humanized the act of divorce, they undermined rather than supported the ideal of lifelong monogamy. Admittedly, trial accounts afforded moralists vivid materials for advocating a return to the inviolability of marriage. But despite the myriad ways in which real-life divorce stories were undoubtedly reshaped and appropriated by diverse communities of readers, it is worth remembering that both the proponents and opponents of divorce believed that by making divorce visible, they emptied it of shame. Writers of sentimental fiction, as we will see, worked to counteract what they viewed as the pernicious effects of these lurid stories by connecting divorce to individual disgrace and collective pollution. In the end, however, even the efforts of antidivorce moralists to put the shame back into divorce were shaped by the very stories they condemned. We turn now to the sensational, open-ended divorce stories chronicled by the press.

WOMEN AS VICTIMS

The plot lines in nineteenth-century divorce pamphlets turned on conflicts between the social freedom of married women and the conjugal authority of married men. As the focus on female adultery in these pamphlets suggests, however, the boundaries between social freedom and sexual freedom were unclear. Determining them could fall to the deliberations of a jury, which was forced to balance the new ideal of male benevolence against the all-important standard of female chastity.

In the Dunham case, where Eliza Dunham first sued for a bed-and-board divorce based on her husband's cruelty, only to be countersued on the basis of her alleged adultery, the problem of setting appropriate limits on the behavior of both husbands and wives provided the central motif. Although Thomas Dunham appealed to a husband's traditional right to monitor his wife's behavior, public sympathy, according to news accounts, lay with Eliza Dunham. So much was at stake for this woman—who was fighting for her honor in the court of public opinion as well as before the jury—that her situation was perilous. Despite damaging testimony by neighbors and servants, reporters portrayed her as a much-maligned woman trapped by the legal machinations of an obsessively jealous husband. A similar bias toward female defendants in other suits based on adultery arose, in part, from a sense of the terrible injustice of subjecting a possibly innocent woman to so harrowing an ordeal. As attorneys well understood, it was the woman-as-victim theme as it was played out in the predicament of the accused wife that resonated with jurors and spectators alike. In presenting Eliza Dunham as the hapless victim of a vindictive spouse, her counsel produced tears throughout the courtroom, and they reportedly flowed "without distinction of Sex."[13]

Eliza Dunham's role, then, was that of damsel in distress. Emphasizing the luminescence of her lovely young face, and implicitly linking the beauty of this beleaguered heroine to her inherent innocence, the pamphlet reporter avowed that every person in attendance would have acquitted her at once, had they the opportunity to serve as her jurors. Her husband's capacity to destroy her life with a single accusation loomed large in testaments to her innocence. Evidence of his readiness to use the law punitively surfaced in the testimony of a defense witness who alleged that when he asked Thomas Dunham if he believed his wife really had committed adultery, Dunham responded that he did not know but was determined to make her suffer. The jury was as sympathetic as the spectators. Thomas Dunham's suit was dismissed, and his wife was awarded a bed-and-board divorce with custody of their two sons.[14]

Given what we know of Victorian adherence to the double standard, the Dunham divorce pamphlet is remarkable for the compassion it exhibited toward a woman who, at the very least, bent the rules of propriety with a physician accused of taking liberties with other female patients. She was not too sick, according to one disapproving witness, to play the accordion for her doctor when he came to her bedside several times a day. One would have expected newsmen to chastise Eliza Dunham for lapses in conduct; instead, it was Thomas Dunham who emerged as a man bent on exacting punishment at any cost. When viewed through the lens of idealized gender roles, he had violated the benevolence that symbolized Victorian manhood more conclusively than she had violated the compliance that symbolized Victorian womanhood. And even though the double standard regarding sexual fidelity went unchallenged—indeed, precisely because it went unchallenged—it generated compassion for the women caught in its web. Reporters perceived female defendants battling against adultery charges as legal and social underdogs. Deemed especially vulnerable to false accusations and dangerously imperiled by a rush to judgment, women consistently received the benefit of the doubt.

In the 1840s and 1850s, a period marked by the spread of cheap pamphlet novels aided by the new technology of the cylinder press, a spate of sensational divorce cases emerged in which sympathy for the embattled wife was striking. Surfacing even in cases where the wife's transgression of gender etiquette was more definitive than in the Dunham case, it flowed from the humanitarian perception that the underlying dependency and relative powerlessness of a woman whose chastity was being challenged entitled her to public compassion. The scenario of female suffering, a compelling motif in both sentimental fiction and antebellum reform literature, was calculated to arouse "spectatorial sympathy." Small wonder that journalists eager to exploit the pathos of divorce before the broadest possible readership focused their attention on female litigants. Divorce was sentimental drama, and in sentimental drama, as Karen Halttunen has observed, the tableau of the passive, suffering female gratified the audience's penchant for voyeurism.[15]

What better tableau of passive female suffering than that of a possibly innocent woman being sued for divorce on the ground of adultery? Yet even the most creative efforts to flatten flesh-and-blood defendants into sentimental stereotypes were foiled by their patently rebellious conduct. Though female defendants might swoon in court much like their theatrical counterparts, other actions belied their passivity. In their readiness to leave hearth and home for the world at large, to socialize independently with members of the opposite sex, and to partake of the intoxicating pleasures of urban "high life," they complicated the archetypes of feminine innocence. Free-wheeling, pleasure-loving, iconoclastic, and independent, they in fact turned those archetypes upside down.

The legal rules for fault divorce, moreover, inadvertently encouraged an enlightened approach to the wife's social freedom by requiring the lines between merely unconventional behavior and truly illicit sex to be drawn with precision. Flirting by a woman was one thing, adultery another; to conflate the two was to permit a husband to cast off his wife on the flimsiest of pretexts. Fault, then, coincidentally challenged the doctrine of separate spheres in these sharply contested cases. As defense attorneys struggled to distinguish a harmless flirtation from outright adultery, they legitimated the notion of a woman moving beyond the confines of the domestic circle to socialize in public with members of the opposite sex. It was the public nature of the socialization, they argued, that rendered it harmless.

Rufus Choate, who had represented the plaintiff-husband in the Dunham case and went on to represent the defendant-wife in the Dalton case, was obliged to justify Helen Dalton's flirtation in order to distinguish it from infidelity. Choate's high visibility in portraying one client as a justly outraged husband and another as an unjustly maligned wife reveals not only how attorneys deftly manipulated gender stereotypes in ways that benefited their clients but also how they were compelled to reinvent them. This was particularly true for Choate's moving portrayal of Helen "Nellie" Dalton, who began what he characterized as a series of innocent meetings with William Sumner only five months after her marriage.

Choate's defense rested on drawing the line between indiscretion and immorality as finely as possible. It was inconceivable to him that this blushing young bride who was not yet eighteen when she wedded Frank Dalton and who had "enjoyed the instruction of a Christian family" could have been party to anything more than a casual flirtation. She was "comely, of remarkable modesty," he avowed, echoing the virginal imagery evoked by his opponent in the Dunham case, and "pure as a falling flake of snow." Yet because her young husband was tied up with the demands of earning a living, and she, residing at a Boston boarding-house, was not yet "at housekeeping," she was lonely and adrift. She met Sumner occasionally together with her married sister, Fanny Coburn, and Josiah Porter, an attorney who was Sumner's cousin. If she was guilty of anything, Choate argued, it was only of naïveté and poor judgment. The foursome, the two married women and the two unmarried men, carried on an altogether harmless relationship that was, according to Choate, a familiar feature of contemporary urban life. Their conduct was neither unusual nor immoral. Sumner, moreover, the alleged paramour, could hardly be cast as the libertine when he was "little more than a boy" and without any evidence of being "a seducer by profession or design." No, all that occurred in these meetings were occasional refreshments at local saloons, together with a few sociable rides on the omnibus to Cambridge. Perhaps there was some attraction there, Choate admitted, acknowledg-ing the possibility of Nellie's inchoate desire for a man other than her hus-band, but it was always constrained by her true feelings of love for her husband. As a consequence, Nellie "never came to love young Sumner with that impulsive, absorbing, and increasing love that endangers virtue and conquers chastity."[16]

Choate's efforts to paint Nellie's conduct as unexceptional and to dis-tinguish the sexual attraction she may have felt for young Sumner from the act of adultery exemplify the subversive threads woven through these trials, which typically drew female spectators. At the very least, such arguments familiarized both female spectators and female readers with real-life alternatives to the straight and narrow. Adopting a stance that ran against the grain of every conventional conduct manual, Choate devoted much of his defense to demonstrating how a young married woman might derive fleeting pleasure from a casual dalliance without being touched by what he called the "sentiment of dangerous love" (76). To anyone familiar with the literature of seduction, it should be evident that he was revamping the traditional image of the coquette—painting her still as vain and foolish, but differentiating her sharply from the ranks of the disreputable and the unchaste.

Nevertheless, in the process of distinguishing what he regarded as mere style in the conduct of women from moral substance, he was blur-ring and complicating the criteria that defined a virtuous woman. The "tens of thousands" of wives, he insisted, who behaved like Nellie Dalton "could never justly be suspected of having taken the last final step." It was foolhardy and unjust to equate a woman's social freedom with her sexual freedom: the former was the modish hallmark of a newly affluent lifestyle, while the latter constituted moral chaos. The slippage implicit in Choate's argument was rendered all the more acceptable by virtue of his appeal to the social conventions of urban elites. Fashionable women, he observed, regularly attended parties without their husbands, only to return to them at midnight, "conscious of a truer pleasure when they lie down by their sides" (76).

Chastity, ran his argument, remained the insurmountable barrier that separated the innocent from the fallen. Women would spurn any female member of their social set who they believed had violated the vow of marital fidelity. The verdict, then, which would ineradicably shape the balance of Nellie Dalton's life, placed a formidable burden on the jurors. Drawing on images of the lonely fate of Hester Prynne, heroine of *The Scarlet Letter,* Choate beseeched them to consider the dire consequences of finding this young woman guilty. It was already too late for her to recapture the easy equanimity she once had enjoyed. A verdict of innocent could neither restore the bliss she had experienced at the start of her marriage nor "enable her to recall the days of folly, of frivolity, and vanity without a blush and without a tear." But a verdict of guilty would send her out into the unforgiving world "with the scarlet letter upon her brow" and "publicly stri[ke] her from the roll of virtuous women" (59). A prelude to a life of shame and dishonor, it would sever her from the affection of her female friends and deliver her into the hands of libertines.

As one might expect, Richard Henry Dana, the renowned writer and attorney who represented Frank Dalton, was unwilling to separate style from substance in the treacherous realm of relations between the sexes. He assumed a traditional stance toward the dangers of coquetry, which only intensified, he seemed to suggest, with the requisites of a modernizing society. In a rapidly changing world where the slightest deviation from appropriate conduct might unleash erotic impulses, there was no substitute for adhering faithfully to the proprieties of gender etiquette. "It is dangerous," Dana asserted, "for a young married woman to be a coquette." Neither the loving influence of Nellie Dalton's family nor the formal strictures of her Christian upbringing were sufficient to insulate her from the pitfalls of a flirtation. Not only were men ever ready to indulge in their passions at every deviation from propriety, but women, too, could be rendered vulnerable as a result of the compromising circumstances in which they placed themselves. The dangers of desire were everywhere. Nellie Dalton, like so many other women impervious to the import of strict codes of social conduct for their sex, "dallied with the tempter a moment too long" (94). Her fall was an old and familiar story that ran across class lines and placed her in the same category as an urban prostitute. The ruined women who walk the streets of our cities, he insisted, came, as Nellie did, from families where their virtue once mattered and where hopes for them ran high.

The debate between the two attorneys turned on the relative influence of a seductive new social freedom on a married woman's chastity. Did Nellie Dalton's ride on the omnibus or her stop at the saloon place her in the moral category of a streetwalker? To frame the question in broader terms, did women of the urban gentry suffer the dire consequences of situating themselves in an immoral and polluted realm when they went out in public? If we view the case as a battle over the truth of Nellie Dalton's adultery and its relation to possible shifts in gender etiquette, we find that the conventional picture of a gender-segregated society that demonstrated its prudery regarding the public socializing of "respectable" men and women by covering up piano legs has been complicated. *Complicate* rather than *replace* is the operative word here, with special emphasis on well-to-do urban families. The social freedom of married women remained controversial, but it did so now in the new context of the expanding possibilities of an urban landscape in which consumerism and desire were linked, a development historians have tended to attribute to a later period.[17]

Questions about the nature and scope of Frank's jealousy were no less controversial and no less emblematic of the ambiguities unleashed by social and legal changes. How was an outraged husband of the mid-nineteenth-century urban gentry to respond to behavior such as Nellie's—with the power of his fists, or with the sanctions of the law? Frank Dalton resorted to both, thereby demonstrating his allegiance to a private remedy as well as a public one. After inveigling William Sumner into a meeting and savagely beating him, he forgave Nellie for her liaison and continued to live with her, either believing in her fundamental innocence or condoning her actual adultery. But he subsequently changed his mind and opted for the courts. Even more important, from the perspective of investing an already emotionally charged case with an additional dollop of sensationalism, was the fact that Frank's divorce suit intersected a manslaughter trial in which both he and his brother-in-law were tried for thrashing their respective wives' suitors and physically injuring Sumner. Although Sumner expired under ambiguous medical circumstances with bruises on his throat three weeks later, he failed even on his deathbed to confess to adultery with Nellie. This point was made emphatically by Rufus Choate, who, insisting that the truth will out in the final throes of death, used it to bolster Nellie's shaky defense.[18]

Nellie's defense was seriously compromised by allegations about an abortion, which Dana held out as evidence of her having taken the final step. His argument relied on the idea that reproductive differences accounted for the double standard and the need to keep women close to hearth and home. Divorce trials like the Dalton case implicitly pitted the allure of an extramarital liaison against the fact that in the absence of reliable birth control, sexuality and reproduction could not be effectively separated. It was Dana's task as attorney for the plaintiff to underscore the perils posed by an unwanted pregnancy. Female readers may have been tempted by the details of Nellie's whirlwind romance to imagine themselves in an impassioned affair, but they were undoubtedly chastened by Dana's appraisal of the price she paid. As he saw it, finding herself pregnant and unsure of the identity of the father, she sought the help of her family in securing an abortion: a subversive resolution of the paternity dilemma and a clear sign of her lack of chastity. Choate boldly countered that Nellie was already pregnant when she met Sumner, a fact that explained her restless behavior, and that she subsequently had experienced a miscarriage. Family members, then, were merely aiding her at a time of medical stress rather than abetting her in a shameless deception.[19]

Both families figured prominently in attorneys' presentations of the case. Frank Dalton's family, according to Choate, pressed him to divorce Nellie to quiet public criticism of his behavior, which failed to comport with prevailing concepts of male honor. Well into the nineteenth century and beyond, a man who assaulted and even murdered his wife's paramour in an act of unpremeditated passion was likely to enjoy the support of juries. Support for the jealous husband suggests the persistence of the notion that men own women, a concept that coexisted uneasily with the idea of women's moral responsibility but was quite compatible with the possessive aspects of romantic love. The problem here was not so much Frank's readiness to avenge the affair outside the courts as the calculating and even cowardly way in which he confronted Sumner and then boasted about it to the Boston newspapers.[20] But whereas Choate portrayed Frank as having fallen under the influence of apprehensive kinfolk eager to shore up his damaged image, Dana stressed the readiness of Nellie's family to cover her tracks at all costs. A cross-examination of her father revealed that he was so anxious to patch up her disintegrating marriage and save her failing reputation that he offered Frank, a salesman in a firm of Boston merchants, $10,000 in goods and $500 in cash to go west with Nellie and establish himself in his own business. There is even a suggestion that Nellie's father attempted to bribe some of the jurors (47).

Nellie's defense was further weakened by a series of written exchanges. They created a stir when introduced into evidence because they raised the possibility of erotic intimacy beyond the boundaries of marriage. Letters of passion, a prominent feature in trial pamphlets, were often touted by publishers on the covers. That Sumner was captivated by this young and beautiful married woman and was engaged in some kind of relationship with her was not at issue; how far he went with her was. Although his earnest verses professing his feelings for his beloved Nellie reputedly set courtroom spectators agog, they were basically an ode to the couple's innocence:

> So innocent is the joy we then sip
> So little of wrong is there in it
> That I wish all my errors were lodged on your lip,
> And I'd kiss them away in a minute

Was Sumner celebrating an amorous relationship that was innocent because it was sexually unconsummated—a still-shocking assertion in view of Nellie's marital status—or was he declaring in opaque Victorian doggerel that what he and Nellie did represented a higher morality beyond the strictures of law or religion? His meaning is unclear. Far more damaging to the defense was a letter Nellie addressed to Frank while he was serving time for the Sumner beating. "Frank, I have done wrong, very wrong," she admitted. "Young as I was, I was led astray. I was tempted, and in a moment yielded to the tempter." Choate was undaunted. He questioned the reliability of the confession; basing his defense on both Frank Dalton's condonation and Nellie Dalton's innocence, he argued that Frank had already forgiven Nellie for a crime she never had committed (10, 57).

The final outcome was a hung jury, but the popular "Shawmut edition" of the trial, published by the *Boston Bee,* was rushed into print even before the verdict was known. The legal fate of Nellie Dalton presumably had less effect on sales than the vivid tableau of her suffering, which she herself played out in a series of effusive, self-pitying letters to a now unforgiving husband. Yet any reader who followed the trial closely would have difficulty fitting the adventurous Nellie into the classic stereotype of damsel in distress. Indeed, Nellie's private response to Sumner's death and the alleged abortion shows her employing a far less sentimental idiom. "I remember her saying on one occasion," a servant testified, bent on blunting the wave of sympathy Nellie evoked, "that she wished the d——d men were both in their graves before she saw them, for they had caused her suffering enough" (21).[21]

SYMPATHY VERSUS ACCOUNTABILITY

Popular sympathy for the plight of the female defendant sprang from the conviction that men and women did not face each other in court as equals, even though the largely gender-neutral framework of American divorce law construed them as such. Nor were they perceived as equals in marriage despite the egalitarian implications of the companionate ideal. Admittedly, some female defendants exhibited behavior so deviant that they lost the sympathy that flowed from assumptions of their vulnerability. But as long as observers regarded a female defendant as oppressed by the power and authority of her husband either at home or in the courtroom, and as long as they were reluctant to accord her any real agency, humanitarian sensibilities mandated giving her the benefit of the doubt. Commentary on the Dalton case suggests that even when a woman's family of origin expended its wealth and influence to balance the scales of justice on her behalf, she could remain a victim in the public imagination.

Nowhere was public sympathy for the well-financed female defendant more effusive or better documented than in the Burch trial, an 1860 Chicago suit of sufficient magnitude to attract New York journalists to the scene. Here, as in the Dalton case, the defendant had written incriminating statements that belied her protestations of innocence and undercut her legal defense. Here, too, was the gnawing uncertainty about her guilt that permitted readers to engage in sexual fantasies as they filled in the blanks. Journalists, of course, were quick to promote titillating elements in the suit. The opening pages of the trial pamphlet collated by a *New York Times* reporter promised the "confession" of Mrs. Burch (in quotation marks to stress its uncertainty), letters offered in evidence but ruled out by the court, and depositions from numerous women of ill fame in St. Louis, Cincinnati, and other cities visited by the well-traveled plaintiff.[22]

The cast of characters was dazzling. Embodying the mobility and affluence now possible in the age of rail and steam, the cosmopolitan Burches captured public interest by revealing the details of an opulent lifestyle that afforded diverse opportunities for extramarital affairs. The complainant, Isaac Burch—a prominent Chicago banker and community leader—accused his wife of "the very worst kind of domestic crime" and fought for the custody of the couple's two children. The defendant, Mary Burch—a Chicago and New York socialite who was the niece and heir of railroad magnate Erastus Corning—accused her husband, in turn, of adultery with numerous prostitutes and of carrying on an affair with a female houseguest. And in a society that esteemed husbands as loving companions and stalwart providers, she charged him with marrying her for her future fortune, an accusation that painted him as doubly lacking. Corning himself attended the trial that catapulted his niece into the nation's newspapers, and he hired the expensive battery of attorneys who represented her.

The fact that Isaac's suit came hard on the heels of a rift he had with Corning not only bolstered the defense's claims that Isaac browbeat Mary into signing an adultery confession but also contributed to the outpouring of sympathy for this undeniably privileged female defendant. In the world of nineteenth-century divorce pamphlets, observers could favor an affluent female defendant over an ambitious male plaintiff if they suspected he was discarding her because she no longer served his financial purposes. In a robustly democratic culture, divorcing for money was an act even more reprehensible than marrying for money; and cued by persuasive newsmen, the public responded accordingly. Journalists depicted Mary Burch as the quintessential damsel in distress, a role she played flawlessly and may very well have internalized. In the words of the *Times* trial report, she was "weak," "excitable," and "of a naturally nervous and lively temperament" (6)—a woman, in other words, who was inherently vulnerable to the demands of a corrupt and powerful spouse. Because Isaac's power reputedly extended to the Chicago courts, the trial was moved at the request of Mary's counsel to the town of Naperville, some thirty miles away.

Journalists knew a good story when they saw one. They flocked to the little prairie town to exploit the scenario of female suffering embodied in a woman accused of having sex in her own home with her husband's friend. The pathos of her struggle to deny her adultery with David Stuart, a prominent Chicago lawyer and an intimate of the Burch family, suffused their reports. Whether or not her denial is true, ventured the

Times correspondent in an unconvincing stab at neutrality, "it is certainly one of the most affecting and thrilling statements of a woman's suffering and a man's wrongs which was ever penned." Fact or fiction, it was the narrative of suffering that counted here, and thus he kept on in his indeterminate vein: "If we believe it untrue, it is a most masterly fiction. If we believe it true, it is most heartrendingly terrible." Moreover, he had his audience clearly in mind: "Who but a woman can understand and appreciate" it, he queried rhetorically, appealing to the sensibilities of his female readers, "and who but a woman can write the story of the following two weeks?" he continued, ignoring the absence of female reporters (5).

Virtually every page of the Burch trial report suggests that as newsmen constructed the case, they emphasized the scenario of suffering over considerations of guilt. The assumption of moral accountability that lay at the heart of fault divorce was obfuscated and sentimentalized by the discourse of victimization. That Mary Burch wrote a letter to her pastor asking him to encourage her husband to pray "for the love he once bore his erring wife" was less significant than her pathetic depiction of herself as "an outcast—a poor lone wanderer upon the earth—shunned by all and loved by none." The avowals she made regarding her own "iniquity" receded before her plea that she was "utterly lost and undone." Yet even a reader ready to believe that she was coerced by her husband into signing a witnessed confession might find it difficult to accept her counsel's dismissal of her agonized self-assessment as "merely penitential," an expression of "contrition in general terms" (9, 81).

Like the newsmen who framed the case in the idiom of sentimental culture, Mary Burch's counsel spoke more to the manifestations of her suffering than to the evidence of her innocence. Arguing that the pathos of her predicament encompassed her entire family, he beseeched the jury to find her innocent for the sake of her children, who would otherwise be shadowed by their "mother's infamy and disgrace." He even urged jurors to consider Mary's mother, "whose grey hairs you bring with sorrow to the grave if you indorse this unrighteous judgment against her suffering daughter." Outlining the consequences of a guilty verdict, he shifted the focus from the defendant to the jurors, who bore a sacred responsibility, in his view, not to contribute further anguish to this already anguished woman. As he entrusted this "poor, frail, timid, trembling, and crushed little woman" into the hands of the twelve men selected to decide her fate, he warned them that if they wished to die in peace and without remorse, they would have to find her innocent (81).

Underscoring the broad social ramifications of so nationally visible a case, Isaac Burch's counsel also exhorted the jurors to understand and accept their formidable responsibility. He, of course, objected vigorously to the terms in which his opponent appealed to the children, urging jurors instead not to entrust them to a guilty mother at the expense of an innocent father. But by far the most revealing tack in his summation was his heroic attempt to counter "the sympathies of a whole community in favor of the wife in any contest." With those words, he delineated where popular sympathy lay in this suit and others like it. Although he empathized, he confessed, with the impulse "to side with the weak against the strong," he reminded jurors of their obligation to adhere faithfully to "the spirit and reason of the law." Implicit in his appeal to the all-male jury evaluating Mary Burch's sexual conduct was the notion that every woman's vow of sexual fidelity was a critical component of male contractualism. Marriage, the sacred contract that underpinned all other contracts, rested on the unalloyed chastity of women, and women must be held accountable in this regard. Addressing the jury man to man, he asked every juror to imagine his feelings "if the wife of your bosom had betrayed your honor and trampled your rights." But in a final effort to counter allusions to the defendant's weakness and to blunt the spectacle of her suffering, he conflated her identity with her uncle's almost as if she were unable to stand on her own as an adversary. He exhorted the jury to consider the sheer power in the cadre of high-priced attorneys who were hired by Erastus Corning. Working to tie the status of this allegedly pathetic little defendant ever more firmly to that of her rich and influential uncle, he contrasted the democratic simplicity of the members of the Naperville jury with the men who "like the feudal barons of old . . . come with their bands of retainers at their heels and with a show of power and influence seek to overcome us" (81–83).

His appeals first to rationalism, then to contractualism, and finally to populism went unheeded by the men to whom they were addressed. As inquisitive crowds jammed the local hotels and assembled in the streets, the jury delivered a unanimous verdict in favor of the defendant. People celebrated animatedly in both Naperville and Chicago. According to the *Chicago Journal,* applause broke out in the courtroom when the foreman announced the verdict, and everyone "was crazy with joy."[23] Jury members later visited Mary Burch at the house where she was staying; unable to control their emotions, they ended up "weeping like children." They went on to carouse with the rest of the townspeople at a local inn while a marching band serenaded Mary from the street. On the following morning, a large group accompanied Mary, her mother, and her attorneys as they left Naperville to catch the train to Chicago. Meanwhile, Chicagoans were investing the occasion with the trappings of a national holiday. When the crowd at Tremont House heard about the verdict, their enthusiasm "was equaled only by the excitement of a Presidential election." As the news spread through the streets of the city, fireworks were set off and bonfires blazed. Mary Burch, "indorsed by the jury and the sympathies of the great popular heart," returned at last to the warm welcome of her Chicago friends (102, 116).

THE NEW DOUBLE STANDARD

Shaped as they were by newsmen's accounts, "the sympathies of the great popular heart" were extended to litigants on sharply gendered terms. Sympathizers could tolerate uncertainty about a woman's conduct by endowing her with an almost paralytic passivity even when the evidence pointed to her volition. Conversely, male litigants were held more strictly accountable in popular trial accounts because their authority and autonomy were assumed. Admittedly, sex with prostitutes or even servants was a type of adultery that, despite the zealous opposition of moral reformers, was tacitly accepted with the understanding that men will be men. Trial correspondents mirrored the widespread impulse to calibrate the immorality of extramarital sex according to the form it took.

Sex with a woman of the middle or upper classes, or even worse, a family friend or relative, constituted a far more ominous form of adultery than a visit to a brothel. Any impassioned male-female relationship carried on without a cash nexus outside the bonds of matrimony threatened marriage in ways that prostitution did not. As Karen Lystra has noted, Victorian men and women valorized male-female intimacy so long as it occurred within marriage. But the intimacy of an extramarital affair represented romantic love in its most erotic and anarchic form. If we construe marriage as the principal social institution for ordering sexuality—its most significant function in the Victorian era—then we can appreciate the degree to which the increasingly powerful ethos of romantic love complicated the moral assessment of male litigants.[24]

Adultery, however, was *not* a focal point in the moral assessment of male litigants in popular trial accounts, an observation that only serves to underscore the public obsession with the topic of female adultery. The occasional emphasis on men's participation in extramarital affairs focused typically on alleged paramours rather than on male defendants. Nonetheless, representations of husbands in sensational divorce suits reflected the intensifying strains of a society committed to lifelong monogamy on the one hand and romantic love on the other. Slated now to fill the often conflicting roles of provider and companion, a husband had two major fronts on which he could fail miserably in the court of public opinion. Whereas the husband as provider still loomed large in both the legal culture and the popular culture, his role as loving companion was making its way into formal complaints, attorneys' summations, and reporters' comments. The law itself required a modicum of kindness on the part of husbands. In recognizing marital cruelty as a ground for divorce, state statutes were, in effect, placing it on a par with adultery. Contested divorces, which provided an important public forum in which contemporary antipathy to cruelty could appear, point to a shift in moral consciousness regarding the responsibilities of men.

Whether it took the form of wife beating or more subtle types of punishment, marital cruelty constituted lovelessness in its most extreme and patriarchal form. In the spectatorial world of publicized divorces, reporters could detect a penchant for cruelty in the grim visage of a male defendant. In the Bennett divorce, a New Haven case in which Mary Bennett accused her doctor-husband not only of attempting to force her into an abortion but of almost killing one of their children with an overdose of laudanum, a *New York Times* reporter revealed where the guilt lay by presenting contrasting portraits of the litigants. Mary Bennett was "very pretty . . . small in stature, lively in expression," with "a silvery voice, brilliant dark eyes, very dark hair, delicate hands, and regular features." Partially deaf and somewhat older, George Bennett suffered severely in the comparison. He was "a little man, with jet black hair standing up all over his head, a heavy black beard and moustache, a restless small black eye," and a voice that sounded as if he had "a sponge in his throat." Several days later, even after Mary Bennett's newly acquired male companion was subpoenaed to testify on the nature of his relationship with her, the reporter speculated "that public sympathy still leans toward the lady."[25] If public opinion did lean toward the lady, the reporter had done his part in generating it.

Newspapers demonstrated their partiality toward beleaguered women in a variety of ways. Under the sardonic rubric "A Model Man," the *New York Times* devoted an editorial to George Bennett's brutality in which it nervously balanced the obligatory benevolence of men against the newly organized insurgency of women. "Few, we imagine, are aware how noble a thing a model husband may be, even in this Nineteenth Century, and in this land of woman's rights, of Bloomerism, and Female Conventions," it stated. Significantly, the traditional tyrannies of patriarchy were seen to outweigh the novel dangers of feminism. The doctor, the paper observed facetiously, had done whatever he could for his wife by giving her philters and poisons, by trying to relieve her of the burdens of her maternity, by kicking her and boxing her ears, and by preventing her from indulging in extravagance. Indeed, he "did everything that any husband, from Bluebeard down to Punch, ever did or could do, to restrain her wandering affections, tame her undisciplined desires, and educate her into a just subservience to himself."[26]

The *Times* was expressing its adherence to the new double standard: the requisite compliance of women now was being balanced by the obligatory benevolence of men. George Bennett was so distressed by the paper's spin on his marital conduct that he addressed a letter to the editor, noting that a newspaper of wide circulation was likely to be read daily by the very judge who was to decide his case and determine the custody of his children. Whatever "infirmities of temper" he may have exhibited in his marriage, he averred, they occurred only under the most extreme provocation. To make matters worse, newspaper coverage of the trial had placed his livelihood at risk. He denounced the paper for calling him a "quack," a term used to derogate "irregular" physicians, and went on to defend the pills he sold in his medicine business as being at least as good as those of Dr. Brandreth, his principal competitor.[27] As his letter suggests, newsmen then as now were key players in these contests, at least in determining their impact on the public.

How are we to understand the meaning of this widespread impulse to view wives as perennial victims in popular trial accounts? Surely we should not reject out of hand the reformist implications of a gender-conscious humanitarianism or ignore its role in reshaping attitudes toward marital conduct. Indeed, the woman-as-victim theme, a compelling motif in temperance and abolitionism, was undeniably the starting point for midcentury feminist agitation. But to read the sympathy exhibited for women in these sharply contested cases as marking a drive toward gender equality is to miss the point. It was a response to real structural inequalities in marriage, and the cult of sensibility and the penchant for spectatorship directed attention to the plight of female litigants. Divorce pamphlets developed in the marketplace, however, and their emphasis on women's victimization came closer to an aggressive exploitation of the double standard than a reformist effort to correct it.

In this genre, seeing women as marital victims meant obscuring women as individual agents.

At the same time, to acknowledge the exploitative drive behind trial reports is not to deny the transgressive currents running throughout the genre. The truly destabilizing elements displayed in the genre—the fine-grained details that pushed flesh-and-blood wives out from behind gender stereotypes—controverted the motif of female victimization and created a new, man-as-victim theme that challenged the double standard. It was the haunting possibility that seemingly respectable women denied the authority of their husbands precisely where it mattered most that rendered the genre so subversive.

A WOMAN BEYOND THE PALE

As we have seen, reporters typically handled legal challenges to female chastity by endowing the defendant with weakness and passivity even when the evidence suggested otherwise. Such treatment in the face of contradictory evidence inadvertently resulted in female characters who were more complex and more ambiguous than the sentimental stereotypes that framed them. But a few wives exhibited behavior so deviant that they were denied the latitude regularly extended to female litigants. Women with "a roving and unhallowed lust," to quote the words of plaintiff's counsel in the Beardsley case, evinced a sexual aggressiveness that placed them beyond the pale of public sympathy. And just as a man's grim visage could reveal his cruelty, so too a woman's physical appearance could alert readers to the depravity that lurked beneath her good looks. Although Mary Beardsley, the daughter of a prominent Brooklyn Methodist minister, was "fair as alabaster . . . with a vermilion blush that a shepherd in the fabled Arcadia might envy," her "exquisite shape" was "shown off by a tight-fitting jacket and by such other ornaments of dress as a showy woman of means might be supposed to select."[28]

Although the portrait of Mary Beardsley reveals some ambivalence on the part of the trial reporter, his description of her daily habits left less room for doubt. The history of the case, as it was developed in the opening pages of the trial pamphlet, emphasized her dangerous fondness for promenading Broadway without her husband. No sooner did Alfred Beardsley leave Brooklyn Heights for work in the morning than his wife set off as well to enjoy the amusements of the city. Boldly eating in Thompson's saloon, coyly dropping rosebuds on the street, brazenly picking up a man with whom she visited Barnum's museum—these were the actions of a woman bent on pursuing selfish pleasures without regard for either the sanctity of her marriage or the welfare of her small son. Her excursions provided perfect fodder for the press. "HOW ACQUAINTANCES ARE MADE IN THE METROPOLIS—THE BROADWAY FASHIONABLE SALOONS—ROSES, LOVE, AND ROMANCE," read the headline for the opening of the defendant's case (10).

What distinguished Mary Beardsley from the female defendants who were given the benefit of the doubt was the flagrant deception she brought to her trysts. If her husband is to be believed, when she left Brooklyn Heights for her outings in the city, she created an entirely new identity for herself in which she had no husband or son. Then, using her invented identity to enter a new union, this proper Methodist minister's respectable daughter committed bigamy by marrying Thomas Mahon, an Irish physician she met on Broadway. This was no ordinary tale of bigamy involving remarriage after an informal separation or long absence: this was bigamy with a vengeance. Sleeping with two husbands simultaneously represented an offense even more anarchic than engaging in an extramarital affair. Because romantic love assumed an inner self to be revealed only to one's lover, the ensuing tale of how Mary sustained a double life in her relations with two men subverted the ideal of marital intimacy in deeply provocative ways. Beyond the question of determining to which man Mary Beardsley had bared her soul and committed her body was a more fundamental issue: who, in fact, was she when she went to bed with her respective husbands? Observers agreed that here was a case where fact was infinitely better than fiction. "History has thrown down the gauntlet to imagination," claimed the reporter as he quoted plaintiff's counsel, "and won in the strife" (7).

Alfred Beardsley alleged that his wife invented a persona calculated to win over the footloose physician, who had flirted jauntily with her as she strolled about the city. When the two went on to experience together the delights of Barnum's museum, a site that exemplified the social possibilities on the urban landscape, she identified herself as Miss Emma Evaline Seymour, daughter of Admiral Sir John Seymour of Halifax, Nova Scotia. She was presently living with friends in Brooklyn, she explained, so that she could complete her education at a fashionable institution in the city. Her father, however, was a disciplinarian of the old school whose wishes she honored faithfully since acts of disobedience on her part might interfere with her "dower" (dowry), which was large enough to encourage her strict compliance. Inspired by her description of high social standing and impressive wealth, the enterprising

Mahon married her before a Catholic priest who later verified their union in court and remembered securing a bishop's dispensation for the reading of the banns.

What turned the trial reporter against Mary Beardsley was the extravagance of her duplicity: she appropriated an entire new identity while she went about the business of maintaining her regular life. The anarchic power of a woman's imagination here was directed toward the malignant purpose of deceiving two men simultaneously. With the illicit marriage consummated, he observed, "with the bridal kiss upon her lips and the marriage ring upon her finger," she returned to the bedside of her lawful husband. The reporter was aghast at the audacity of her hoax. That a married woman would devise such a scheme is "incredible," he remarked, and "how she could impose herself on a man of the world for an heiress, or on a doctor as a maiden, is equally strange" (7).

Mary's defense consisted of a series of countercharges that were no less fantastic than the accusations she faced. Not only did she accuse her husband of adultery with her best friend as well as with numerous prostitutes, but she claimed that Thomas Mahon, her alleged second husband, was a party to a conspiracy devised by Alfred to rid himself of her and marry her friend. Chauncey Shaffer, her counsel, argued that the obvious snag in Alfred's version of the story was the lack of motive. Why would Mary Beardsley pursue an older, debt-ridden, Irish physician at the expense of her young American husband? Has it come to this, he exclaimed disgustedly as he drew on anti-Irish sentiment, "that American women will leave ambrosia to feed on garbage!" (59). Then Shaffer turned to the woman-as-victim appeal as he tried to strip his client of any vestige of autonomy. He emphasized the physical vulnerability of the pale and slender defendant, "who with blood crimsoning her lips was borne out of the Court on her father's arm." He pointed to the dire consequences of finding her guilty, suggesting that it might even drive her to suicide. And he exhorted jurors as "fathers of manly sons and chaste daughters . . . to crush a conspiracy deep and damning as ever was forged in the pit of hell itself" (67).

That both partners might have committed adultery posed a serious problem for the plaintiff. Inasmuch as Shaffer had little difficulty in confirming Alfred's activity with prostitutes, a finding that essentially nullified the charge against Mary, it remained for Alfred's counsel to differentiate for the jury between types of extramarital sex. In both his opening remarks and his summation, Richard Busteed upheld the continuing legitimacy of the double standard, especially as it related to prostitution. Although the law failed to distinguish between the sexes in defining the fault of adultery, he deemed it unreasonable to assume that Alfred Beardsley had lived in New York "without seeing its sights—without having a look at the elephant," as he put it (11–12). But Busteed, who was understandably eager in this case to hold women to a stricter standard of chastity than men, simultaneously deplored another result of the double standard: the sympathy given to accused women. "At no time or place, and under any circumstances is it desirable to be the accuser of a woman," he complained, underscoring the tactical disadvantage under which he labored in the courtroom. Whereas Albert had demonstrated the ordinary drives of manhood, Mary was hopelessly depraved. A woman of "insatiable sexual appetite," she was guilty of "the treble crime of bigamy, adultery, and hypocrisy" (70, 75).[29]

Hypocrisy, the masking of one's authentic self, loomed large in Busteed's assessment of the pain Mary had inflicted on Alfred. It was Alfred, not Mary, he insisted, who was the hapless victim here; and though Alfred could never be restored to his former state of domestic bliss, the jury needed to come to terms with the enormity of Mary's deception. They needed to understand that Alfred's life was forever dimmed by the scorn and suffering he experienced at the hands of his duplicitous wife. "His Lares and Penates [household gods] are broken in pieces," intoned Busteed, "and trail in the dust" (75).

The trial reporter pronounced the summation "one of the best forensic displays ever heard in the court of justice," but the jurors were less impressed. They found Alfred guilty of adultery despite Busteed's appeal to the propriety of the double standard. They found Mary guilty of adultery as well but innocent of entering into an illicit marriage, thereby saving her from a criminal prosecution for bigamy. The paradox of finding her guilty of adultery but innocent of bigamy, despite compelling testimony to the contrary, suggests that even when the female defendant subverted monogamy in a particularly provocative way, the lines between woman as sexual predator and pathetic victim were not always clear.

That the long-separated couple remained in legal limbo as a result of the decision passed without comment from the pamphlet reporter. Nor did he address the issue of support or child custody, which the judge presumably determined at a later date.[30] Such practical concerns were not as engaging as playing the freedom of a married woman against the authority of her husband, with both set against the backdrop of urban life and its burgeoning diversions. They did not slake the contemporary thirst for voyeurism as effectively as juxtaposing the details of a woman's sexual misconduct with the poignant tableau of her suffering.

To be sure, adultery was not the only theme in divorce pamphlets to exploit the spectacle of female suffering. Marital cruelty did so as well but ran as a distant second to female adultery, not only because the mere possibility of female adultery was more titillating but because it tested the limits of conjugal authority as no other story line could. As for male adultery, although it was the object of formal condemnation, it was hardly newsworthy. To put it another way, female compliance in the all-important area of chastity was far more central to the Victorian ideology of marriage than either male compliance or male benevolence. Female compliance was also problematic. While the ideal of female chastity buttressed the new double standard as visibly as it had the old one, it did so now in the face of an urban social life that augmented opportunities for relations between the sexes. Indeed, it was the tensions between the traditional ideal of chastity and the novel temptations of the city that animated popular midcentury trials.

TESTING THE JURORS' SYMPATHY

Few suits represented those tensions more dramatically than that of Catherine Forrest against Edwin Forrest, the renowned American tragedian. Although Catherine was no match for her husband in terms of financial resources, she was his intellectual superior, and she brought a cosmopolitan worldview to their contests in the courtroom. Here was a woman who moved easily in New York's elite literary circles and also evinced a fondness for Fourierism and feminism. An audacious, free-thinking plaintiff who was transformed into a defendant by virtue of her husband's countercharges, she sorely tested the sympathy jurors typically exhibited toward the accused woman.

Edwin was, in fact, the original plaintiff in a series of suits that moved across state lines. An agreement the couple signed in 1850 following their separation stipulated that Catherine would not oppose Edwin's quest for an out-of-state divorce, provided the suit did not impeach her virtue. When Catherine discovered Edwin was attempting a legislative divorce in Pennsylvania on the ground of her adultery, she applied to the Supreme Court of New York for an injunction restraining him from pursuing the Pennsylvania suit.[31] She subsequently sued him for divorce in New York on the basis of his adultery.

Starting in December of 1851, the New York City trial of *Forrest v. Forrest* provided readers with thirty-two days of spellbinding court coverage that was "sold wholesale in every corner of the land." This trial was one battle in a long war of attrition in which Edwin appealed the verdict five times, giving up only after eighteen years of costly litigation. Of the $64,000 Edwin paid out to Catherine, it is estimated that $59,000 went for the legal fees run up by her attorney, Charles O'Conor, a leading state Democratic politician and a prominent member of the New York bar. It was the 1851 trial, however, which followed on the heels of the Astor Place riot, that exposed the Forrests' marital problems to the full glare of national publicity.[32]

Ripples from the Astor Place riot spilled over into the courtroom. In May of 1849, a rowdy group of Bowery Boys—or "Forresters," as Edwin's devoted working-class fans were called—stoned the Astor Place Opera House in order to stop the performance of William Macready, an English actor who was Edwin's archenemy. As Iver Bernstein has observed, the confrontation that ensued pitted a patrician urban elite against the plebeian supporters of the revered American actor. The police and militia called up by the mayor to protect the threatened English performer fired point-blank into the crowd, killing twenty-two persons.[33] Catherine, who had disapproved of Edwin's headstrong handling of his feud with Macready, attributed her husband's marital disaffection to the harsh criticism he faced following the riot and to the attendant ebbing of his popularity. Connections between the bloody riot and the bitter divorce suit extended to the list of Catherine's alleged paramours. Edwin's altercation with the writer Nathaniel P. Willis, one of several men he accused of having sexual intercourse with Catherine, began with his anger at Willis's criticism of his feud with Macready. The Forresters enlivened the legal proceedings with zealous expressions of loyalty when they attended the trial to support their embattled hero, hissing and cheering at the appropriate junctures.

Ironically, Edwin did not receive top billing here, although it was his celebrity that had attracted press coverage in the first place: he was far better known than his wife. If the trial pamphlet collated by the *New York Herald* can serve as a gauge, his role was nowhere near as important as hers. Accordingly, it was her portrait that adorned the cover of the pamphlet. And though Catherine served as the legal plaintiff, press coverage focused on Edwin's countercharge of her adultery. It was Catherine, then, who stood at center stage throughout the *Herald* version of the proceedings, and it was doubts about her chastity that put her there.

Given the difficulty of producing hard evidence of Catherine's adultery, Edwin's counsel, John Van Buren, produced a stream of witnesses to document her loose morals and ultraist beliefs. He filled out his portrait of Catherine's radicalism by reading from a letter she had written professing her admiration for Fourierism and woman's rights and her skepticism about bourgeois marriage norms. In the letter, she denounced the economic dependency of women, insisting that men could never hope to be free unless women were free as well. Even more shocking was her assertion that a wife should not blame her husband "for seeking after new fancies" if she herself had been insensitive to his desires. This letter, which Van Buren read with such gusto to the attentive crowd in the courtroom, revealed in no uncertain terms that Catherine found relations between the sexes in need of total reform.[34]

The most sensational piece of evidence, however, was the much-heralded Consuelo letter, whose full contents were promised to readers on the cover of the *Herald* pamphlet. Written by George Jamieson, one of Edwin's fellow actors, and discovered by Edwin among Catherine's possessions, the letter allegedly addressed Catherine as Consuelo, a character in a George Sand novel. Although O'Conor protested that the heroine of the Sand novel was a morally exemplary woman, the problem of Jamieson's ardent language remained; he had few options beyond suggesting there was no proof that the real-life Consuelo was Catherine Forrest. The power of the Consuelo letter lay in the lyricism with which it celebrated erotic love. "It will be found," promised Van Buren in his opening statement, "that in that letter, he addressed her in a language of deep affection, and that it contained admissions of criminality. It will be found that that letter speaks of the realization of a voluptuous enjoyment" (14). The letter, which wedded tenderness together with eroticism, was the centerpiece of Van Buren's case because it glorified the presence of romantic love outside the bonds of matrimony. "[H]ave we not known real bliss?" Jamieson queried his beloved Consuelo; "have we not experienced the truth that ecstasy is not a fiction?" (74).[35]

The balance of Van Buren's case against Catherine took the form of witnesses, mostly servants, who described her as a "segar" smoker and brandy drinker accustomed to giving all-night parties when her husband was on the road. O'Conor tried to defend her social habits by arguing that she was obliged to mix in New York literary society in order to maintain her husband's position. But witnesses noted that a great many gentlemen and a few ladies visited Catherine while Edwin was gone, often staying until the early hours of the morning. Curious readers were

duly introduced to the cadre of writers, actors, and musicians who consumed the alcoholic beverages, smoked the cigars, played the drawing
room games, and were found from time to time in sexually compromising positions. A waiter testified that he saw Nathaniel Willis and Catherine Forrest in the living room while they were "lying on each other,"
and later found "some hairpins and an elastic garter." The testimony of
the same witness, who alleged he also saw Catherine's sister lying on the
floor with a man, was cut off with the prim observation that "here the
witness's testimony is unfit for publication" (28).

Van Buren concluded by urging jurors to see Edwin as a wounded husband instead of as a famous actor. The focus of his summation, however,
was the countercharge against Catherine, which was proven, he insisted,
by her immodest social habits, including her readiness to entertain men
who were unknown to her husband. This practice, he argued, placed her
beyond the pale of "the sickly sentimentality that sometimes pervades the
jury box when a female party is on one side." "How," he asked, "do you
explain this desire to know men whom her husband did not know—this
determination to associate with them?" (143, 156). It was the trait that
showed her for what she was to the men who would decide her fate, separating her life from the lives of respectable, middle-class jurors. "This is
quite going ahead of my time," he said, referring to Catherine's flamboyant soirees, "and I doubt whether any of the jurors ever happened to
have in their own household a frolic like that" (148).

O'Conor, of course, appealed to "the sickly sentimentality" that Van
Buren feared would undo his case. Here was a "helpless and friendless"
woman, he told the jurors, pitted against a man of vast financial
resources who was insane with jealousy and intent on dishonoring her
at any cost, including the bribing of witnesses. Naturally, it was Edwin
who was the focal point of his summation. In an effort to challenge the
validity of Edwin's apparent suffering, he highlighted the theatrical life
that Van Buren tried to downplay. His point was a simple one: given
Edwin's years of experience on the stage, how could he be trusted to
expose his true feelings in another forum (157)? O'Conor was driving a
wedge between the visible signs of Edwin's anguish in the courtroom and
the Victorian ideal of transparency. Edwin's tears, according to O'Conor,
were not a signifier of his sincerity.

The jurors were evidently inclined to trust O'Conor's narrative over
Van Buren's. They found Edwin guilty, Catherine innocent, and set
alimony at a hefty $3,000. Although both Forrests were cheered as they
left the building through different exits, spectators in the courtroom

applauded the foreman's responses to the fifth and eighth questions posed by the judge, which established Catherine's innocence and set the amount of her alimony. To be sure, class (as well as race) was undoubtedly a factor in the sympathy extended to Catherine. As Christine Stansell has suggested, middle-class men traditionally exhibited sexual antagonism in response to any slip in the conduct of working-class (or nonwhite) women.[36] Nonetheless, in light of Catherine's embrace of feminism and Fourierism along with her avant-garde lifestyle, the willingness of male jurors to find her innocent compellingly demonstrates the resonance of the woman-as-victim theme. It confirms just how powerful a symbol the powerless woman was.

At the same time, the figure that emerges from the trial embodies a good deal more than woman as victim. The competing depictions of Catherine fuse female stereotypes in a way that obscures simple distinctions between passivity and power and innocence and guilt. Romantic love, moreover, with its volatile blend of spirituality and desire, surfaces here detached from the safety of conjugal moorings. Small wonder that both the opponents and proponents of divorce believed that divorce pamphlets took the shame out of divorce; in fact, they did far more. Divorce stories like the Forrest case went beyond picturing either the grim details of a failed marriage or the liberating prospect of the second chance. In depicting scenes of heterosexual intimacy outside the boundaries of marriage, they were helping to detach sexuality from the realm of procreation.[37] Although that split could only be fully realized with the development of effective birth control, it was presaged by the eroticism of romantic love, which pressed hard against the constraints of lifelong monogamy.

EROS VERSUS ORDER: SENTIMENTAL FICTION

Popular awareness of divorce underwent a significant transformation in the middle decades of the nineteenth century as divorce stories proliferated. The divorce question came to the fore, often in tandem with the woman question, amid a profusion of individualizing narratives that spoke with greater immediacy than did the abstractions and exhortations of public debate. The spread of divorce stories helps us understand the process whereby people made sense of divorce and assessed its long-term effects; not surprisingly, different stories elicited different assessments. On the one hand, trial reports took some of the shame out of divorce through their open-endedness, their sheer repetitiveness, and their sympathetic representations of accused women; on the other hand, sentimental novelists, who began appropriating divorce as a subject in the late 1840s, worked to put the shame back in.[38]

Although there can be no denying the influence of popular trials on sentimental fiction—or, for that matter, sentimental fiction on popular trials—fictional narratives of divorce were essentially cautionary tales for a middle-class female audience, whose social status and economic survival depended on marriage. Men needed marriage too, but their capacity to replace the unpaid and therefore invisible labor of their wives exceeded their wives' corresponding capacity to replace the earnings of their husbands.[39] The fundamental disparity between the marital circumstances of men and women shaped the stance that most fiction writers took and stood in uneasy tension with claims about women's moral autonomy. Temperance literature is a case in point. In indicting intemperance in the endemic moral failure of men, Timothy Shay Arthur could endorse separation in the face of a husband's alcoholism while stressing the price women invariably paid for severing the bonds of matrimony.

Sentimental novelists valorized formulas for shoring up marriage, the institution that defined and embodied the bourgeois ethos. They typically paired appeals to masculine benevolence, an ideal that assumed the husband's authority but recommended affection, with encouragement for feminine acquiescence, a prescription that balanced the wife's moral independence against her economic vulnerability. What to do, though, when spouses failed to adhere to the terms of the new double standard, which was reshaping gender roles to support the synergy of Victorian marriage? What to do with cruel and indifferent husbands and selfish and headstrong wives? The answer was *not* divorce.

Most sentimental novels framed divorce in unequivocally bleak terms. Not only did they lack the inevitable ambiguity of trial reports, which provided two versions for each case of marital breakdown, but they stood as a bulwark against the transgressive implications of those reports. The contrasts between the two genres, then, are striking. Where trial reports unveiled the erotic underside of Victorian society's intensifying commitment to romantic love, novelists modified the concept of romantic love with a didacticism that was the hallmark of evangelical culture. And where trial accounts inadvertently complicated the moral assessment of women by virtue of their cross-grained stories and competing stereotypes, sentimental novelists simplified the moral issues by extolling resignation and self-control. Fictional women, like notable litigants, were victims and even martyrs, but either they lacked the penchant for rebelliousness that ran beneath the surface of trial accounts or else they paid dearly for it.

Because duty always outweighed love in the sentimental calculus of values, novelists typically qualified their tributes to love with the caveat that both women and men had a great deal to lose in pursuing love without a corresponding sense of responsibility. Admittedly, love was important—indeed imperative—in the quest for a happy union. Mid-nineteenth-century stories, like late-eighteenth-century stories, showed how young people pressed into advantageous unions by ambitious parents were deprived of the transcendent emotion that bound women and men together. As a young woman in T. S. Arthur's *Love in High Life* admonished a cousin about to enter a loveless union, "In matters of the heart you must be free."[40]

Yet the balance of Arthur's novel vividly demonstrates that freedom in matters of the heart was effectively foreclosed once a loveless union was solemnized; it thus departs from the post-Revolutionary tolerance for the idea of the second chance. For both male and female protagonists, there were no viable second chances. Remarriage was an even more explosive issue than divorce itself. While the legitimation of divorce held out the hope of finding happiness in a new union, a prospect that sustained liberal thinkers from Tom Paine to Elizabeth Cady Stanton, sentimental novelists blunted that prospect by investing second unions with unrelenting misery, irredeemable shame, and social ostracism. In the universe of sentimental fiction, regardless of the circumstances surrounding the first union or the statutory provisions of the law, remarriage after divorce was a signifier of illicit sex.

Nowhere was the sinfulness of remarriage spelled out more boldly than in Lady Charlotte Bury's English version of the divorce narrative, which appeared under the imprimatur of T. B. Peterson, one of the giants in nineteenth-century American publishing. Bury's 1853 novel *The Divorced,* a heavy-handed parable, provides us with a crude but transparent example of the antidivorce bias in sentimental fiction. It is by no means clear how Bury's fictional aristocrats managed to end one marriage and start another at a time when divorce was virtually unattainable in England. No matter; Bury detailed for American readers the terrible price paid by the impetuous Lady Howard, a woman who gave up custody of her son when she left her first husband, the marquis of Vernon, to elope with Lord Howard.

The story, which begins many years after the divorce, chronicles the deaths of Lady Howard's son and daughter by her second marriage, the suicide of her disaffected second husband, and her own decline into a disinherited and dying widow dependent on the kindness of the son she long ago abandoned. As the plot indicates, novelists took readers— white, middle-class, female readers, to be more exact—beyond the point where trial reports stopped to the ensuing consequences. The prying eyes and malicious tongues that Lady Howard confronts reflect society's abhorrence of a divorced woman, and the deaths of the members of her second family are linked to the sin of remarriage. Death, which is literally and metaphorically everywhere, extends to the figure of Lady Howard, whom one character describes as "a white sepulchre, fair outside, but foul within."[41]

The Divorced presents a worst-case scenario in which a married woman chooses desire over duty and thereby places herself beyond the compass of feminine friendship. Bury is not uncritical of the social code that permits Lord Howard to circulate freely despite his role as the paramour while it precludes Lady Howard from socializing with the women of her class. Nonetheless, it is the double standard, she contends, that causes Lord Howard to lose affection and respect for the woman he once loved, and it is the double standard that all women must confront regardless of its unfairness.

"You must remember," Lord Howard tells his wife unfeelingly, "that you knew when you left your first estate, the consequences, the humiliating consequences which in spite of my tender care, must become your portion." But she has not suffered alone, and he blames his wife for the sea of misfortune engulfing them; "the man who ties a mill-stone about his neck cannot expect to swim on the surface." Although Lady Howard understands now that her husband's aversion to her is retribution for what she has done, she cannot resist pointing out their shared responsibility. Yet the lion's share of the responsibility here is hers. The story stands as a cautionary tale about the pitfalls of female desire. Do not imagine, warns the author in a final aside on the dangers of illicit pleasure, that this "is a fiction or an exaggerated description of the consequences which occurred from Lady Howard's crime."[42]

Sentimental novelists countered the ambiguities in trial reports with a definition of love that left no room for second chances. Not only did Lady Howard's elopement represent deeply deviant behavior, but the Howards' subsequent estrangement proves that the eroticism that animated their union was really not love at all. One way sentimental fiction attempted to resolve the tensions between romantic love and marital duty was by emptying love of its eroticism, its involuntary and anarchic component, thereby rendering it compatible with "passionlessness" and self-control. As Nancy Cott has noted, passionlessness, or women's supposed lack of interest in sex, promoted women's status and self-esteem; and self-control was an important corollary for nineteenth-century men. Easy divorce, however, provided out-of-control spouses with a form of escape that ignored their obligations to their partners and imperiled society at large.[43]

Individual and collective experience were inseparable in the nineteenth-century divorce novel, a genre that through its didactic narratives and authorial asides contributed to the notion that divorce was a national dilemma. Writers who deployed marriage as a trope for the trust implicit in other forms of contract conflated the preservation of lifelong monogamy with the well-being of the nation. If marriage was the contract that underpinned all others, then the traditional commitment it carried to lifelong fidelity could not be abrogated without undermining the general value of promise keeping. *Traditional*, of course, is the implicit qualifier applied here to a society that had long since accepted dissolutions for serious breaches of marital conduct and was moving toward ever more flexible terms. Nonetheless, the marriage contract, conceived in a way that privileged Scripture over law, could set the standard for fidelity in the world of market relations. "We fail to impress the duty of FIDELITY upon our children," lamented E. D. E. N. Southworth in *The Deserted Wife*, "and hence irregularity and unfaithfulness in business, embezzlement of funds, &c., and hence broken marriage faith and deserted families."[44]

Marriage, the marketplace, and the nation, in this view, were all of a piece. But in collapsing the conventional opposition between home and the world, Southworth exposed the vulnerability of a wife forced to confront the world without a husband. If the husband decides to go to sea or go west, she warned, stressing the enhanced mobility of antebellum men, and "his wandering fancies fix upon some younger, fresher, fairer, or some *new* form," then he can manipulate the law into releasing him from his marriage vows.[45] Southworth understood the difficulties faced by Hagar, the heroine she created in *The Deserted Wife*, all too well; her own husband had abandoned her when she was pregnant with her second child. Hagar, who is left with three young children to support, is compelled, as Southworth was, to pursue an independent career. Yet Southworth provides Hagar with a fictional resolution that departs from her own experience: Hagar's husband returns to her.[46] After shamelessly pursuing a young woman who turns out miraculously to have been his sister, and after living beyond his means and subjecting Hagar's house to creditors' claims, he blithely resumes married life with the woman he had deceived and deserted.

Southworth's stand against divorce mirrored the reservations of those woman's rights advocates who viewed marriage as society's principal instrument for reining in men and imposing order on eros. Although much midcentury domestic fiction presented the same view, there were notable exceptions. In *Mary Lyndon,* Mary Sargeant Nichols, who embraced Spiritualism and its harmonial philosophy, construes divorce as an instrument for liberating women. And in *Christine,* Laura J. Bullard, a prominent woman's rights activist, denounces the legal system for its restrictive divorce provisions.

But in confronting the conflict between eros and order, Bullard's novel also teaches the important lesson that love is not enough to bind a man to a woman. When the paramour of Annie Howard, the unhappy wife of the novel's subplot, assures Annie that "in God's sight" the pseudo-marriage they are about to enter into "would be sacred and . . . he would always consider it so," we know we cannot trust him. He subsequently deserts her to marry a wealthy woman, the child from their union dies, and Annie, after taking up prostitution to support her remaining child, dies as well. Bullard does not absolve Annie of responsibility for the selfish gratification she sought in her first marriage or her indifference to her marriage vows. Only in death can Annie achieve redemption. If marriage functioned to protect women from male license, then license in a woman was infinitely more dangerous because it belied the sway of passionlessness and collapsed "natural" differences between the sexes. As editor of the *Revolution,* Bullard would argue that "the elevation of marriage" was the way "to prevent a floodtide of license from sweeping through society."[47]

Annie was clearly guilty of failing to uphold the sanctity of marriage. What, then, of the wrongly accused wife, the figure who dotted the pages of trial pamphlets and preoccupied hard-pressed jurors? On this account, she demonstrated her moral superiority by the fortitude with which she endured her harrowing encounter with male authority. As Jane Tompkins has argued, sentimental fiction approached the problem of male power from a religious perspective that invested women with authority through sacrifice rather than rebellion. In emphasizing the weight carried by the nineteenth-century reader's conviction that the meek shall inherit the earth, Tompkins provides us with a provocative alternative to voyeurism as an explanation for the woman-as-victim theme. Her argument may account for the prominence of female victims in these novels; more precisely, it may explain how changing perceptions have transformed yesterday's heroines into today's victims.[48] We may conclude that novelists appropriated voyeuristic narratives of female suffering from the consumer-oriented penny press, but we can also see how evangelical Christianity provided both writers and readers with a religious framework that supported the melodrama of female suffering. Though contemporary feminist scholars debating the uses of and motivations for the theme of female victimization make important distinctions between Christian sacrifice and exploitative voyeurism as explanatory models, they seem to blur when we scrutinize nineteenth-century print culture.

What is clear is the prominence of female suffering in both fictional and nonfictional narratives of divorce. T. S. Arthur's *Divorced Wife* reads like the scenarios drawn by defense counsels in high-profile cases. "Friendless, almost heart-broken, the poor cast-off wife who had no living relative to take up her cause" was left without a remedy unless her husband reconsidered her guilt. Arthur, however, brings closure to the story of the accused wife by producing the deathbed confession of an Irish servant who swore falsely against the wife because she had charged him with stealing. Although "a blasting suspicion had fallen upon the young wife, and proofs of her infidelity were presented in such a black array" that a divorce was decreed, she is saved from living out her life as a wrongly accused woman deprived of her children. This is Arthur's notion of a happy ending. In this updated version of Patient Griselda, he creates an innocent victim, subjects her to a terrible ordeal, and then reunites her with the man responsible for it. The husband, chastened now after his heartless rush to judgment, and the wife, reformed now of provocative slips in gender etiquette, remarry. For Arthur, who dwelled on the divorce question throughout his literary career, putting the divorced couple back together was an ending he particularly liked, for it obviated the legal effects of the divorce and reconciled the spouses to "the higher law obligations which were upon them."[49]

Law paled before the higher authority of religion, which accorded marriage the sanctity commensurate with its place in society. Radical feminists, according to Arthur, misunderstood the sacred role of marriage when they turned women against men. In *Out in the World*, a novel in which he demonstrated the precarious position of a wife who dared to align herself with other women in opposition to her husband, he spelled out his contempt for ultraists, Spiritualists, and the advocates of free love. The mind of the heroine, Madeline, had been "poisoned" by radicals who did not understand the true relations of husband and wife. Neither, admits Arthur, did Madeline's husband Carl, who was selfish "as all men are."[50] But Carl's selfishness, an endemic problem of men, is not as critical in the failure of the marriage as Madeline's transgression, which is entrusting herself to the dubious influence of radical women.

The rift between Madeline and Carl reflects the gendered contests Arthur regularly profiled between cold and insensitive men and warm but headstrong women. Yet despite the couple's shared responsibility in failing to achieve a spirit of concession, the consequences of the divorce are strikingly uneven. Although both partners suffer emotionally, Madeline is devastated financially because it is she who leaves Carl. A friend making a last-ditch effort to save her from penury extols marriage as a garden whose walls insulate women from the dangers and demands of economic survival. "Go back, and quickly," she urges Madeline, "into the old safe regions where you know your landmarks; where your strong tower stands—where your walled gardens are safe from intruders, where enemies cannot find you!"[51] The message is clear: a woman without a husband is a woman in danger. Admittedly, when Carl remarries—a clear violation of his sacred vows to Madeline—no good can come of it. His second wife is coarse and selfish with no system of government, and their children, bereft of proper maternal influence, grow up wild. In the end, as a dying invalid, having committed "a great life error" beyond the power of correction, Carl wants only to catch a last glimpse of Madeline, now an impoverished seamstress who is dying as well. The disparate sites from which the ill-fated lovers view one another could not have been lost on the reader: he sits in a horse-drawn carriage looking up at her window; she stands in a cold, rented room.

If the clutch of divorce trials that captured the public imagination left its impress on sentimental fiction, it did so by providing women with a warning flag about risqué behavior. Few authors responded to the implicitly subversive influence of lurid trials more heatedly than Harriet Beecher Stowe, who condemned the marital follies of the urban gentry. In *Pink and White Tyranny,* published in 1871, a time when organized activity to roll back divorce statutes was well under way, she denounced the women who smoked cigarettes, summered in Newport, spent too much on fashion, and went to balls without their husbands—all activities faithfully recorded in the news coverage of sensational divorce trials. These were the kind of women who, like Stowe's deeply flawed protagonist, Lillie, "marry where they cannot love, to serve the purposes of selfishness and ambition, and then make up for it by loving where they cannot marry."[52]

What drives the story line in *Pink and White Tyranny* is the man-as-victim theme, which places the moral responsibility for marriage squarely on the shoulders of women. John, Lillie's honest but indulgent husband, is undone by his selfish, pleasure-loving wife, who demonstrates her lack of character by her restless social climbing and incessant flirting. In highlighting Lillie's discontent with Springdale, an honest country town, and disparaging her love for New York, the hub of French fashions and loose mores, Stowe connects transgressive behavior to the snares of city life. Indeed, in Stowe's hands, urban high life becomes urban low life; and whether Lillie is truly adulterous or simply outrageously indiscreet, Stowe paints her as a moral invalid incapable of nourishing either her husband or her children. But when stoic John finally laments to his sister about the misery Lillie is causing him, she admonishes him that despite his great unhappiness, he is still responsible for his wife. His constancy in marriage is no less important than the probity he has demonstrated in business: a deal is a deal. "John," she advises him, "if you stand by a business engagement with this faithfulness, how much more should you stand by that great engagement which concerns all other families and the stability of society."[53]

John must bear what will come because, as his sister puts it, "I am sure that you will think it better to be a good man than a happy one." Stowe's message, however, is not addressed to husbands struggling to endure selfish wives but to prodivorce feminists, who "clamor for having every woman turned out helpless." All along Scripture has provided them with an answer that they persist in rejecting; all along Christianity has understood that a woman's dependency in marriage is a corollary of her natural weakness. "It was because woman is helpless and weak," Stowe avers, "and because Christ was her great provider, that he made the law of marriage irrevocable."[54]

Stowe, of course, was obscuring what women's divorce petitions eloquently demonstrated: women were not always protected in exchange for their dependency on the providers they had chosen to fulfill Christ's law. Equally notable is her opposition between goodness and happiness. In the world of sentimental fiction, which Stowe so ably represented, divorce was the pursuit of happiness run amok, a reading that translated into the triumph of eros over order. It remained for William Dean Howells to show in exquisite detail how a society that no longer constructed itself on the sturdy pillars of lifelong monogamy was a society in decline.[55]

Stowe's scriptural construction of marriage, however, is deceptively communitarian. Because she apprehended the pitfalls of making marriage more like other contracts, and by extension the problematic nature of contractualism, her message has not been without appeal to feminist critics of liberalism. Yet in asserting that promise keeping in marriage was the source of promise keeping in business, a tack taken by E. D. E. N. Southworth as well, she was putting Scripture at the service of nineteenth-century capitalism and its gendered division of labor. And in imputing a sacrificial republicanism to marriage and a selfish liberalism to divorce, she was denigrating the possibilities suggested by an autonomous female subject.

The divorce stories in the two genres examined in this chapter warrant a few final observations. If they reveal a common thread, it is the underlying instability of the Victorian marriage synthesis. They all turn on the gaping contradictions of a society devoted to romantic love on the one hand and lifelong monogamy on the other.[56] In doing so, they raise the vexing question of what would happen to a society where love broke away from the old moorings of responsibility and moderation and the romantic self loomed as a wellspring of anarchy. That women are the ones typically standing at the center of that apocalyptic vision as either powerless victims or selfish transgressors is no accident. The reason is this: the great nineteenth-century conflict between individual autonomy and social authority distilled so potently in the symbol of divorce was also a conflict between the individual autonomy of women and the social authority of men.

❖ Epilogue ❖

By the 1870s, when antidivorce sentiment coalesced into a national movement to roll back divorce, the legal framework for modern American divorce was already well defined. Using various lenses, I have attempted to capture the world in which that framework was first set into place and was subsequently tested and contested. Despite the press of growing numbers of litigants, it proved remarkably durable. Divorce would continue to exhibit the same basic lineaments until the advent of no-fault in the late 1960s. Now, more than a century after the drive for national divorce reform emerged, a new movement is under way to roll back divorce by reinstituting fault or imposing extended waiting periods for no-fault. It is spearheaded not only by the Christian right but also by some influential moderates and feminists. And in a world at once far removed from the one I have depicted here but still intimately connected to it, a new debate is taking shape over the proper ground rules for divorce.[1]

Although I do not believe that history teaches its lessons in narrowly didactic ways, the period devoted to framing American divorce affords a historical context for the current debate. Admittedly, the disparate and competing narratives I have created to probe the range and complexity of "the divorce question" do not lend themselves to a metanarrative. Yet because they collectively exemplify the sheer weight of the moral, economic, and political freight that divorce has carried, they provide reference points for today's divorce question.[2] And although they are hardly conducive to a tidy then-and-now overview that accounts for the sameness and otherness of the past, they exhibit some stunning parallels with the contemporary debate.

Some continuities are crystal clear. Commentators routinely appended political positions, moral stances, and whole systems of belief to the positions they took on divorce. When a contemporary journalist asks how divorce "start[ed] looking like the seed of America's destruction," history yields answers.[3] We can locate the notion in seventeenth-century Anglo-American political culture and point to the ardor with which royalist defenders of Charles I equated Parliament's rebellion with the anarchy of divorce. We can see it was a sentiment ready to hand when it was evoked by Benjamin Trumbull in the late eighteenth century, and that it was advanced ever more zealously and acquired sharper definition in the debates of the 1850s and 1860s. We can find it played out in the novels of T. S. Arthur, Harriet Beecher Stowe, and William Dean Howells, all of whom deployed divorce as a symbol of national decline. Given the role it played in these varied genres and contexts, we should not be surprised to find it surfacing now in the rhetoric of "family values" or in the avowals of the "Promise Keepers."

What has linked such diverse critics of divorce across the centuries is their reliance on the deep and historic interplay between family and polity, which was often fused with appeals to evangelical Christianity. This combination of familial political imagery and religious fundamentalism was especially powerful in the hands of the Victorian American moralists who used it to make what they believed was a last-ditch effort to stem the tide of divorce. Thus, when they exposed the perils of subjecting marriage to perennial rather than onetime consent, an outcome they anticipated with uncanny prescience, they advanced their argument by using marriage as a signifier of law and order and by equating divorce with political chaos. And when they championed the self-sacrificing communitarianism of marriage against the selfish individualism of divorce, they defined their campaign as nothing less than a contest between Christians and infidels. Their polarizing definition of themselves and their opponents exemplifies how they translated the divorce question into a symbolic focal point for competing worldviews. That the opposition between Christians and infidels, between order and anarchy could play so compelling a role in the acrimonious debates of the 1850s and 1860s suggests divorce was a lightning rod for deep-seated political anxieties that revolved around the positive and negative implications of freedom.[4]

The role of gender in those anxieties, however, was typically obscured. It is worth remembering that the type of divorce that royalist defenders of Charles I equated with anarchy was a divorce by a woman. Although late-eighteenth-century observers could acknowledge that gender was at the heart of legitimating divorce—a testimony perhaps to their confidence in the stability of the gender system as much as to the influence of the Revolution—the issue disappeared from subsequent discourse. Not until the emergence of the woman's rights movement do we hear again about the gendered nature of divorce, and then it is largely from divorce critics. Gender, then, owed its exposure less to the proponents of divorce than to its opponents, who underscored the economic perils it posed for women and pointed up the dangers of custody battles. Then as now, it was the critics of divorce who highlighted the problem of male inconstancy that was being unleashed by the ease with which a husband could trade in his wife for a younger model.

Divorce critics' focus on gender, however, came at a considerable price. Although they apprehended the very real asymmetry of marital power—a problem all too evident in county court records—they constructed women as passive members of the weaker sex who were "naturally" dependent on the support and protection of their male partners—an assumption belied in county court records. Critics, moreover, tended to displace the problem of economic dependency by valorizing feminine sacrifice, a motif that was pervasive in sentimental fiction. We should not discount the role these critics played in discouraging middle-class women from resorting to divorce. In the face of daunting legal changes, they did their part to shore up the sanctity of marriage by investing divorce with shame. But they did so at the expense of recognizing women as independent subjects with legal rights they could enforce against their husbands.

T. S. Arthur's image of marriage as a walled garden is a revealing example of how deftly gender was exploited once it made its way into the debate. In the well-ordered universe Arthur imagined, that enclosure would have kept the heedless heroine of *Out in the World* safe from the perils of wage earning while it divested her of agency. By dooming her in the wake of a divorce to loneliness, penury, and finally death, Arthur's punishing conclusion demonstrates that the "naturalness" of female dependency was not only a critical component of the melodramatic narrative; it was an integral part of the assault on divorce.

And what of prodivorce legislators? They took divorce, an adversarial contest between a man and a woman, and buried its gendered dimensions in universalist oppositions that they then collapsed. Thus they juxtaposed the need to redress individual but gender-neutral suffering against the larger interests of the state and found them to be compatible. Their rhetorical strategies suggest that a woman's role as an autonomous legal agent in an action to end her marriage needed to be obscured at all costs. At issue here is their striking reluctance to take any note of divorce's effects on relations between the sexes, not even dismissing them with assurances that they were negligible. Yet they did issue such assurances about the (gender-neutral) consequences of broad grounds. Divorce, they alleged, was a purely derivative phenomenon, no better or worse than the society it mirrored. Clearly, if prodivorce legislators were to succeed at making divorce more accessible, they needed to avoid gender and downplay the social consequences.

Radicals, by contrast, like the Spiritualist leader Andrew Jackson Davis and the former utopian socialist Robert Dale Owen, not only supported divorce as a much-needed social option but put a prodivorce spin on the interplay between family and polity by invoking the Declaration of Independence. Linking the political ideology of a just revolution to the liberating potential of a just divorce code, they staked their support for divorce on the legitimacy of the second chance, a principle inscribed in the Declaration of Independence. It remained for prodivorce feminists like Elizabeth Cady Stanton and Ernestine Rose, who were undeterred by the paradox of demanding equality and insisting on difference, to apply the same logic to gender relations. Instead of reading lifelong monogamy as a way of reining in men, an assumption that guided the reservations of antidivorce feminists, they seized on the heady precedent of the second chance as a tool for liberating women.

The liberal feminist embrace of divorce also came at a price: it slighted the inadequacy of alimony and child support so evident in court records. But the vision it projected was so radically egalitarian and so politically expansive that it helps explain the nervous intensity of the divorce debate. Because liberal feminists believed that divorce had the capacity to transfigure marriage, the principal institution through which men dominated women, more was at stake here than the status of women as wives. As Lynn Hunt has persuasively argued and some woman's rights advocates fervently believed, liberal political theory and the exclusion of women did not fit neatly together. Divorce, as prodivorce feminists saw it, destabilized the "sexual contract" (to borrow Carole Pateman's phrase); and in so doing, it posed a formidable challenge to the arrangement whereby men excluded women from the imagined community of the social contract.[5]

The radicalism of their position suggests why divorce generated moral panic among the Victorians. It helps us understand why legislators could broach class in considering divorce legislation but needed to sidestep gender. It helps account for how they could invest wives with a measure of legal autonomy and then ignore it or obscure it. And it helps us see that even as the post-Revolutionary legitimation of divorce reflected a reorganization of the gender system—an attempt to come to terms with the prevalence of self-divorce, the growing emphasis on female wage earning, and the flowering of romantic love—it was a threat to the very same gender system unless it was construed in highly limited terms. Fault divorce, then, was a compromise of two sorts: it created a strict official code while tolerating a lax unofficial one, and it invested women with a legal independence that the larger culture either obfuscated or debased.

I cannot convey the lesson I believe that compromise offers us with anywhere near the moral assurance of my Victorian predecessors who framed the dangers of a lax divorce code in loaded oppositions like order versus anarchy, and duty versus love. For one thing, I know that husbands and wives lived in the spaces between those oppositions. And though my bias lies with the so-called infidels, largely because I appreciate the initial shock of applying the liberal notion of the individual to the corporate institution of marriage, I cannot invoke the Declaration of Independence as a panacea for the asymmetry of marital power. On the contrary, I remain aghast at the paucity of support provisions in nineteenth-century divorces. Nonetheless, I am convinced that what we can learn from the Victorian compromise is the high cost of obfuscating the relationship between the ground rules for divorce and the social construction of gender. Contemporary feminists should be wary of banding together with conservatives to roll back no-fault: not only is the effort doomed to failure but it also represents an anachronistic drive to return a newly destabilized gender system to the model of the breadwinner husband, the dependent wife, and the heterosexual union.

As critics of divorce well know, representations matter. If in the end Victorian crusaders lost their legal battle against divorce, they more than held their own in the culture wars. Their readiness to construe women as passive victims in need of masculine protection denigrated whatever independence divorce provided wives. For that reason among others, we should recognize wives as independent legal subjects, and we should resist the impulse to restrict the time-honored precedent of the second chance.

Notes

PROLOGUE

1. William Dean Howells, *A Modern Instance* (1882), ed. William M. Gibson (Boston: Houghton Mifflin, 1957), vii.

2. Tony Tanner, *Adultery in the Novel: Contract and Transgression* (Baltimore: Johns Hopkins University Press, 1979), 15. For insights on the nature of the marriage contract, see Carole Pateman, *The Sexual Contract* (Stanford: Stanford University Press, 1988); Linda K. Kerber, "A Constitutional Right to Be Treated Like American Ladies: Women and the Obligations of Citizenship," in *U.S. History as Women's History: New Feminist Essays,* ed. Linda K. Kerber, Alice Kessler-Harris, and Kathryn Kish Sklar (Chapel Hill: University of North Carolina Press, 1995), 20–23; Nancy F. Cott, "Giving Character to Our Whole Civil Polity: Marriage and the Public Order in the Late Nineteenth Century," in ibid., 107–21; and Hendrik Hartog, "Marital Exits and Marital Expectations in Nineteenth-Century America," *Georgetown Law Journal* 80 (1991): 95–129. On marriage as a metonym for the social order, see Joseph Allen Boone, *Tradition, Counter Tradition: Love and the Form of Fiction* (Chicago: University of Chicago Press, 1987), 7. The marriage contract was, as nineteenth-century jurists put it, "*sui generis*" and "*publici juris,*" and therefore "regulated and controlled by the sovereign power of the state." See "Obligation of Contracts," *American Jurist and Law Magazine* 24 (1841): 260–61.

3. Quantification may very well have begun with Benjamin Trumbull's assessment of the divorce rate in New Haven County, Connecticut; see *An Appeal to the Public, Especially to the Learned, with Respect to the Unlawfulness of Divorces (in All Cases except Incontinency)* (New Haven: J. Meigs, 1788), 49; and Linda K. Kerber, *Women of the Republic: Intellect and Ideology in Revolutionary America* (Chapel Hill: University of North Carolina Press,

1980), 179. In the 1880s, Congress funded a national statistical survey of marriage and divorce that was compiled by Carroll D. Wright; see *A Report on Marriage and Divorce in the United States, 1867–1886* (Washington, D.C.: Government Printing Office, 1889).

4. On my periodization for divorce, see Michael S. Hindus and Lynne E. Withey, "The Law of Husband and Wife in Nineteenth-Century America: Changing Views of Divorce," in *Women and the Law: A Social Historical Perspective,* ed. D. Kelly Weisberg, 2 vols. (Cambridge, Mass.: Schenkman Publishing, 1982), 2:133–53. Debate over divorce, however, intensified from the end of the century into the Progressive Era. See William O'Neill, *Divorce in the Progressive Era* (New Haven: Yale University Press, 1967).

5. On Roman, Anglo-Saxon, and Germanic models, see Frances and Joseph Gies, *Marriage and the Family in the Middle Ages* (New York: Harper and Row, 1987), 23–25, 33–42, 108, 135, 245, 300–302. On Puritan divorce, see Henry S. Cohn, "Connecticut's Divorce Mechanism, 1636–1969," *American Journal of Legal History* 14 (1970): 35–54; Nancy F. Cott, "Divorce and the Changing Status of Women in Eighteenth-Century Massachusetts," *William and Mary Quarterly,* 3d ser., 33 (1976): 586–614; and Cornelia Hughes Dayton, *Women before the Bar: Gender, Law, and Society in Connecticut, 1639–1789,* published for the Institute of Early American History and Culture (Chapel Hill: University of North Carolina Press, 1995). Studies of self-divorce, customary divorce, "besom divorce," and wife-sale include Samuel Pyeatt Menefee, *Wives for Sale: An Ethnographic Study of British Popular Divorce* (New York: St. Martin's Press, 1981); Gerhard O. W. Mueller, "Inquiry into the State of a Divorceless Society: Domestic Relations, Law, and Morals in England from 1660 to 1857," *University of Pittsburgh Law Review* 18 (1957): 545–78; and John R. Gillis, *For Better, for Worse: British Marriages, 1600 to the Present* (New York: Oxford University Press, 1985), 98–100. On Native Americans see, for example, Anon., *An Essay on Marriage; or, The Lawfulness of Divorce* (Philadelphia: Z. Poulson, Jr., 1788), 20–21.

6. On the important role hypocrisy played in the Victorian compromise on divorce, see Lawrence M. Friedman, "Notes toward a History of American Justice," in *American Law and the Constitutional Order: Historical Perspectives,* ed. Lawrence M. Friedman and Harry M. Scheiber, enlarged ed. (Cambridge, Mass.: Harvard University Press, 1988), 13–26.

7. On the problem of credibility in conflicting legal narratives, see Laura Hanft Korobkin, "The Maintenance of Mutual Confidence: Sentimental Strategies at the Adultery Trial of Henry Ward Beecher," *Yale Journal of Law and Humanities* 7 (1995): 1–48; on the stark simplicity of legal stories, see James Boyd White, *The Legal Imagination,* abridged ed. (Chicago: University of Chicago Press, 1985), 114.

8. The absence of appellate court cases, for example, represents my rejection of a body of sources that constitute the customary stuff of legal history. That decision reflects my belief that divorce was a legal regime that took shape incrementally in the countless suits adjudicated in courts of original jurisdiction. For a brilliant example of shifting the point of view from person to person, see James Goodman, *Stories of Scottsboro* (New York: Pantheon, 1994).

9. On regional variations, see Glenda Riley, *Divorce: An American Tradition* (New York: Oxford University Press, 1991), 34–44, 85–86; on Tennessee, see Lawrence B. Goodheart, Neil Hanks, and Elizabeth Johnson, "An Act for the Relief of Females: Divorce and the Changing Legal Status of Women in Tennessee, 1716–1860," *Tennessee Historical Quarterly* 44 (1985): 318–39. On the South, see Peter W. Bardaglio, *Reconstructing the Household: Families, Sex, and the Law in the Nineteenth-Century South* (Chapel Hill: University of North Carolina Press, 1995), 153; and Stephanie McCurry, *Masters of Small Worlds: Yeoman Households, Gender Relations, and the Political Culture of the Antebellum South Carolina Low Country* (New York: Oxford University Press, 1995), 86–91.

10. In the decade since I began this study, additions to the literature on the history of divorce include Lawrence Stone, *Road to Divorce: England, 1530–1987* (New York: Oxford University Press, 1990); Roderick Phillips, *Putting Asunder: A History of Divorce in Western Society* (New York: Cambridge University Press, 1988); Riley, *Divorce;* Richard H. Chused, *Private Acts in Public Places: A Social History of Divorce in the Formative Era of American Family Law* (Philadelphia: University of Pennsylvania Press, 1994); and Michael Grossberg, *A Judgment for Solomon: The D'Hauteville Case and Legal Experience in Antebellum America* (New York: Cambridge University Press, 1996). For an insightful overview of the mounting tensions between overarching narratives and postmodern theory, see Dorothy Ross, "Grand Narrative in American Historical Writing: From Romance to Uncertainty," *American Historical Review* 100 (1995): 651–77. For a pragmatic approach to the dilemma of historical epistemology, see Joyce Appleby, Lynn Hunt, and Margaret Jacob, *Telling the Truth about History* (New York: W. W. Norton, 1994), and James T. Kloppenberg, "Pragmatism: An Old Name for Some New Ways of Thinking?" *Journal of American History* 83 (1986): 100–138. On the iconography of the woman-as-victim theme, see especially Judith Walkowitz, *City of Dreadful Delight: Narratives of Sexual Danger in Late-Victorian London* (Chicago: University of Chicago Press, 1992).

CHAPTER 1. INAUGURATING THE RULES, 1770–1800

1. Master's Report, Sarah Everitt v. William Everitt (1787), BA, E-1, Archives of the Supreme Court of New York County.

2. Decree, in ibid.

3. On links between marriage and government, see especially Carole Pateman, *The Sexual Contract* (Stanford: Stanford University Press, 1988). Studies of self-divorce, customary divorce, "besom divorce," and wife-sale include Samuel Pyeatt Menefee, *Wives for Sale: An Ethnographic Study of British Popular Divorce* (New York: St. Martin's Press, 1981); Gerhard O. W. Mueller, "Inquiry into the State of a Divorceless Society: Domestic Relations, Law, and Morals in England from 1660 to 1857," *University of Pittsburgh Law Review* 18 (1957): 545–78; and John R. Gillis, *For Better, for Worse: British Marriages, 1600 to the Present* (New York: Oxford University Press, 1985).

4. Evidence of such extralegal alternatives appears in the file papers of legal divorces. Witnesses who described an extralegal union as "passing as man and wife" were underscoring the permanence and outward respectability of the union while simultaneously acknowledging its illegality.

5. With the single ground of adultery, New York was restrictive with regard to grounds. In raising these questions, I am referring here also to other states that recognized divorce in the post-Revolutionary era.

6. Quoted in Roderick Phillips, *Putting Asunder: A History of Divorce in Western Society* (New York: Cambridge University Press, 1988), 176.

7. Ibid., 175–84; Joan B. Landes, *Women and the Public Sphere in the Age of the French Revolution* (Ithaca: Cornell University Press, 1988).

8. On Connecticut, see Cornelia Hughes Dayton, *Women before the Bar: Gender, Law, and Society in Connecticut, 1639–1789*, published by the Institute of Early American History and Culture (Chapel Hill: University of North Carolina Press, 1995), 105–56; Henry S. Cohn, "Connecticut's Divorce Mechanism, 1636–1969," *American Journal of Legal History* 14 (1970): 35–55; and Marylynn Salmon, *Women and the Law of Property in Early America* (Chapel Hill: University of North Carolina Press, 1986), 60–70.

9. Linda K. Kerber, *Women of the Republic: Intellect and Ideology in Revolutionary America* (Chapel Hill: University of North Carolina Press, 1980), 161.

10. Thomas Meehan, "Not Made out of Levity," *Pennsylvania Magazine of History and Biography* 92 (1968): 441–64, citation on 444.

11. William Renwick Riddell, "Legislative Divorce in Colonial Pennsylvania," *Pennsylvania Magazine of History and Biography* 57 (1933): 175–80, citations on 177, 178; see also Salmon, *Women and the Law of Property*, 61; Phillips, *Putting Asunder*, 149–50.

12. Jefferson's notes supporting divorce were developed in conjunction with the possible legislative divorce of Dr. James Blair of Williamsburg, who retained him as a lawyer-legislator in the event that his wife, from whom he was separated, should insist on a separate maintenance. Blair, however, died in December of 1772 before Jefferson had an opportunity to try out his arguments. See Frank L. Dewey, "Thomas Jefferson's Notes on Divorce," *William and Mary Quarterly*, 3d ser., 39 (1982): 212–23, citation on 218. On the influence of local and state declarations and the members of Congress on the Declaration of Independence, see Pauline Maier, *American Scripture: Making the Declaration of Independence* (New York: Alfred A. Knopf, 1997). Cursory guidelines were laid down for alimony and the distribution of marital property in the Northwest Territory. See *Laws of the Northwest Territory, 1788–1800,* ed. Theodore Calvin Pease (Springfield, Ill.: Trustees of the Illinois State Historical Library, 1925), 258–59.

13. *Acts of Tennessee, 1799,* chap. 19; the Alabama Territories provided for divorce in 1803, Arkansas in 1807, and Kentucky in 1809. See Phillips, *Putting Asunder,* 154–55.

14. Phillips, *Putting Asunder,* 230–31; on the suit for criminal conversation and the social status of the men who petitioned Parliament, see Lawrence Stone,

Road to Divorce: England 1530–1987 (New York: Oxford University Press, 1990), 231–345.

15. On independence as a prototype for divorce, see Kerber, *Women of the Republic,* 10, 84.

16. Natalie Zemon Davis, *Society and Culture in Early Modern France* (Stanford: Stanford University Press, 1975), 127; Jean Jacques Rousseau, *The Social Contract* (1762), trans. and ed. G. D. H. Cole (New York: E. P. Dutton, 1950), 4–5.

17. Pateman, *The Sexual Contract,* passim; on divorce, see 183–84. Divorce, however, constitutes an anomaly in Pateman's powerful argument.

18. Jan Lewis, "The Republican Wife: Virtue and Seduction in the Early Republic," *William and Mary Quarterly,* 3d ser., 44 (1987): 689–721. Other explorations of the familial paradigm include Philip J. Greven, Jr., *Four Generations: Population, Land, and Family in Colonial Andover, Massachusetts* (Ithaca: Cornell University Press, 1970); Winthrop D. Jordan, "Familial Politics: Thomas Paine and the Killing of the King, 1776," *Journal of American History* 60 (1973): 294–308; Jack P. Greene, "An Uneasy Connection: An Analysis of the Preconditions of the American Revolution," in *Essays on the American Revolution,* ed. Stephen B. Kurtz and James H. Hutson (Chapel Hill: University of North Carolina Press, 1973), 32–80; Jay Fliegelman, *Prodigals and Pilgrims: The American Revolution against Patriarchal Authority* (New York: Cambridge University Press, 1982); Melvin Yazawa, *From Colonies to Commonwealth: Familial Ideology and the Beginnings of the American Republic* (Baltimore: Johns Hopkins University Press, 1985); Cynthia S. Jordan, "'Old Words' in New Circumstances: Language and Leadership in Post-Revolutionary America," *American Quarterly* 40 (1988): 491–521; and Kerber, *Women of the Republic.* For an insightful Freudian reading of the French Revolution, see Lynn Hunt, *The Family Romance of the French Revolution* (Berkeley: University of California Press, 1992).

These interpretations vary considerably. Whereas Yazawa, who argues that the bonds of filial affection gave way to a new emphasis on individual attachment to the state, posits an erosion of the familial paradigm, both Fliegelman and Lewis find a new emphasis on matrimonial bonds. Lewis, moreover, notes as does Kerber that republicanism presented women with a quasi-political role, but she locates that role primarily in wifehood while Kerber underscores motherhood. Cynthia Jordan, however, views the post-Revolutionary use of the paradigm as a manipulative variant of patriarchy. On the status of women, see also Nancy F. Cott, "Divorce and the Changing Status of Women in Eighteenth-Century Massachusetts," *William and Mary Quarterly,* 3d ser., 33 (1976): 586–614; Mary Beth Norton, *Liberty's Daughters: The Revolutionary Experience of America Women* (Boston: Little, Brown, 1980); and Joan Hoff Wilson, "The Illusion of Change: Women and the American Revolution," in *The American Revolution: Explorations in the History of American Radicalism,* ed. Alfred F. Young (DeKalb: Northern Illinois University Press, 1976), 383–445.

19. On consent in marriage, see Sir William Blackstone, *Commentaries on the Laws of England in Four Books,* ed. Thomas Cooley, 2 vols., 4th ed.

(Chicago: Callaghan, 1899), 1:374–75. On the problematic nature of regarding marriage as a contract, see Amy Dru Stanley, "Conjugal Bonds and Wage Labor: Rights of Contract in the Age of Emancipation," *Journal of American History* 75 (1988): 471.

20. Henry Ferne, *Conscience Satisfied that there is No Warrant for the Armes Taken up by Subjects* (Oxford, 1643), 12, cited in Phillips, *Putting Asunder,* 117. See also Mary Lyndon Shanley, "Marriage Contract and Social Contract in Seventeenth-Century English Thought," *Western Political Quarterly* 32 (1979): 79–91; and Gordon Schocket, *Patriarchalism in Political Thought* (New York: Basic Books, 1975).

21. Hunt, *The Family Romance of the French Revolution,* xiii. For an analysis of metaphor in ethnography, see Clifford Geertz, *The Interpretation of Cultures: Selected Essays* (New York: Basic Books, 1973), 210–11.

22. From John Lind, *An Answer to the Declaration of the American Congress* (London, 1776), cited in Carl L. Becker, *The Declaration of Independence: A Study in the History of Political Ideas* (1922; reprint, New York: Vintage Books, 1942), 229.

23. Gordon S. Wood, *The Creation of the American Republic, 1776–1787* (Chapel Hill: University of North Carolina Press, 1969), 259–73; John W. Gough, *The Social Contract: A Critical Study of Its Development* (Oxford: Clarendon Press, 1957), 142–44; Peter Charles Hoffer, *The Law's Conscience: Equitable Constitutionalism in America* (Chapel Hill: University of North Carolina Press, 1990), 71–76, citation on 72.

24. Becker, *The Declaration of Independence,* 237–38.

25. John Milton, *Doctrine and Discipline of Divorce,* 2d ed. (London, 1644), 3–4; John Locke, *Two Treatises of Government* (1690), ed. Peter Laslett (Cambridge: Cambridge University Press, 1963), 339; on Abigail Strong's petition, see Sheldon S. Cohen, "To Parts of the World Unknown: The Circumstances of Divorce in Connecticut, 1750–1787," *Canadian Review of American Studies* 11 (1980): 289; Andrew Jackson Davis, *The Great Harmonia; Concerning Physiological Vices and Virtues, and the Seven Phases of Marriage,* 4 vols. (Boston: Sanborn, Carter, and Bazin, 1856), 4:404. See also Kerber, *Women of the Republic,* 18; Lawrence Stone, *The Family, Sex, and Marriage in England, 1500 to 1800,* abridged ed. (New York: Harper and Row, 1979), 164.

26. Gilbert Imlay, *The Emigrants,* intro. by Robert R. Hare (1793; reprint, Gainesville, Fla.: Scholars' Facsimiles and Reprints, 1964), ii; it is likely that this novel attributed to Mary Wollstonecraft's American lover was written by Wollstonecraft herself. For a fine description of this literature and its meanings in a Revolutionary and post-Revolutionary context, see Lewis, "The Republican Wife," 691–93; on the permeability of eighteenth-century legal concepts, see Hendrik Hartog, "Distancing Oneself from the Eighteenth Century: A Commentary on the Changing Pictures of American Legal History," in *Law and the American Revolution and the Revolution in the Law,* ed. Hendrik Hartog (New York: New York University Press, 1981), 242–43. On the seductions of novel reading, see especially Cathy N. Davidson, *Revolution and the Word: The Rise of the Novel in America* (New York: Oxford University Press, 1986), 45–46.

27. Fliegelman, *Prodigals and Pilgrims,* 126.

28. [Thomas Paine], "Cupid and Hymen," *Pennsylvania Magazine*, April 1775, 159–61.

29. [Thomas Paine], "Reflections on Unhappy Marriages," *Pennsylvania Magazine*, June 1775, 264–65. On the role of Genesis in marriage and divorce, see Elaine Pagels, *Adam, Eve, and the Serpent* (New York: Random House, 1988), 8, 13–14, 22. According to the New Testament, Jesus drew on Genesis to respond to the Pharisees' queries about the legitimate grounds for divorce. Not only did he rule out divorce altogether, thereby departing from Mosaic law, but he went on to suggest that celibacy may be preferable to marriage. Reinterpretations of the doctrine of divorcelessness focused on Matthew, especially 5:27–31 and 9:10–13.

30. "On Marriage," *The General Magazine and Impartial Review of Knowledge and Entertainment*, July 1778, 41–45. Paine's version of the perfect partnership also conveniently leaves out the same-sex partnerships Aristophanes offers in Plato's *Symposium*. On moving beyond reading gender only as a metaphor for power, see Ruth Bloch, "A Culturist Critique of Trends in Feminist Theory," *Contention* 2 (1993): 79–106. Bloch argues that gender constructs a culture's most fundamental debates over the meaning of intimacy and interconnectedness.

31. "Essay on Love and Marriage," *Boston Magazine*, November 1783, 15–17; "The Unreasonableness of the Law in Regard to Wives," *Columbian Magazine*, May 1788, 243–46, continued in January, 22–27; February, 61–65; March, 126–30; April, 186–89; and "Expostulation with the Married," *Desert to the True American*, July 21, 1798, n.p.

32. "The Matron," *Gentlemen and Ladies Town and Country Magazine*, December 1784, 581–83.

33. "The Bad Effects of an Improvident Matrimonial Connection," *Desert to the True American*, January 12, 1799, n.p. See also "On Marriage," *General Magazine and Impartial Review of Knowledge and Entertainment*, July 1778, 41; and "Three Days after Marriage, or the History of Ned Easy and Mrs. Manlove," *Gentlemen and Ladies Town and Country Magazine*, February 1789, 19–21.

34. "The Directory of Love," *Royal American Magazine*, May 1774, 190.

35. Imlay, *The Emigrants*, v–vi, 35. On licentiousness, seduction, and the double standard, see "Unhappy Women," *Gentlemen and Ladies Town and Country Magazine*, July 1789, 311–12; "The Seduction of Young Women," *Boston Magazine*, October 1783, 18–19; and "Suicide," *Desert to the True American*, April 20, 1799, n.p.

36. "Curious Queries with Regard to Bigamy," *Gentlemen and Ladies Town and Country Magazine*, July 1784, 116.

37. Anon., *Amelia; or, The Faithless Briton* (Boston: Spotswood and Wayne, 1798);"Divorce in Pennsylvania," *Portfolio* 10 (1813): 489; Kenneth Silverman, *A Cultural History of the American Revolution* (New York: T. Y. Crowell, 1976), 497–99. On the problem of desertion in early America and its role as a ground in Pennsylvania, see Merril D. Smith, "Breaking the Bonds: Marital Discord in Pennsylvania, 1730–1830" (Ph.D. diss., Temple University, 1989); on bigamy and the problem of shifting identity in a rapidly expanding society, see

"Trial for Bigamy," *American Law Journal* 1 (1808): 70–80. For a private bill passed by the territorial legislature of Indiana validating a wife's technically bigamous marriage, see An Act for the Relief of Catherine Moore, *Laws of Indiana Territory,* 1808, chap. 3.

38. See, for example, "Answers to the Queries on Marriage," *Pennsylvania Magazine,* December 1775, 558; "The Marriage Ceremonies of Different Countries Compared," *Columbian Magazine,* June 1787, 491–97. On statutory concerns, see "Address of Thomas M'Kean," *Pennsylvania Archives,* 4th ser. (1802), 4:500–506, which advised the Pennsylvania Assembly on the "utility of revising the ancient laws relative to clandestine marriages"; see also "A Law to prevent forcible and stolen marriages, and for punishment of the crime of Bigomy [*sic*], Adopted from the Virginia code," *Laws of Indiana Territory,* 1803, chap. 6. On links between the emergence of divorce and the decline in viewing marriage as an exchange of property, see Randolph Trumbach, *The Rise of the Egalitarian Family* (New York: Academic Press, 1978), 290.

39. For the definitive treatment of so-called common law marriage and other American redefinitions of marriage, see Michael Grossberg, *Governing the Hearth: Law and the Family in Nineteenth-Century America* (Chapel Hill: University of North Carolina Press, 1985), 69–102. See also Ariela R. Dubler, "Governing through Contract: Common Law Marriage in the Nineteenth Century," *Yale Law Journal* 107 (1998): 1885–1920.

40. The Rhode Island statute of 1798, for example, gave courts the authority to decree a divorce for "gross behavior and wickedness in either of the parties, repugnant to and in violation of the marriage covenant." See Nelson Manfred Blake, *The Road to Reno: A History of Divorce in the United States* (New York: Macmillan, 1962), 50. On the importance of causality in Revolutionary thinking, see Gordon S. Wood, "Conspiracy and the Paranoid Style: Causality and Deceit in the Eighteenth Century," *William and Mary Quarterly,* 3d ser., 39 (1982): 401–41; on contract, see Patrick S. Atiyah, *Promises, Morals, and Law* (New York: Oxford University Press, 1981), 142. On the moral importance of fault and the need to punish the guilty, see Hendrik Hartog, "Marital Exits and Marital Expectations in Nineteenth-Century America," *Georgetown Law Journal* 80 (1991): 121.

41. Anon., *An Essay on Marriage, or the Lawfulness of Divorce* (Philadelphia: Z. Poulson, Jr., 1788), 17–24.

42. Hannah Foster, *The Coquette; or, The History of Eliza Wharton* (Boston: Samuel Etheridge for E. Larkin, 1797), 28, 254; on marital ground rules, see "The Marriage Ceremonies of Different Countries Compared," *Columbian Magazine,* June 1787, 491–97.

43. "The Married Man," *Boston Magazine,* January 1784, 133–34.

44. "Selling of Wives," *Mirror of Taste* 2 (1810): 432–34; *(New York) Daily Advertiser,* June 25, 1817.

45. On Tennessee, see Gale W. Bamman and Debbie W. Spero, *Tennessee Divorces, 1797–1858* (Nashville, Tenn.: Gale W. Bamman, 1985), 33. On Pennsylvania, see Salmon, *Women and the Law of Property,* 59.

46. As Michael A. Bellesiles has written, "Traditionally historians have seen law and order as generated principally from above. More recently some have

written of the direct transportation of common law to the American frontier as though every settler carried a copy of Blackstone in his luggage." See "The Establishment of Legal Structures on the Frontier: The Case of Revolutionary Vermont," *Journal of American History* 73 (1987): 895–915, citation on 897. On the lawfulness of settlers, see John P. Reid, *Law for the Elephant: Property and Social Behavior on the Overland Trail* (San Marino, Calif.: Huntington Library, 1980). There is good reason to see the transition from divorcelessness to divorce in the post-Revolutionary era as encompassing many of the same issues raised by "frontier justice," regardless of the locale.

47. *Laws of New York,* chap. 69; forfeiture of property by the guilty spouse was spelled out in *Laws of New York 1813,* chap. 102. On the decline of prosecution for adultery, see William E. Nelson, "Emerging Notions of Modern Criminal Law in the Revolutionary Era: An Historical Perspective," in *American Law and the Constitutional Order: Historical Perspectives,* ed. Lawrence M. Friedman and Harry N. Scheiber, enlarged ed. (Cambridge, Mass.: Harvard University Press, 1988), 165–72.

48. Benjamin Trumbull, *An Appeal to the Public, Especially to the Learned, with Respect to the Unlawfulness of Divorces (in All Cases except Incontinency)* (New Haven: J. Meigs, 1788), 45. Trumbull's pamphlet, an important exception to the acceptance of divorce, failed to reform Connecticut divorce statutes.

49. Meehan, "Not Made out of Levity," 442.

50. On the principle of personal autonomy in the late eighteenth century, see Rhys Isaac, *Transformation of Virginia, 1740–1790,* published for the Institute of Early American History and Culture (Chapel Hill: University of North Carolina Press, 1982), 113.

51. On feminist critiques of the French Enlightenment, see especially Landes, *Women and the Public Sphere,* and Lieselotte Steinbrugge, *The Moral Sex: Women's Nature in the French Enlightenment,* trans. Pamela E. Selwyn (New York: Oxford University Press, 1995); on the United States, see Carroll Smith-Rosenberg, "Dis-Covering the Subject of the 'Great Constitutional Discussion,' 1786–1789," *Journal of American History* 79 (1992): 841–73; on the possibility and rejection of a radical alternative that envisioned wives as independent partners and responsible citizens, see Linda K. Kerber, "The Paradox of Women's Citizenship in the Early Republic: The Case of *Martin vs. Massachusetts,* 1805," *American Historical Review* 97 (1992): 349–78.

52. On the import of a woman's right to sue for divorce, see Cott, "Divorce and the Changing Status of Women." For nineteenth-century California, see Robert L. Griswold, *Family and Divorce in California, 1850–1890: Victorian Illusions and Everyday Realities* (Albany: State University of New York Press, 1982), 78. On rising marital expectations on the part of women, see Kerber, *Women of the Republic,* 163–64.

CHAPTER 2. REFINING THE RULES, 1800–1850s

1. "D'Arusmont v. D'Arusmont," *Western Law Journal* 8 (1850–51): 549. Wright, who had first filed for divorce in Tennessee, wanted an injunction against her husband's transactions on property that was originally hers.

2. On Wright and the Enlightenment, see Anthony F. C. Wallace, *Rockdale: The Growth of an American Village in the Early Industrial Revolution* (New York: W. W. Norton, 1978), 275–77, 342, 345.

3. On the quantification of divorce prior to the government survey of 1867, see Glenda Riley, *Divorce: An American Tradition* (New York: Oxford University Press, 1991), 78–79; Carl Degler, *At Odds: Women and the Family in America from the Revolution to the Present* (New York: Oxford University Press, 1980), 165–67; and Roderick Phillips, *Putting Asunder: A History of Divorce in Western Society* (New York: Cambridge University Press, 1988), 458–64. We have no comprehensive numbers before 1867. Both anecdotal evidence and state statistics, however, support the notion of a steady increase in the number of divorces over the first six decades of the nineteenth century. The *Western Law Journal* (1 [1843]: 175) charted a 200 percent increase in divorce suits before the Ohio Supreme Court between 1833 and 1843, against a 62 percent increase in population. Yet the numbers remain small by today's standards. As noted by Degler, who sees the nineteenth-century increase in divorce more as the mark of a new sense of marital discontent than as a function of legal change, even in 1867, the first year of comprehensive statistics, the total number of divorces nationwide was under 10,000.

4. Christopher L. Tomlins, *Law, Labor, and Ideology in the Early American Republic* (New York: Cambridge University Press, 1993), 21. Tomlins does not find the diffuse and decentralized nature of state courts a significant bar to the power of legal discourse. On law as an instrument of social change, see especially Morton J. Horwitz, *The Transformation of American Law* (Cambridge, Mass.: Harvard University Press, 1977). On the constitutive nature of law, see also Michael Grossberg, *A Judgment for Solomon: The D'Hauteville Case and Legal Experience in Antebellum America* (New York: Cambridge University Press, 1996), xi, 235.

5. On the spread of the storytelling techniques of frontier revivalists, see David S. Reynolds, *Beneath the American Renaissance: The Subversive Imagination in the Age of Emerson and Melville* (New York: Alfred A. Knopf, 1988), 20–22.

6. Timothy Dwight, *Theology Explained and Defended in a Series of Sermons,* 5 vols. (Middletown, Conn.: Clark and Lyman, 1818), 4:273–74. Statistics for all of France are unavailable. Although the number of divorces in Paris and other cities was undeniably impressive by late-eighteenth-century standards, the initial surge in the use of divorce probably reflected the pent-up demand created by divorcelessness. Use of the divorce process declined in subsequent years. See Phillips, *Putting Asunder,* 258–59.

7. "A Turnpike and a Divorce," *Locomotive,* November 26, 1853.

8. The idea that men were inherently more licentious than women made its way into a few statutes that afforded male defendants greater latitude for the ground of adultery. On gender-neutral statutes and their exceptions, see Robert L. Griswold, *Adultery and Divorce in Victorian America, 1800–1900,* Legal History Program Working Papers, ser. 1 (Madison, Wis.: Institute for Legal Studies, 1986), 3–4. North Carolina, Texas, and Kentucky stipulated that the husband had to be living in a state of adultery in order for a wife to use adultery as a ground.

9. On the hybrid nature of American divorce law, see "Law of Marriage and Divorce," *American Quarterly Review* 2 (1827): 71–72. On the distinction between Parliament and state legislatures acting in a judicial capacity, see "Jones v. Jones," *American Law Journal* 9 (1850): 401; on the foundations for judicial review, see John Philip Reid, "Another Origin of Judicial Review: The Constitutional Crises of 1776 and the Need for a Dernier Judge," *New York University Law Review* 64 (1989): 963–89.

10. Dwight, *Theology Explained,* 4:273. On the growing divergence between law and Scripture in post-Revolutionary Connecticut, see Benjamin Trumbull, *An Appeal to the Public, Especially to the Learned, with Respect to the Unlawfulness of Divorces* (New Haven: J. Meigs, 1788); on fears about nineteenth-century cities, see Paul Boyer, *Urban Masses and Moral Order in America, 1820–1920* (Cambridge, Mass.: Harvard University Press, 1978).

11. Michael Grossberg, "Crossing Boundaries: Nineteenth-Century Domestic Relations Law and the Merger of Family and Legal History," *American Bar Foundation Journal* (1985): 819–23; see also Neil R. Feigenson, "Extraterritorial Recognition of Divorce Decrees," *American Journal of Legal History* 34 (1990): 119–67.

12. Phillips, *Putting Asunder,* 440, 442; on Massachusetts, see also Michael S. Hindus and Lynne E. Withey, "The Law of Husband and Wife in Nineteenth-Century America: Changing Views of Divorce," in *Women and the Law: A Social Historical Perspective,* ed. D. Kelly Weisberg, 2 vols. (Cambridge, Mass.: Schenkman Publishing, 1982), 2:133–53.

13. "Divorce," *DeBow's Commercial Register* 2 (1846): 155–64; on divorce in the Napoleonic Code, see also *American Law Journal* 2 (1809): 477, and *Southern Quarterly Review* 26 (1854): 332–55. In 1816, France prohibited complete divorces altogether. On the South in general, see Jane Turner Censer, "Smiling through Her Tears: Ante-bellum Southern Women and Divorce," *American Journal of Legal History* 25 (1981): 26–27.

14. Citation in *National Era,* September 8, 1859, 142. On the sanctity of marriage as a component of southern social status, see Bertram Wyatt-Brown, *Southern Honor: Ethics and Behavior in the Old South* (New York: Oxford University Press, 1982), 298–304. See also Peter W. Bardaglio, *Reconstructing the Household: Families, Sex, and the Law in the Nineteenth-Century South* (Chapel Hill: University of North Carolina Press, 1995).

15. Michael Stephen Hindus, *Prison and Plantation: Crime, Justice, and Authority in Massachusetts and South Carolina, 1767–1878* (Chapel Hill: University of North Carolina Press, 1980), 50–53; Marylynn Salmon, *Women and the Law of Property in Early America* (Chapel Hill: University of North Carolina Press, 1986), 65, 75–76. On South Carolina, see also Stephanie McCurry, *Masters of Small Worlds: Yeoman Households, Gender Relations, and the Political Culture of the Antebellum South Carolina Low Country* (New York: Oxford University Press, 1995), 86–91.

16. Joel Prentice Bishop, *Commentaries on the Law of Marriage and Divorce and Evidence in Matrimonial Suits* (Boston: Little, Brown, 1852), chap. 15, sec. 268. See *Iowa Revised Statutes, 1843,* chap. 100. The state's omnibus clause authorized a divorce when "it is apparent to the satisfaction of the Court that

the parties cannot live in peace or happiness together, and that their welfare requires a separation between them." On other omnibus clauses or "discretionary divorce," see Bishop, chap. 20, secs. 542–47.

17. On the problem of progress and decay in late-eighteenth-century thought, see Drew R. McCoy, *The Elusive Republic: Political Economy in Jeffersonian America* (Chapel Hill: University of North Carolina Press, 1980), 13–47. Stephen A. Siegel argues that although Bishop was a "classical" jurist who conceived of law as an autonomous discipline, he believed it was "deeply connected to society and rooted in morality"; see "Joel Bishop's Orthodoxy," *Law and History Review* 13 (1995): 215–59, citation on 217.

18. On the difficulty of getting a divorce in the first half of the century, specifically in Virginia, see Suzanne Lebsock, *The Free Women of Petersburg: Status and Culture in a Southern Town, 1784–1860* (New York: W. W. Norton, 1984), 68–70; on the sex of legislative petitioners, see *Pennsylvania House of Representatives Journal, 1847*, vol. 1, 21–23. For an important study of legislative divorce in Maryland, a jurisdiction where judicial divorce was unavailable until 1841, see Richard H. Chused, *Private Acts in Public Places: A Social History of Divorce in the Formative Era of American Family Law* (Philadelphia: University of Pennsylvania Press, 1994). Chused finds that women made up a majority of the petitioners to the legislature and were, in fact, more successful than men. Legislators, he notes, were unable to resist individual tales of misfortune.

19. Citations, in order of appearance, in *American Jurist and Law Magazine* 2 (1829): 392, and 3 (1830): 181; *Pennsylvania Constitutional Convention, 1837–1838, Debates and Proceedings*, vol. 9, 4–5, 15; Auguste Carlier, *Marriage in the United States*, 3d ed., trans. B. Joy Jeffries (Boston: Devries, Ibarra, 1867), 107. See also "Legislative Divorces," *American Law Journal* 9 (1850): 419–25.

20. On the importance of narrow grounds in legislative discretion, see *New York Assembly Documents, 1849*, vol. 2, no. 66, January 30, 1–2; legislators argued to no avail that the single ground of adultery should result in greater legislative discretion to grant divorces instead of a constitutional prohibition. On Owen's remarks, see *Indiana State Sentinel*, February 20, 1851.

21. Governor P. D. Vroom, *New Jersey General Assembly Journal, 1829–31*, January 7, 1830, 82.

22. *New York Revised Statutes, 1829*, vol. 2, sec. 8, tit. 1, reiterated verbatim in the state's 1846, 1852, 1859, and 1875 revisions. Longwood's petition is in *New York Assembly Documents, 1833*, vol. 2, no. 47, January 8, 1. See also ibid., vol. 2, no. 332, April 1, 3, which records the judiciary committee's response to the petition of Margaretta Obrigon: the report proudly notes that the only legislative divorce granted in New York since statehood was to Eunice Chapman in 1818, adding, "In several of the States the practice prevails of granting legislative divorces, but we indulge the hope that it may never prevail here."

23. *Laws of Tennessee, 1831*, chap. 20, cited in *American Jurist and Law Magazine* 8 (1832): 444.

24. *Pennsylvania House of Representatives Journal, 1824–25*, vol. 2, no. 170, February 26, 1825.

25. *Ohio House Journal, 1835–36*, 339–40.

26. For similar appeals, see especially Gale W. Bamman and Debbie W. Spero, *Tennessee Divorces, 1797–1858* (Nashville, Tenn.: Gale W. Bamman, 1985).

27. *American Jurist and Law Magazine* 4 (1830): 401; 5 (1831): 380; 6 (1831): 197–98, 436; 7 (1832): 441; 8 (1832): 201; on statistics for legislative divorces in Ohio from 1800 to 1842, see *Western Law Journal* 1 (1844): 282; citation from governor in *New Jersey General Assembly Journal, 1829–31,* January 7, 1830, 82. For similar concern in midcentury England with establishing a unitary, coherent divorce policy, see Mary Poovey, *Uneven Developments: The Ideological Work of Gender in Mid-Victorian England* (Chicago: University of Chicago Press, 1988), 54–55; and Lawrence Stone, *Road to Divorce: England, 1530–1987* (New York: Oxford University Press, 1990), 368.

28. On the constitutionality of legislative divorce, see *Western Law Journal* 6 (1848–49): 368; "Gaines v. Gaines," *American Law Journal* 8 (1849): 555–67; "Jones v. Jones," 401–7; and "Obligation of Contracts," *American Jurist and Law Magazine* 24 (1841): 261. For a discussion of *Maynard v. Hill,* an 1888 Supreme Court case investing the Oregon territorial legislature with the right to grant a divorce, see Nancy F. Cott, "Giving Character to Our Whole Civil Polity: Marriage and the Public Order in the Late Nineteenth Century," in *U.S. History as Women's History: New Feminist Essays,* ed. Linda K. Kerber, Alice Kessler-Harris, and Kathryn Kish Sklar (Chapel Hill: University of North Carolina Press, 1995), 119.

29. *Monthly Law Reporter* 1 (1839): 340; *Maine Legislative Documents, 1844,* House of Representatives Document, no. 43, 5.

30. *Ohio House Journal, 1828,* 408–9; on the continuing problem of legislative divorces, see ibid., *1836,* 399.

31. *Pennsylvania Archives,* 4th series, vol. 5, 847; *Pennsylvania House of Representatives Journal, 1829–30,* vol. 2, no. 160, January 1830.

32. *Pennsylvania House of Representatives Journal, 1847,* vol. 1, 21–23.

33. According to Shunk, there had been 16 decrees in the decade after 1815, 42 in the next decade, and 90 in the past decade. See *Pennsylvania Archives,* 4th series, vol. 7, 117–42, citations on 135. On his vetoes of 1847 and 1848 legislative decrees, see ibid., 177–78, 186, 253–55, 269–70; see also the veto in 1849 of Governor William Freame Johnston of a legislative decree in ibid., 357–58; "Legislative Divorces"; and *In the Matter of the Petition of Edward Middleton to the General Assembly of Pennsylvania, for a Divorce from His Wife* (Philadelphia: n.p., 1850).

34. *Constitution of California, 1850,* art. 4, sec. 26.

35. Lawrence M. Friedman, "Notes toward a History of American Justice," in *American Law and the Constitutional Order: Historical Perspectives,* ed. Lawrence M. Friedman and Harry M. Scheiber, enlarged ed. (Cambridge, Mass.: Harvard University Press, 1988), 17–18, 23.

36. Bishop, *Commentaries,* chap. 15, sec. 286.

37. *New York Assembly Documents, 1849,* vol. 2, no. 66, January 30; ibid., *1855,* vol. 5, no. 119, March 26.

38. Citations in "Oliver Oldschool," *Portfolio* 10 (1813): 483–84; "Law of Marriage and Divorce," 70–102, citation on 100.

39. On the "Lolly doctrine," see Stone, *Road to Divorce,* 358–59.

40. Henry De Saussure, "Effect of Foreign Divorces," *Carolina Law Journal* 1 (1831): 377–83, citation on 377.

41. The report of the Marion County clerk appears in *Locomotive,* October 30, 1858. Conflict of law in divorce cases, which included appeals to out-of-state legislatures, received broad coverage in both professional and nonprofessional journals. New Yorkers figured prominently in migratory divorce because of both the state's narrow statute and the sheer size of its population. On New Yorkers in Pennsylvania, see "Divorces by Act of the Legislature," *Pennsylvania Law Journal* 3 (1844): 293, and "Legislative Divorces," 423–24; on the migratory divorce of New Yorkers in Michigan, see "Freeman v. Freeman," *Western Law Journal* 3 (1844–45): 475, and "Visher v. Vischer," in ibid. 10 (1853): 421; on the problems of comity between other states, see, for example, *American Jurist and Law Magazine* 7 (1832): 345; *Locomotive,* January 23, 1858, and April 28, 1860; and *American Law Register* 12 (1864): 209.

42. Joan Wallach Scott, *Only Paradoxes to Offer: French Feminists and the Rights of Man* (Cambridge, Mass.: Harvard University Press, 1996), 20; Carole Pateman, *The Sexual Contract* (Stanford: Stanford University Press, 1988), 183–84. Pateman argues that feminists who gravitate toward the individualism and contractualism of divorce have missed the utter incompatibilty of feminism and contract; "the individual," she insists, is a patriarchal category. On marriage as a pillar of the state, see Cott, "Giving Character to Our Whole Civil Polity," 107–9.

43. *Locomotive,* July 10, 1858.

44. On women in the courts, see "Divorce Laws of Ohio," *Western Law Journal* 1 (1843): 173; on the gender-neutral appeal to "social duties," see "Divorce," 161. On generalized pollution, see "The Legal Condition of Women," *North American Review* 26 (1828): 331; on divorce as moral theater, see also Griswold, *Adultery and Divorce,* 16.

45. Citations, in order of appearance, in *New Jersey General Assembly Journal, 1837–38,* 200; "Butler v. Butler," *American Law Journal* 8 (1848–49): 397–98; "The Gaines Case," *Southern Quarterly Review* 18 (1843): 293; *New York Assembly Documents, 1833,* vol. 2, no. 322, April 29, 4. For an earlier balancing of individual suffering versus the greater good, see Dwight, *Theology Explained,* 4:266. Dwight, it should be noted, who was still close to post-Revolutionary cultural conventions, addressed gender directly, suggesting it was preferable to be a deserted wife than a divorced one.

46. Thomas W. Laqueur, "Bodies, Details, and the Humanitarian Narrative," in *The New Cultural History,* ed. Lynn Hunt (Berkeley: University of California Press, 1989), 176–204. For a typical prodivorce argument, see *New York Assembly Documents, 1840,* vol. 8, no. 324, April 18, 5; on "legitimate increase," see Bishop, *Commentaries,* chap. 15, secs. 282–83.

47. Citations in De Saussure, "The Effect of Foreign Divorces," 388; Tapping Reeve, *The Law of Baron and Femme,* 3d ed. (Albany, N.Y.: Gould, 1862), 196; *Massachusetts House of Representatives Documents, 1841,* no. 20, 13; *New York Senate Documents, 1856,* vol. 2, no. 40, February 27, 3; "Marriage and Divorce," *Southern Quarterly Review* 26 (1854): 355. On the Christian

nature of American marriage law, see Cott, "Giving Character to Our Whole Civil Polity," 120, and Carole Weisbrod, "Family, Church, and State: An Essay on Constitutionalism and Religious Authority," *Journal of Family Law* 26 (1988): 741–70.

48. On the denial of a cause-and-effect relationship between the availability of divorce and the number of decrees, see *Massachusetts House of Representatives Documents, 1841,* no. 20, 7–8; see also "Law of Divorce," *North American Review* 90 (1860): 426.

49. *California Senate and Assembly Journals, 1851,* doc. [M], 656–59.

50. Ibid., 657–58.

51. Ibid., doc. [N], 665–68, citation on 667.

52. *California Senate Journal, 1851,* 104, 113, 115, 405.

CHAPTER 3. CONTESTING THE RULES, 1850s–1870

1. McFarland had wounded Richardson slightly once before. For an assessment of the trial from the perspective of a series of trials acquitting husbands who murdered their wives' lovers, see Hendrik Hartog, "Lawyering, Husbands' Rights, and 'the Unwritten Law' in Nineteenth-Century America," *Journal of American History* 84 (1997): 67–96. Developments in the trial were covered by both local and out-of-state newspapers and collected in trial pamphlets. Details can be gleaned from *The Trial of Daniel McFarland for the Shooting of Albert D. Richardson, the Alleged Seducer of His Wife,* compiled by A. R. Cazauran (New York: W. E. Hilton, 1870); *The Veiled Lady; or the Mysterious Witness in the McFarland Trial* (Philadelphia: G. W. Alexander, 1870); and *The Richardson-McFarland Tragedy* (Philadelphia: Barclay, 1870). Stanton's "Speech to the McFarland-Richardson Protest Meeting" is reprinted in *Elizabeth Cady Stanton, Susan B. Anthony: Correspondence, Writings, Speeches,* ed. Ellen Carol DuBois (New York: Schocken Books, 1981), 125–38. Ironically, Horace Greeley, a vociferous opponent of easy divorce, arranged for Beecher and Frothingham to preside over the marriage. On Beecher's significance in liberal, northern Protestant culture, see Richard Wightman Fox, "Intimacy on Trial: Cultural Meanings of the Beecher-Tilton Affair," in *The Power of Culture: Critical Essays in American History,* ed. Richard Wightman Fox and T. J. Jackson Lears (Chicago: University of Chicago Press, 1993), 103–32.

2. Stanton, "Speech to the McFarland-Richardson Protest Meeting," 127–28; Elizabeth Clark, "Matrimonial Bonds: Slavery and Divorce in Nineteenth-Century America," *Law and History Review* 8 (1990): 30–54.

3. Stanton, "Speech to the McFarland-Richardson Protest Meeting," 129–30.

4. "The McFarland-Richardson Tragedy," *Revolution,* December 16, 1869, 376–77; Jeanne Boydston, Mary Kelley, and Anne Margolis, *The Limits of Sisterhood: The Beecher Sisters on Women's Rights and Woman's Sphere* (Chapel Hill: University of North Carolina Press, 1988), 292–94, citation from Hooker on 305; citation from Stowe in Mary Kelley, *Private Woman, Public Stage: Literary Domesticity in Nineteenth-Century America* (New York: Oxford University Press, 1984), 237. Hooker could hardly be construed as a conservative on

women's rights; in joining Stanton and Anthony in the New York–based National wing of the movement, she was rejecting her siblings' commitment to the more moderate, Boston-based American wing, thereby setting off a family rift. She argued that if Richardson seduced Abby McFarland before the divorce, both deserved condemnation, but if Abby had cause for divorce, then she had every right to declare her independence.

5. On the autonomy and integrity of the individual in Victorian culture, see James Turner, *Without God, without Creed: The Origins of Unbelief in America* (Baltimore: Johns Hopkins University Press, 1985), 208; on the radicalism of women's moral autonomy, see Carroll Smith-Rosenberg, *Disorderly Conduct: Visions of Gender in Victorian America* (New York: Oxford University Press, 1985), 129–64. On women as both subjects and objects in the legitimation of divorce, see Joan Wallach Scott, *Only Paradoxes to Offer: French Feminists and the Rights of Man* (Cambridge, Mass.: Harvard University Press, 1996), 20.

6. Cauzauran, *The Trial of Daniel McFarland*, 30.

7. Citations in ibid., 28–29; for the influence of "Fourierite vagaries" and "socialistic theories" on the unraveling of the McFarland marriage, see also *Full Particulars of the Assassination of Albert D. Richardson, the Libertine, Shot by the Injured Husband, McFarland* (New York: n.p., 1870), 3.

8. *The Richardson-McFarland Tragedy*, 34.

9. Citation in *History of Woman Suffrage*, ed. Elizabeth Cady Stanton, Susan B. Anthony, and Matilda Joslyn Gage, 3 vols., 2d ed. (Rochester, N.Y.: Fowlers and Wells, 1889), 2:809, hereafter cited as *HWS*. On the underestimated cultural impress of the antebellum women's movement and the ensuing intensification of gender tensions in the postbellum era, see Karen Lystra, *Searching the Heart: Women, Men, and Romantic Love in Nineteenth-Century America* (New York: Oxford University Press, 1989), 249; on the consequences of the shift in the family from a center of production to an agency of capital formation, see Anne C. Rose, *Victorian America and the Civil War* (New York: Cambridge University Press, 1992), 179. See also the debate over a resolution upholding the sanctity of marriage and denouncing free love at the Equal Rights Association meeting in May of 1869 in *HWS*, 2:388–90.

10. Françoise Basch, "Women's Rights and the Wrongs of Marriage in Mid-Nineteenth-Century America," *History Workshop* 22 (1986): 18–40; Carole Pateman, *The Sexual Contract* (Stanford: Stanford University Press, 1988). On links between the marriage contract and the social contract, see, for example, Samual J. May, *The Rights and Condition of Women: A Sermon Preached in Syracuse, Nov. 1845*, 3d ed., Woman's Rights Tract No. 1 (n.p., n.d.), 11. May's was one of ten numbered early woman's rights tracts.

11. On free loveism, see *New York Semi-Weekly Tribune*, May 20, 1853.

12. *HWS*, 1:733.

13. Ibid., 1:735.

14. Ibid., 1:721. For a critique of the ambivalence of feminists toward divorce, see Linus Pierpont Brockett, *Woman: Her Rights, Wrongs, Privileges, and Responsibilities* (Hartford, Conn.: L. Stebbins, 1869), 415

15. *Banner of Light*, May 27, 1865. I am grateful to Ann Braude for guiding me to the life and writings of Elizabeth Packard. See Elizabeth Parson Ware

Packard, *Marital Power Exemplified in Mrs. Packard's Trial and Self-Defense from the Charge of Insanity* (Hartford, Conn.: Case, Lockwood, 1866); *The Prisoner's Hidden Life, or Insane Asylums Unveiled* (Chicago: A. B. Cass, 1868); *Mrs. Packard's Address to the Illinois Legislature on the Passage of the Personal Liberty Bill* (Chicago: V. N. Clarke, 1870); and *Modern Persecution, or Married Woman's Liabilities as Demonstrated by the Action of the Illinois Legislature* (Hartford, Conn.: Case, Lockwood, and Brainard, 1873).

16. Citations in Packard, *Marital Power*, 64, and *Modern Persecution*, 400–401. On the status and security that women derived from marriage, see John C. Spurlock, *Free Love: Marriage and Middle-Class Radicalism in America, 1825–1860* (New York: New York University Press, 1988), 183. On Packard's important distinction between good and bad dependency, see Hendrik Hartog, "Mrs. Packard on Dependency," *Yale Journal of Law and Humanities* 1 (1988): 84. Judith R. Walkowitz discusses the incarceration of Georgina Weldon, a troublesome English Spiritualist wife, in *City of Dreadful Delight: Narratives of Sexual Danger in Late-Victorian London* (Chicago: University of Chicago Press, 1992), 171–89.

17. Packard, *Address to the Illinois Legislature*, 2.

18. *HWS*, 1:587; Elizabeth Oakes Smith, letter in *New York Semi-Weekly Tribune*, February 8, 1853; Elizabeth Oakes Smith, *The Sanctity of Marriage*, Woman's Rights Tract No. 5 (Syracuse, N.Y.: n.p., 1853), 3.

19. "The Marriage Institution," *Lily* 7 (1855): 82.

20. On the self-defeating patterns in melodrama, see Mary Poovey, *Uneven Developments: The Ideological Work of Gender in Mid-Victorian England* (Chicago: University of Chicago Press, 1988), 83. On the uneven economic consequences of divorce, see *On the Responsibilities of Woman: A Speech by Mrs. C. I. H. Nichols, Worcester, October 15, 1851*, Woman's Rights Tract No. 6 (n.p., n.d.), 12–13; see also "Letter of C. I. H. Nichols to Sisters and Friends of Temperance," *Lily* 4 (1852): 38–39, in which Nichols favored a prohibition law over divorce for intemperance.

21. "Editor's Table," *Godey's Lady's Book* 58 (1856): 79; Gail Hamilton [Mary Abigail Dodge], *A New Atmosphere* (Boston: Ticknor and Fields, 1865), 266. On Norton, see also Poovey, *Uneven Developments*, 62–88.

22. "Marriage and Divorce," *Revolution*, October 22, 1868, 249–50.

23. Mary Upton Ferrin, "Address to the Judiciary Committee of the Massachusetts Legislature," in *HWS*, 1:213; and the 1854 Albany resolve in ibid., 1:593.

24. Amelia Bloomer, "The Duty of Drunkards' Wives—Divorce," *Lily* 4 (1852): 69; Nichols, "To Sisters and Friends of Temperance." On legislative reform, see, for example, "Memorial of Mrs. Caroline M. Severance," *Lily* 6 (1854): 66.

25. "Marriage and Divorce," *Ladies' Repository* 30 (1870): 240.

26. "Is It Love or Folly?" *Lily* 8 (1856): 14; "Letter from Mrs. Stanton to the Woman's Temperance Convention," *Lily* 4 (1852): 10; Eleanor Kirk, "A Word to Abused Wives," *Revolution*, June 18, 1868, 381–82.

27. "Man and Woman" (probably written by Paulina Davis), *Una*, September 1855, 135.

28. Advertisement for the *Revolution* in *Hearth and Home,* January 15, 1870, 63; Elizabeth Cady Stanton, "Vashti," *Revolution,* July 22, 1869, 37; Esther Haines, "Marriage—Its Sacredness and Security," *Revolution,* February 10, 1870, 94. On passionlessness, see Nancy F. Cott's thoughtful analysis in "Passionlessness: An Interpretation of Victorian Sexual Ideology, 1790–1850," *Signs* 4 (1978): 219–36; on romantic love, see Lystra, *Searching the Heart.*

29. John B. Ellis, *Free Love and Its Votaries* (San Francisco: A. L. Bancroft, 1870), 453.

30. Rev. Henry Loomis, Jr., "Divorce Legislation in Connecticut," *New Englander* 25 (1866): 436.

31. On the role of marriage in utopian socialism, see John R. Gillis, *For Better, for Worse: British Marriages, 1600 to the Present* (New York: Oxford University Press, 1985), 222–27, citation from one of Owen's followers on 225.

32. On the role of worldly moralism in the decline of religious faith, see Turner, *Origins of Unbelief,* 83–84, 163–65.

33. Ann Braude, *Radical Spirits: Spiritualism and Women's Rights in Nineteenth-Century America* (Boston: Beacon Press, 1989), 46. Spiritualism was linked persistently with free love, but its adherents often distinguished support for liberal divorce from obliterating the "healthy limits and proper barriers to the riot of passion, that . . . would consume us body and soul." See *Banner of Light,* July 10, 1858, 4; citation in ibid., July 17, 1858, 4.

34. Andrew Jackson Davis, *The Great Harmonia; concerning Physiological Vices and Virtues, and the Seven Phases of Marriage,* 4 vols. (Boston: Sanborn, Carter, and Bazin, 1856), 4:398, 403–4. This particular source predates Loomis's postbellum appeal, but Davis defended divorce in postbellum tracts as well.

35. Ibid., 4:418; Andrew Jackson Davis, *The Genesis and Ethics of Conjugal Love* (New York: Progressive Publishing House, 1874), 19. On Davis's personal life and the reference to Mary Fenn Love, his second wife, see Ellis, *Free Love and Its Votaries,* 411–12. Davis's first wife, who died while they were married, had been divorced when she married him, and he subsequently divorced his second wife in 1885 to marry a third time. For a similar position on Scripture and divorce, see "Gerrit Smith on Divorce," *Revolution,* February 10, 1870, 87, which cites a letter written by Smith to the *New York Independent.*

36. Davis, *The Great Harmonia,* 4:419.

37. Braude, *Radical Spirits,* 127–30; citation in Anon., *Slavery and Marriage: A Dialogue* (n.p., 1850), 11. This pamphlet is available at the American Antiquarian Society.

38. On free love as the ultimate radicalism, see Spurlock, *Free Love,* 2.

39. See Nelson Manfred Blake, *The Road to Reno: A History of Divorce in the United States* (New York: Macmillan, 1962), 82–86, 89–92. The tract in question was *Love vs. Marriage* by Dr. M. Edgeworth Lazarus. Quotation in Stephen Pearl Andrews, *Love, Marriage, and Divorce and the Sovereignty of the Individual: A Discussion by Henry James, Horace Greeley, and Stephen Pearl Andrews; Including the Final Replies of Mr. Andrews, Rejected by the Tribune* (New York: Stringer and Townsend, 1853), 9.

40. Andrews, *Love, Marriage, and Divorce,* 19, 48, 87. James, Greeley, and Andrews were all more or less students of Fourier, who had deemed marriage the proper outlet for what he called the passions. But whereas James regarded unalloyed individual sovereignty as misguided, Andrews worked to create a social context for it by collaborating with Josiah Warren in the founding of an anarchist community, Modern Times.

41. Ibid., 52, 115; Ellis, *Free Love and Its Votaries,* 492. Andrews attributed the plight of the millworker to the cruel influence of a public sentiment that could not tolerate the sovereignty of the individual.

42. Anon., *Divorce* (Boston: n.p., 1871), 12, a pamphlet available at the American Antiquarian Society; Theodore Woolsey, "Divorce," *New Englander* 27 (1868): 784–85.

43. George Ellington, *The Women of New York or the Under-World of the Great City* (New York: New York Book, 1869), 346–48. On varied responses to Powers's nude statue, see Jean Fagan Yellin, *Women and Sisters: The Antislavery Feminists in American Culture* (New Haven: Yale University Press, 1989), 99–113.

44. Woolsey, "Divorce," 527, 548, 788–89. His insistence on the preeminence of lower-class litigants in divorce litigation may be exaggerated, but fragmentary evidence from mid-nineteenth-century court records affirms that they were present in substantial numbers. See especially Robert L. Griswold, *Family and Divorce in California, 1825–1890: Victorian Illusion and Everyday Realities* (Albany: State University of New York Press, 1982).

45. Theodore Woolsey, "The Law of Divorce," *Hearth and Home,* January 8, 1870, 40; Loomis, "Divorce Legislation in Connecticut," 452.

46. Ellis, *Free Love and Its Votaries,* 484; Ellington, *Women of New York,* 383–84; "Frequent Divorce in New England," *American Church Review* 20 (1868): 226 (citing an article on Ohio divorce in the *Nation*); "Divorce Legislation in Connecticut," *Catholic World* 4 (1866): 103. New York City divorce records include numerous Catholics whose religious affiliation is confirmed by the documentation of their marriages.

47. See, for example, Woolsey, "Divorce," 540.

48. Michael Grossberg, *Governing the Hearth: Law and the Family in Nineteenth-Century America* (Chapel Hill: University of North Carolina Press, 1985), 90–91; Glenda Riley, *Divorce: An American Tradition* (New York: Oxford University Press, 1991), 108–29; Blake, *Road to Reno,* 138–39. Even before its formal inception, the New England group compiled divorce statistics for the New England states. See, for example, "Frequent Divorce in New England," *American Church Review* 20 (1868): 271–318; Alvah Hovey, *The Scriptural Law of Divorce* (Boston: Gould and Lincoln, 1866), 9.

49. On religious conferences, see "The Divine Law of Divorce," *Ladies' Repository* 28 (1868): 287–91. For "A Canon as to Repulsion in Cases of Divorce," see *American Church Review* 25 (1873): 499; a divorced adulterous spouse was excluded from holy communion for a period of three years.

50. Anon., *Divorce,* 20. See "The Indissolubility of Christian Marriage," *Catholic World* 5 (1867): 687.

51. *Catholic World* 5 (1867): 688; see Woolsey, "Divorce," 768, 770. On the tightening of statutes, see Blake, *Road to Reno,* 131–36.

52. Heinrich Schliemann, *Schliemann in Indianapolis,* ed. Eli Lilly (Indianapolis: Indianapolis Historical Society, 1961), 12–13.

53. Ibid., 18–20, citation on 18–19. Schliemann was probably trying to satisfy provisions in an amendment that required proof of intent to remain in the state, which he supported over the even stricter provisions of the pending divorce bill. The legislative effort to tighten divorce provisions stopped when forty-one Democrats resigned to avoid voting on the Fifteenth Amendment, thereby depriving the legislature of a quorum. Indiana finally revised its divorce code in 1873 by extending residency to two years and demanding adequate proof. The omnibus clause was eliminated, and plaintiffs were forbidden to remarry for two years during which time the case could be reopened. See Blake, *Road to Reno,* 121.

54. Schliemann, *Schliemann in Indianapolis,* 49–63.

55. For satire on New York divorce, see Augustin Daly's 1871 play, *Divorce,* reprinted in *Man and Wife, and Other Plays,* ed. Catherine Sturtevant (Princeton: Princeton University Press, 1942), 75–152. Daly mocks both the motives of the petitioners and the dishonesty of the legal system. On Indiana, see, for example, "Divorce," *Putnam's* 8 (1856): 630–34, a tall tale of a transplanted Yankee lawyer making his living off Indiana's lenient divorce code.

56. Horace Greeley, *Recollections of a Busy Life* (New York: J. B. Ford, 1869), 571. Greeley's editorials and Owen's responses appeared in March and April of 1860 and were reprinted in Greeley's memoirs.

57. Ibid., 573–78, citation on 574. Owen also denounced the strictness of New England divorce laws, referring probably to Massachusetts.

58. Ibid., 579, 586.

59. Ibid., 589, 599.

60. Ibid., 604, 612.

CHAPTER 4. WHEN WOMEN GO TO COURT

1. Frank L. Dewey, "Thomas Jefferson's Notes on Divorce," *William and Mary Quarterly,* 3d ser., 39 (1982): 212–23, citations from Jefferson on 218–19.

2. On glimpsing "lived experience" and the renegotiation of gender through the documents in a divorce suit, see Michael Grossberg's elegant *A Judgment for Solomon: The D'Hauteville Case and Legal Experience in Antebellum America* (New York: Cambridge University Press, 1996). On experience, see also Richard Wightman Fox, "Intimacy on Trial: Cultural Meanings of the Beecher-Tilton Affair," in *The Power of Culture: Critical Essays in American History,* ed. Richard Wightman Fox and T. J. Jackson Lears (Chicago: University of Chicago Press, 1993), 103–32.

3. Cott duly noted the absence of financial support in Massachusetts decrees, but it is her subtle analysis of the links between women's use of the divorce process and a paradigmatic shift in marriage that has had enormous influence on subsequent scholarship. Although that scholarship has been far from monolithic, Cott has largely set the terms for relating divorce to gender. As

a result, scholars have located women's right to divorce on a patriarchal-companionate continuum. See Nancy F. Cott, "Divorce and the Changing Status of Women in Eighteenth-Century Massachusetts," *William and Mary Quarterly*, 3d ser., 33 (1976): 586–614, and "Eighteenth-Century Family and Social Life Revealed in Massachusetts Divorce Records," *Journal of Social History* 10 (1976): 20–43. For unreservedly sanguine views on women and divorce, see Carl N. Degler, *At Odds: Women and the Family in America from the Revolution to the Present* (New York: Oxford University Press, 1980); and Robert L. Griswold, *Family and Divorce in California, 1850–1890: Victorian Illusions and Everyday Realities* (Albany: State University of New York Press, 1982). For bleaker views of divorce in early America, see Linda K. Kerber, *Women of the Republic: Intellect and Ideology in Revolutionary America* (Chapel Hill: University of North Carolina Press, 1980); and Cornelia Hughes Dayton, *Women before the Bar: Gender, Law, and Society in Connecticut, 1639–1789*, published by the Institute of Early American History and Culture (Chapel Hill: University of North Carolina Press, 1995). On the distribution of marital assets in separations and divorces during the same period, see Marylynn Salmon, *Women and the Law of Property in Early America* (Chapel Hill: University of North Carolina Press, 1986), 58–80; on the benefits that divorce provided southern women in a patriarchal context, see Jane Turner Censer, "Smiling through Her Tears: Antebellum Southern Women and Divorce," *American Journal of Legal History* 25 (1981): 24–47, and Lawrence B. Goodheart, Neil Hanks, and Elizabeth Johnson, "'An Act for the Relief of Females . . .': Divorce and the Changing Legal Status of Women in Tennessee," parts 1 and 2, *Tennessee Historical Quarterly* 44 (1985): 318–39, 402–16.

For a refinement of the concept of companionate marriage that emphasizes women's decreasing economic dependence on individual men in their readiness to use the law independently, see Suzanne Lebsock, *The Free Women of Petersburg: Status and Culture in a Southern Town, 1784–1860* (New York: W. W. Norton, 1984). Michael C. Grossberg's overarching study of family law, *Governing the Hearth: Law and the Family in Nineteenth-Century America* (Chapel Hill: University of North Carolina Press, 1985), suggests a decline on one level in the relative autonomy of women with the emergence of what he calls "a judicial patriarchy" in the last decades of the nineteenth century. At the same time, Grossberg's *Judgment for Solomon* profiles the important shift represented by awarding custody of a child to a mother in a sharply contested Pennsylvania suit. On divorce in the Progressive Era, see William O'Neill's pioneering *Divorce in the Progressive Era* (New Haven: Yale University Press, 1967), a work that develops the idea of divorce as a safety valve for marriage. See also Elaine Tyler May, *Great Expectations: Marriage and Divorce in Post-Victorian America* (Chicago: University of Chicago Press, 1980); contrasting divorces in the 1880s with those from the 1920s, May notes a confluence between an improvement in alimony provisions in the 1920s together with women's rising expectations. For an optimistic overview of American divorce suggesting that its historic emphasis on morality diverted attention from a much-needed emphasis on alimony and custody, see Glenda Riley, *Divorce: An American Tradition* (New York: Oxford University Press, 1991). For the problems engendered by contemporary patterns of alimony and child support in no-fault, see Lenore J. Weitzman, *The Divorce Revolution: The Unexpected Social and Economic Consequences for Women and Children in America* (New York: Free Press, 1985); and J. Herbie DiFonzo, *Beneath the Fault Line: The Popular and Legal Culture of Divorce in Twentieth-Century America* (Charlottesville: University Press of Virginia, 1997). Generally, there has been little emphasis by historians on some remarkably similar problems in nineteenth-century fault divorce.

For celebrations of companionate marriage, see especially Lawrence Stone, *The Family, Sex, and Marriage in England, 1500–1800*, abridged ed. (New York: Harper and Row, 1979); Edward Shorter, *The Making of the Modern Family* (New York: Basic Books, 1975); and for the United States, Degler, *At Odds*. For a critical review of this trend in scholarship on marriage, see John R. Gillis, *For Better, for Worse: British Marriages, 1600 to the Present* (Oxford: Oxford University Press, 1985), 3–5. A. James Hammerton, moreover, argues that in Victorian England, the marital authority of husbands was preserved by making it more palatable through "domestication" even as women in fact grew more assertive; in *Cruelty and Companionship: Conflict in Nineteenth-Century Married Life* (London: Routledge, 1992), Hammerton finds the notion of an overarching transition from patriarchy to companionship over the *longue durée* misguided; instead he views them as simultaneous and negotiated. Carole Patemen, whose brilliant assault on patriarchy is waged largely in ahistorical, essentialist terms, links divorce to the growing contractualism of sexuality in which men assert their control over women's bodies; see *The Sexual Contract* (Stanford: Stanford University Press, 1988). For a critique of divorce as a woman's remedy in the larger context of "legal liberalism," see also Joan Hoff Wilson, *Law, Gender, and Injustice: A Legal History of U.S. Women* (New York: New York University Press, 1991).

4. Indiana provided divorce for impotency, bigamy, adultery, abandonment, conviction of a felony, cruelty, and "in any other case, where the court in their discretion, shall consider it reasonable and proper that a divorce should be granted." Divorce was defined officially in 1833 as a proceeding in chancery. The circuit courts sat as both common law and chancery courts with jurisdiction over any county where the complainant resided, regardless of where the cause for the divorce took place. See *Laws of Indiana*, 1831, chap. 31; ibid., 1833, chap. 33; Richard Wires, *The Divorce Issue and Reform in Nineteenth-Century Indiana* (Muncie, Ind.: Ball State University, 1976). The Monroe County Records are available in the Office of the County Clerk, Bloomington Indiana. Marion County divorces are documented in Circuit Court Order Books and the Circuit Court Complete Record, as well as Court of Common Pleas Order Books and Court of Common Pleas Complete Record; they are available in the Office of the County Clerk in Indianapolis.

5. New York County divorces are drawn from "An Index to Matrimonial Actions, 1784–1910," and are located in the archives of the Supreme Court of New York County; they include, as does the index, early chancery cases. My sampling, from roughly the first third of the alphabet, is made up of all A–H matrimonials from 1787 to 1800, 1 of every 3 between 1801 and 1840, 1 of every 4 between 1841 and 1860, and 1 of every 10 between 1861 and 1870. Although divorce was limited until 1848 to courts with equity jurisdiction, those

courts multiplied. Common law and equity were finally merged in the state constitution of 1846. Divorce became available in a variety of local courts such as the superior court, the mayor's court, and the court of common pleas. See Alden Chester, ed., *A Legal and Judicial History of New York*, 3 vols. (New York: National American Society, 1911), 1:333; and "Barbour's Reports on Cases in Chancery," *Hunts Merchant's Magazine* 18 (1847): 392.

6. According to Carroll D. Wright's survey, between 1867 and 1886, 65.8 percent of the divorces in the United States were granted to women. Statewide for the same period, women accounted for 71 percent of the divorces in Indiana and 62.6 percent of those in New York. Although the New York statute may have also discouraged the use of formal divorces, the rate of divorce in New York County exceeded that in all but one other county in the state (Cortland). In New York County in 1870, the average annual number of divorces per 100,000 persons was 28, while in Monroe County, Indiana, it was 85. Estimating the divorce rate in relation to total population is misleading, but given the faulty recording of marriages and the considerable ambiguity over what constituted a marriage, it remains the most accurate available estimate. See Carroll D. Wright, comp., *A Report on Marriage and Divorce in the United States, 1867–1886* (Washington, D.C.: Government Printing Office, 1889), 170; and United States Bureau of the Census, Special Reports, *Marriage and Divorce, 1867–1902*, 2 vols. (Washington, D.C.: Government Printing Office, 1908–1909), 1:95, 148, 165.

7. Bill of Complaint, Mary Warren v. Eli Warren, Final Record, 1830–1849. Mary Warren made no effort to prove her husband's intemperance, but intemperance had been added as a statutory ground to the state's already liberal divorce statute in 1838. See *Laws of Indiana*, 1838, chap. 31.

8. Lawrence Stone, *Road to Divorce: England, 1530–1987* (New York: Oxford University Press, 1990), 19. Similarly, James Boyd White depicts the application of a legal rule to an individual case as resulting in a starkly simple narrative; see *The Legal Imagination*, abridged ed. (Chicago: University of Chicago Press, 1985), 114.

9. Decree, January 1850, Warren v. Warren; Bill in Chancery for Dower (March 1850), Final Record, 1838–1849. The disposition of the family dwelling is unclear from this evidence, but it likely went to Mary.

10. On southern migration, see Eric Foner, *Free Soil, Free Labor, Free Men: The Ideology of the Republican Party before the Civil War* (New York: Oxford University Press, 1984), 131–39. Many New York matrimonials specifically link the disappearance of a husband to "the west." Mary Jane Cordier was remarried and had five children from her second union when her first husband, who she claimed "died in the mines," reappeared and successfully sued her for divorce. On appeal, the court held that her search for him was not sufficiently diligent. Jean Hyacinth Cordier v. Mary Jane Cordier (1864), GA-121, C-3, and (1866), GA-114, C-2.

11. On plowing and fieldwork, see John Mack Faragher, *Women and Men on the Overland Trail* (New Haven: Yale University Press, 1979), 49–53.

12. The cost of divorce in New York may very well have been defrayed by statutory provisions enabling poor litigants to sue without court costs or attorneys' fees in civil suits. The judgment rolls do not indicate if a plaintiff sued under

the special provisions for the impoverished. See "Of the Bringing and Maintaining of Suits by Poor Persons," *New York Revised Statutes,* 1829, vol. 2, chap. 8, tit. 1, reiterated verbatim in the state's 1846, 1852, and 1875 revisions. On "hotel evidence," see "Divorce Made Easy," *New York Times,* October 10, 1869; and Nelson Manfred Blake, *The Road to Reno: Divorce in the United States* (New York: Macmillan, 1962), 190–91.

13. Complaint, Mary Hermann v. Nicholas Hermann (1857), GA-268, H-2.

14. Examination, Anna Maria Steinbinger, Hermann v. Hermann. Most defendants failed to appear or to be represented, and after testimony by witnesses, their guilt was established "pro confesso," as if they had confessed. Because service of a summons was often not possible, it was satisfied in both New York and Indiana by the publication of the impending suit for a period of weeks in the local press.

15. Answer, Nicholas Hermann, Hermann v. Hermann.

16. Decree, in ibid. The prohibition against remarriage was customarily reiterated in New York decrees. If Nicholas had remarried in New York and subsequently had the validity of his marriage tested in the state courts, it would have been deemed illegal. Given the state of record keeping, however, and the religious nature of marriage rites, there was little to prevent marriage in another state or even within the state. Isabella Eddy, who was guilty of adultery in a divorce, remarried in the state only to be exposed when her second marriage failed, and her second husband won an annulment on the basis of her guilt and her subsequent remarriage; see Edward Eddy v. Isabella Eddy (1865), GA-131, E-1. On passing as man and wife, see, for example, Martha Haines v. Ezra Haines (1849), AL-618, Lib-232; Theresa Girarden v. Emil Girarden (1858), GA-271, G-2; Emma Broome v. John Broome (1852), GA-9, B-2; Louisa Haskin v. William E. Haskin (1855), GA-212, H-1; and Cary Harris v. Mary Harris (1853), GA-104, H-1. A spate of other cases involved defendants who assumed aliases in their second unions. As Wright noted, even by the 1880s, very few states had a comprehensive system for recording marriages. In Maryland marriages celebrated far exceeded marriage licenses issued because marriage could take place either under a license or with the publication of banns. See *A Report on Marriage and Divorce, 1867–1886,* 18–19.

17. Frederick Geisenhower, who served also as a witness, testified on cross-examination that Nicholas gave bad breath as an explanation for his desertion. John Boswell notes that bad breath was permitted as a cause for divorce in the thirteenth-century crusader kingdom of Jerusalem; see *The Kindness of Strangers* (New York: Random House, 1988), 346–47 n. 83.

18. The evidence includes allusions to aliases, transfers of property out of state, and documentation of long-term second unions.

19. Martha Codd v. Matthew Codd (1833), BA, C-40. On the importance of women's assets in nineteenth-century divorces, see also Paula Petrik, "Not a Love Story: Bordeaux v. Bordeaux," *Montana: The Magazine of Western History* 41 (1991): 32–46.

20. Lavinia Moore v. John Moore (August 1850), Final Record, 1838–1849; Samuel R. Caring v. Harriet Caring (1822), Civil Order Book, 1819–1827. On customary notions of separate property, see Gillis, *For Better, for Worse,* 199.

21. Sarah McConnell v. Joseph McConnell, Complete Record, Marion County Court of Common Pleas [A], 1849–1852, 80–88.

22. Sophia Dandy v. Timothy Dandy (1821), BA, D-299. On alimony as nourishment, see Salmon, *Women and the Law of Property*, 58–59. *Indiana Revised Statutes*, 1852, vol. 2, chap. 4, sec. 22 stipulated: "The decree for alimony to the wife shall be for a sum in gross and not for annual payments, but the court in its discretion, may give a reasonable time for the payment thereof, by instalments, on sufficient security being given."

23. On the forms private separation agreements took, see Joseph S. Ferrell, "Early Statutory and Common Law of Divorce in North Carolina," *North Carolina Law Review* 41 (1961): 620–21.

24. Sabrina H. Anderson v. Thomas H. Anderson (1860), GA-11, A-1.

25. Clementine Durchsprung v. Gottlieb Durchsprung (1864), GA-149, D-1.

26. Answer, Emma D. Barron v. John M. Barron (1864), GA-62, B-3.

27. Referee's Report, Barron v. Barron; *Trow's New York City Directory*, 1865, vol. 78, Commercial Register, 58.

28. Answer, Barron v. Barron.

29. Lydia Catlin v. Charles Catlin (1866), GA-93, C-1.

30. Dandy v. Dandy.

31. Trust Deed, Exhibit A, Peter Bolenbacher v. Amelia Bolenbacher (August 1850), Final Record, 1838–1849. Exhibit B is a copy of a special legislative act sent by the Indiana secretary of state to the clerk of the Monroe County Court permitting Peter to file for divorce "without regard to the length of time the said Bolenbacher has been a resident citizen of this state." Bolenbacher's petition acknowledged that Amelia brought $300 in cash to their marriage.

32. Complaint, Bill of Exceptions, and Decree in Matilda Langdon v. Samuel Langdon (1847), Final Record, 1838–1849.

33. On deserting husbands, see Paula Petrik, "If She Be Content: The Development of Montana Divorce Law, 1865–1907," *Western Historical Quarterly* 18 (1987): 261–91. For women's alignment with and reliance on kin in the divorce process, see Marilyn Ferris Motz, *True Sisterhood: Michigan Women and Their Kin* (Albany: State University of New York Press, 1983), 122–24. On the range of litigants, see Griswold, *Family and Divorce in California,* and Lawrence M. Friedman and Robert V. Percival, "Who Sues for Divorce? From Fault through Fiction to Freedom," *Journal of Legal Studies* 5 (1976): 69.

34. Mary Jane Humphrey v. Silas Humphrey (1844), Final Record, 1838–1849. New York plaintiffs consistently cited desertion, intemperance, and cruelty in divorce petitions although they were not statutory grounds. What is particularly convincing in many allegations of desertion is the specificity with which plaintiffs and their witnesses documented desertion, especially when it entailed a long-term relationship with a paramour.

35. On cruelty, see Robert L. Griswold, "Law, Sex, Cruelty, and Divorce in Victorian America," *American Quarterly* 38 (1986): 721–45. On custody, see Michael Grossberg, "Who Gets the Child? Custody, Guardianship, and the Rise of Judicial Patriarchy in Nineteenth-Century America," *Feminist Studies* 9 (1983): 235–60. On the prevalence of desertion as a ground, see Wright, *A*

Report on Marriage and Divorce, 1867–1886, 168–69. The absence of children may reflect the brevity of some marriages and the long duration of others, but there is no distinct pattern in either jurisdiction with respect to the number of years litigants had been married.

36. Henrietta Heine v. Solomon Heine (1841) BA, H-256. On the reluctance of Connecticut judges to undermine a husband's authority in early American cases, see Dayton, *Women before the Bar,* 154.

37. Jette Ball v. Michael Ball (1860), GA-44, B-2.

38. Louisa Haskin by Frederick Moses her next friend v. William E. Haskin (1855), GA-212, H-1; Eleanor Camp v. Charles H. Camp (1867), GA-76, C-1.

39. Hammerton, *Cruelty and Companionship.*

40. Letter in Mary H. Crane by her next friend William Stuart v. John W. Crane (1859), GA-160, C-3. On love, see, for example, Phoebe Hatfield v. Peter Hatfield, Jr. (1822), AL-3822, Lib-370; and Charlotte Lukens v. Samuel H. Lukens, Complete Record, Marion County Court of Common Pleas, [A] 1849–1852, 70–72.

41. See Amy Champlin v. Guy Champlin, alias dictus Elisha Hinman, alias dictus Henry Hull (1827), BA, C-10.

42. Charles Henry Edwards v. Amanda M. F. Edwards (1842), BA, E-75; Charles Augusthuys v. Rachel Augusthuys (1854), GA-7, A-1.

43. Copy of letter, Mary Ann Helen Bunner v. F. Charles Bunner (1835), BA, B-32. On departures from "the breadwinner ethic" in the post-1950s, see Barbara Ehrenreich, *The Hearts of Men: American Dreams and the Flight from Commitment* (Garden City, N.Y.: Anchor Press/Doubleday, 1984); it seems the trend Ehrenreich depicts was already something of a problem by the middle decades of the nineteenth century.

CHAPTER 5. WHEN MEN GO TO COURT

1. Family Record, Isaiah Thomas Papers, American Antiquarian Society, box 7, folder 4; diary of Isaiah Thomas, *Transactions and Collections of the American Antiquarian Society,* vol. 9 (1909): 408; vol. 10 (1909): 23. On Thomas's marriages, see also Anne Russell Marble, *From Prentice to Patron: The Life Story of Isaiah Thomas* (New York: D. Appleton, 1935); and Clifford K. Shipton, *Isaiah Thomas: Printer, Patriot, and Philanthropist, 1749–1831* (Rochester, N.Y.: Leo Hart, 1948).

2. Benjamin Franklin Thomas, *Memoir of Isaiah Thomas* (Boston: Albany, Munsell, 1874), 27; Libel of Isaiah Thomas against Mary Thomas, Isaiah Thomas Papers, box 1, folder 4.

3. Libel of Isaiah Thomas against Mary Thomas.

4. Memorandum of an Agreement between Isaiah Thomas and Rebecca his wife, May 17, 1822, Isaiah Thomas Papers, box 7, folder 6; diary of Isaiah Thomas, *Transactions and Collections of the American Antiquarian Society,* vol. 10, 75, 113.

5. Memorandum of an Agreement between Isaiah Thomas and Rebecca his wife. On Massachusetts divorce statutes, see Michael S. Hindus and Lynne E. Withey, "The Law of Husband and Wife in Nineteenth-Century America:

Changing Views of Divorce," in *Women and the Law: A Social Historical Perspective,* ed. D. Kelly Weisberg, 2 vols. (Cambridge, Mass.: Schenkman Publishing, 1982), 2:133–53.

6. Thomas House v. Betsy House (1824), Civil Order Book, 1818–1828; James Scoby v. Ruth Scoby (1825), Final Record, 1819–1827; Samuel Glenn v. Mary E. Glenn (1870), GA-199, G-1.

7. Zachariah Mann v. Ann Mann (1850), Complete Record, Book N, Circuit Court, Marion County, 205–6.

8. Aaron Wright v. Julia Ann Wright (1850), Complete Record, Book N, Circuit Court, Marion County, 95–97.

9. Charles Henry Edwards v. Amanda M. F. Edwards (1841), BA, E-75.

10. A. James Hammerton, *Cruelty and Companionship: Conflict in Nineteenth-Century Married Life* (New York: Routledge, 1992), 78.

11. Eliza Von Cort v. Charles Von Cort (1845), BA, V-172.

12. Sarah Brown and her next friend Caleb M. Littell v. Matthias A. Brown (1831), BA, B-13.

13. John Lewellen v. Nancy Lewellen (1849), Final Record, 1838–1849.

14. Jacob F. Bird v. Anna R. Bird (1865), GA-54, B-2.

15. Alfred Cole v. Clarissa Cole (1863), BA-132, C-3.

16. Thomas W. Egan v. Marie Egan (1866), GA-149, E-1.

17. Thomas H. Gilhooley v. Sarah Gilhooley (1860), GA-241, G-1. On women and public space, see especially Mary P. Ryan, *Women in Public: Between Banners and Ballots, 1825–1880* (Baltimore: Johns Hopkins University Press, 1990), 58–94.

18. The People ex rel. Eliza Fowler agt. William Fowler (1857), WR-F, 1295.

19. Harriet E. Butler by her next friend William N. Benedict v. Thomas Butler (1857), GA-67, B-2.

20. John Goff v. Margaret Ellen Goff by Matthew Spittle, her next friend (1854), GA-138, G-1; Henry Hurst v. Susanna Hurst (1864), GA-246, H-1; Casper Florence v. Lena Florence (1867), GA-147, F-1.

21. George Barnes v. Sarah Jane Barnes (1857), GA-96, B-3.

22. William B. Coan v. Ada S. Coan (1859), GA-152, C-3.

23. Cary Harris v. Mary Harris (1853), GA-104, H-1.

24. James B. Atwood v. Sarah Atwood (1822), Civil Order Book, 1818–1829.

25. William Harvey v. Kassandra Harvey (1847), Final Record, 1838–1849.

26. Thomas Collins v. Sabrina Collins (1857), GA-143, C-2.

27. Francis N. Crussel v. Mary A. Crussel (1860), GA-146, C-2.

28. Joshua B. Hyatt v. Margaret F. Hyatt (1859), GA-323, H-2; Samuel A. Gathright v. Mariah Gathright, Marion County Court of Common Pleas Order Book, 1849–1852, 95, 105, 160.

29. James Emmens v. Mary Ann Emmens (1855), GA-124, E-1; Henry C. Foster v. Malinda B. Foster (1862), GA-285, F-2.

30. Julia Ann Dredger v. William Dredger (1864), BA-137, D-1. For a similar set of circumstances in which a husband living in a long-term relationship with a paramour was awarded custody with permission for the wife's visitation rights, see Mary Emelia Eaton v. John A. Eaton (1869), BA-186, E-1.

31. Carole Pateman, *The Sexual Contract* (Stanford: Stanford University Press, 1988), 34; Michael Fotcher v. Louisa Fotcher (1866), BA-184, F-2.

32. Jacob Blackwell v. Maria Blackwell (1869), GA-28, B-1.

33. Ira S. Elkins v. Jane Ann Elkins (1865), GA-128, E-1.

34. William Bayer v. Theresa Bayer (1858), GA-83, B-3.

35. Abner Duryea by Peter Duryea (his guardian) v. Marietta Duryea (1850), BA-48, D-1.

36. Ann Couch v. George Couch (1859), GA-137, C-2.

37. George Bunte v. Minna Bunte (1867), GA-74, B-3.

38. Ibid.

CHAPTER 6. DIVORCE STORIES

1. *Important Trial Petition for Divorce on the Ground of Adultery of Thomas Dunham* (Boston: J. L. Homer, 1842), 31.

2. *The Dalton Divorce Case,* Shawmut ed. (Boston: Boston Bee, 1857), cover.

3. Daniel A. Cohen, *Pillars of Salt, Monuments of Grace: New England Crime Literature and the Origins of Popular Culture, 1674–1860* (New York: Oxford University Press, 1993), 38. Although Cohen estimates the cost of murder trial pamphlets at six or seven cents, twenty-five cents is marked on three of the divorce pamphlets I have surveyed, and there is a fifty-cent edition of the Forrest case. The rest are without a price. On the cost of printed materials in general, see Ronald J. Zboray, "Antebellum Reading and the Ironies of Technological Innovation," in *Reading in America: Literature and Social History,* ed. Cathy N. Davidson (Baltimore: Johns Hopkins University Press, 1989), 190. On the information revolution, see especially Richard D. Brown, *Knowledge Is Power: The Diffusion of Information in Early America, 1700–1865* (New York: Oxford University Press, 1989). For eighteenth-century English accounts of popular adultery trials, see David A. Ferris and Mary L. Person, *Trials of Love: A Valentine's Day Exhibition at the Harvard Law Library* (Cambridge, Mass.: Harvard Law School, 1994). American accounts of divorce trials, however, should be distinguished from English accounts of adultery trials, which belonged to a larger late-eighteenth-century body of erotica. Even at their most erotic, popular American accounts could be considered only a form of "soft porn."

4. On the rise of mass marketing as an alternative to traditional publishing, see Janice A. Radway, *Reading the Romance: Women, Patriarchy, and Popular Literature* (Chapel Hill: University of North Carolina Press, 1984), 21–22. On the female readership of newspapers, of which divorce pamphlets were an extension, see Brown, *Knowledge Is Power,* 281.

5. *Report of the Beardsley Divorce Case* (New York: Robert M. De Witt, 1860), 5. On the Jarvis case, see *The Great Divorce Case! A Full and Impartial History of the Trial of the Petition of Mrs. Sarah M. Jarvis for a Divorce from Her Husband, the Rev. Samuel F. Jarvis, D.D., L.L.D.* (New York: n.p., 1839), 3–4. Sometimes celebrity alone was enough to generate newspaper coverage. Charles Sumner, the famous champion of antislavery, managed to obtain a civ-

ilized divorce in the Supreme Court of Massachusetts. Yet newspapers speculated shamelessly on the cause of the dissolution, raising the possibility of his
impotency and suggesting his wife's infidelity. On the civilized nature of Sumner's divorce, see Elias Nason, *Life of Charles Sumner* (Boston: B. B. Russel,
1874), 312; on incessant newspaper speculation regarding Sumner's impotency
and his wife's fidelity, see Frederick J. Blue, "The Poet and the Reformer: Longfel-
low, Sumner, and the Bonds of Male Friendship, 1837–1874," *Journal of the
Early Republic* 15 (1995): 290.

6. *(Indianapolis) Indiana State Sentinel,* June 6, 1850; Charles Cowley,
Famous Divorces of All Ages (Lowell, Mass: Penhallow Printing, 1878), 193.

7. "Charles Dickens and His Wife," *Banner of Light,* July 10, 1858, 4. For
ads, see, for example, the back cover of *Report of the Beardsley Divorce Case.*

8. *Petition for Divorce of Thomas Dunham,* 7, 11.

9. *Report of the Proceedings on the Petition of Mrs. Sarah M. Jarvis for a
Divorce from Her Husband, Rev. Samuel F. Jarvis, D.D., L.L.D.* (Hartford,
Conn.: Review Press, 1839), 3, 116. For a New York paper's insistence that it
was better able to get at the truth than Connecticut locals, see *The Great Divorce
Case!* 3–4. As part of their efforts to assure readers of the accuracy of their
accounts, editors enlisted litigants to affirm the reliability of the editions. The
so-called certified edition of the long-lasting Forrest divorce trial carried an
endorsement from Edwin Forrest, the popular tragedian, who deemed the report
"faithful and comprehensive" and the only one of several that was "unpreju-
diced and complete." See *Report of the Forrest Divorce Case,* Herald Certified
ed. (New York: Robert M. De Witt, 1852), back cover.

10. *New York Times,* May 11, 1870. On "manly emotionality," see Lewis
Perry, *Intellectual Life in America: A History* (Chicago: University of Chicago
Press, 1989), 242

11. *Petition for Divorce of Thomas Dunham,* 28.

12. *Boston Daily Advertiser,* November 18, 1842; Cohen, *Pillars of Salt,*
251. For a brilliant analysis of the use of sentimental and antisentimental discourses to tell two conflicting stories, see Laura Hanft Korobkin, "The Maintenance of Mutual Confidence: Sentimental Strategies at the Adultery Trial of
Henry Ward Beecher," *Yale Journal of Law and Humanities* 7 (1995): 1–48.
Korobkin's article, with its sensitivity to alternative discourses, is an important
contribution to the burgeoning law and literature movement, which addresses
law *as* literature and law *in* literature. See, for example, Ian Ward, *Law and Literature: Possibilities and Perspectives* (New York: Cambridge University Press,
1995); "Symposium on Law, Literature, and the Humanities," *Cincinnati Law
Review* 79 (1994): 1–402. On feminists' narratives and the challenge they pose
to legal objectivity, see Kathryn Abrams, "Hearing the Call of Stories," *California Law Review* 79 (1991): 971–1052. Although I allude here to the discursive
strategies of attorneys who played on the melodrama of the accused wife as well
as those of their opponents who invoked legal objectivity, I am interested less in
lawyering than the competing images of the female defendant emanating from
the genre of the trial pamphlet.

13. *Petition for Divorce of Thomas Dunham,* 31.

14. Ibid., 25, 28.

15. On pamphlet novels, see David S. Reynolds, *Beneath the American Renaissance: The Subversive Imagination in the Age of Emerson and Melville* (New York: Alfred A. Knopf, 1988), 208; on female suffering and "spectatorial sympathy," see Karen Halttunen, "Humanitarianism and the Pornography of Pain in Anglo-American Culture," *American Historical Review* 100 (1995): 307.

16. *The Dalton Divorce Case,* 60–61; all citations, hereafter given parenthetically in the text, are to this edition. The trial, which was recounted in pamphlet form by the *Boston Bee,* generated several "extras," or very short pamphlets, which were printed (also by the *Bee*) in the midst of the trial.

17. I am thinking here particularly of Elaine Tyler May's chronologically comparative study of divorce, *Great Expectations: Marriage and Divorce in Post-Victorian America* (Chicago: University of Chicago Press, 1980), which locates the links between divorce and consumerism in the early twentieth century. These nineteenth-century trials, of course, profiled an exceptional segment of the urban population. On the problematic periodization of consumerism, see Paul G. E. Clemens, "The Consumer Revolution: Now, Only Yesterday, or A Long Time Ago," *Reviews in American History* 23 (1995): 574–81. On the problem of women in public spaces, see Richard Sennett, *The Fall of Public Man* (New York: Cambridge University Press, 1973), 23; and Judy R. Walkowitz, *City of Dreadful Delight: Narratives of Sexual Danger in Late-Victorian London* (Chicago: University of Chicago Press, 1992), 46.

18. On the beating, referred to in the divorce trial as "the Shawmut affair" after the site where it took place, see *Complete Report of the Trial of Edward O. Coburn and Benjamin F. Dalton, for the Manslaughter of William Sumner* (Boston: Burnham, Federhen, 1857). Dalton was found guilty of manslaughter and sentenced to five months in jail, during which time he evidently reconsidered the question of his wife's chastity.

19. Dana's personal file on the case suggests he had little faith in his abortion argument, because abortion was so common among respectable married women. I am grateful to Scott Sandage for forwarding me the file, which he found in the attic of the Worcester, Massachusetts, court archives. See Richard Henry Dana Papers, Attic Storage Room No. 2, Law Library, Worcester County Court House.

20. A forthright murder of passion might have been more acceptable than the clandestine beating arranged by Frank Dalton and his brother-in-law. See Henrik Hartog, "Lawyering, Husbands' Rights, and 'the Unwritten Law' in Nineteenth-Century America," *Journal of American History* 84 (1997): 67–96. For an avenging husband who killed his wife's lover, was acquitted by a jury that deliberated only seventy minutes, and went on to live with his wife, see *Trial of the Hon. Daniel E. Sickles for Shooting Philip Barton Key, Esq.* (New York: Robert M. De Witt, 1859). Sickles, a New York congressman, shot and killed Key, a U.S. district attorney, in President's Square in Washington. For a similar verdict, see also *The Richardson-McFarland Tragedy* (Philadelphia: Barclay, 1870).

21. The jury voted 10 for the libellant and 2 for the respondent, which indicates that they collectively doubted Nellie's version of the story. For the verdict, see the *Boston Bee*'s extra of May 1857, *Judge Merrick's Charge to the Jury, in the Dalton Divorce Case.*

22. *The Only Complete Report of the Burch Divorce Case* (New York: Robert M. De Witt, 1860), cover, 4, 6. Although the report was compiled by a *New York Daily Times* reporter, he excerpted coverage both from local Chicago and from other New York papers for the days he was unable to attend. All citations, hereafter given parenthetically in the text, are to this edition, but see also *Arguments in the Case of Isaac H. Burch v. Mary W. Burch by C. Beckwith, Esq. and the Hon. O. W. Browning* (Chicago: Scott, 1861).

23. On courtroom applause for a similar verdict on behalf of a female defendant whose minister husband accused her of "genteel prostitution" while her counsel claimed the reverend married her for her property, see the case of *Reverend Richard Cox v. Ellen Catherine Cox*, covered in the *New York Times*, March 18, 19, 20, and 28, 1856.

24. On Victorian masculine values, see Karen Lystra, *Searching the Heart: Women, Men, and Romantic Love in Nineteenth-Century America* (New York: Oxford University Press, 1989), 131–39.

25. *New York Times*, December 10 and 18, 1858.

26. *New York Times*, December 6, 1858.

27. For the Bennett letter dated December 30, 1858, see *New York Times*, January 1, 1859; on the verdict, see January 5, 1859; see also the report the *Times* reprinted on January 6, 1859, from the New Haven *Journal and Courier*. On similar responses to marital cruelty, see *The Great Divorce Case!*, the New York edition of the Jarvis case; there, the irony of a prominent Connecticut minister being accused of abusing his wife proved irresistible to newsmen.

28. *Beardsley Divorce Case*, 8; further citations will be given parenthetically in the text.

29. Busteed, something of a media celebrity, also represented Wildes Walker in a famous divorce suit that was tried in New York City but focused on evidence accumulated in Maine and Massachusetts. Busteed's verbal assault on the conduct of Catherine Walker, a plaintiff countercharged by her husband with adultery, was similar to the tack he took in the Beardsley case. See *A Full and Accurate Report of the Celebrated Trial of Walker vs. Walker* (New York: C. C. Childs, 1854).

30. The D'Hauteville case constitutes a significant exception to the inattention to custody issues in these sensational American divorce trials, which focused essentially on stories of sexual transgression. The D'Hauteville case was a battle over child custody in the midst of a separation; moreover, the report, as Michael Grossberg tells us, was published in an expensive, leatherbound edition, in contrast to the cheap productions of the trials under discussion. See *Report of the D'Hauteville Case* (Philadelphia: William S. Martien, 1840); and Grossberg, *A Judgment for Solomon: The D'Hauteville Case and Legal Experience in Antebellum America* (New York: Cambridge University Press, 1996), 175.

31. On the Pennsylvania suit, see Anon., *The Recorder or Any Body's Book* (Boston: Fay, 1850), 14–18, where the cost of paying the "lobbyers" and carrying the bill through Harrisburg was estimated at $10,000.

32. William Rounseville Alger, *Edwin Forrest: The American Tragedian*, 2 vols. (Philadelphia: J. B. Lippincott, 1877), 2:496–99, citation on 496–97; on legal expenditures, see also Henry Sedley, *Mr. O'Conor and the Forrest Case: A*

Letter Published in the New York Times, April 18, 1876 (New York: n.p., 1876). On the scope of national coverage, see, for example, the African American *National Era,* February 19, 1852. I am grateful to Shane White for bringing this citation to my attention. Journalists focusing on the Pennsylvania suit could not resist quoting from Othello, one of Edwin Forrest's favorite roles; see, for example, the *Indiana State Sentinel,* June 6, 1850.

33. Iver Bernstein, *The New York City Draft Riots: Their Significance for American Society and Politics in the Age of the Civil War* (New York: Oxford University Press, 1990), 148–49; see also Perry, *Intellectual Life in America,* 241–42.

34. *Report of the Forrest Divorce Case,* 62–63, citation on 63; further citations will be given parenthetically in the text.

35. On the joining of eroticism with tenderness in Victorian love, see Peter Gay, *The Tender Passion* (New York: Oxford University Press, 1986).

36. Christine Stansell, *City of Women: Sex and Class in New York, 1789–1860* (New York: Alfred A. Knopf, 1986), 23–25.

37. On the separation of sexuality and reproduction, see John D'Emilio and Estelle B. Freedman, *Intimate Matters: A History of Sexuality in America* (New York: Harper and Row, 1988).

38. On the emergence of the divorce novel, see James Harwood Barnett, *Divorce and the American Novel, 1858–1937: A Study in Literary Reflections of Social Influences* (New York: Russell and Russell, 1968); and Warren French, "Timothy Shay Arthur's Divorce Fiction," *Texas University Studies in English* 33 (1954): 90–96. My own search for titles that suggest divorce as a theme reveals an earlier start than Barnett indicates. On the influence of news accounts of divorce on writers of fiction, see Timothy Shay Arthur, "Wives Who Are Not Wives," *Hearth and Home* 2 (1870): 522.

39. On the invisibility of women's labor, see especially Jeanne Boydston, *Home and Work: Housework, Wages, and the Ideology of Labor in the Early Republic* (New York: Oxford University Press, 1990). For a more sanguine view of the economic prospects of divorced women in the nineteenth century, see Robert L. Griswold, *Family and Divorce in California, 1850–1890: Victorian Illusions and Everyday Realities* (Albany: State University of New York Press, 1982), 81–86

40. Timothy Shay Arthur, *Love in High Life: A Story of the "Upper Ten"* (Philadelphia: T. B. Peterson, 1849), 18. On the import of love for both sexes, see Peter N. Stearns, "Girls, Boys, and Emotions: Redefinitions and Historical Change," *Journal of American History* 80 (1993): 50–51.

41. Lady Charlotte Bury [Susan Maria Campbell], *The Divorced* (Philadelphia: T. B. Peterson, 1863), citation on 57.

42. Ibid., 18, 67, 74, 88.

43. Nancy Cott, "Passionlessness: An Interpretation of Victorian Sexual Ideology, 1790–1850," *Signs* 4 (1978): 219–36.

44. Emma D. E. Nevitt Southworth, *The Deserted Wife* (New York: Appleton, 1850), 5–6.

45. Ibid., 7.

46. On Southworth's desertion, see Mary Kelley, *Private Woman, Public*

Stage: Literary Domesticity in Nineteenth-Century America (New York: Oxford University Press, 1984), 313; for a similar authorial stand against divorce in sentimental fiction, see Augusta Evans Wilson, *Vashti, or "Until Death Do Us Part"* (New York: Carleton, 1869), 371.

47. Laura J. (Curtis) Bullard, *Christine; or Woman's Trials and Triumphs* (New York: De Witt and Davenport, 1856), citations on 297; on Bullard's argument in the *Revolution,* see William Leach, *True Love and Perfect Union: The Feminist Reform of Sex and Society* (New York: Basic Books, 1980), 190. On *Christine,* see also Reynolds, *Beneath the American Renaissance,* 393–94.

48. Jane Tompkins, *Sensational Designs: The Cultural Work of American Fiction, 1790–1860* (New York: Oxford University Press, 1985). For a very different reading of sentimental fiction, see Ann Douglas, *The Feminization of American Culture* (New York: Alfred A. Knopf, 1977).

49. Timothy Shay Arthur, *The Divorced Wife* (Philadelphia: T. B. Peterson, 1850), citations on 24, 51. For similar endings, see "Twice Married," *Arthur's Home Magazine* 4 (1854): 330–36; and "After the Storm," in ibid. 15 (1860): 221–36, 285–302, 348–54.

50. Timothy Shay Arthur, *Out in the World* (Philadelphia: John E. Potter, 1864), 6.

51. Ibid., 133.

52. Harriet Beecher Stowe, *Pink and White Tyranny* (1871; reprint, Boston: Roberts Brothers, 1885), 237.

53. Ibid., 316.

54. Ibid., 316–17, 320.

55. I am obviously referring here to *A Modern Instance.* Although Howells's personal stance in the novel remains controversial among literary scholars, I am convinced he belongs squarely in Stowe's camp. On his fears about divorce, see John W. Crowly, *The Mask of Fiction: Essays on W. D. Howells* (Amherst: University of Massachusetts Press, 1989), 49.

56. On the conflict between romantic love and lifelong monogamy that is symbolized in divorce, see Norma Basch, "Marriage, Morals, and Politics in the Election of 1828," *Journal of American History* 80 (1993): 890–918.

EPILOGUE

1. On efforts to repeal no-fault, see "The Divorce Debate," *New York Times,* February 15, 1996; and Hanna Rosin, "Separation Anxiety," *New Republic,* May 6, 1996, 14, 16–18. On Louisiana's move to provide couples with the option of "covenant marriage," see Amitai Etzioni, "Marriage with No Easy Outs," *New York Times,* August 13, 1997. On the emergence of no-fault in a comparative perspective with emphasis on the problem of unilateral divorce, see Mary Ann Glendon, *Abortion and Divorce in Western Law: American Failures, European Challenges* (Cambridge, Mass.: Harvard University Press, 1987); and J. Herbie DiFonzo, *Beneath the Fault Line: The Popular and Legal Culture of Divorce in Twentieth-Century America* (Charlottesville: University Press of Virginia, 1997). See also William A. Galston, "Needed: A Not-So-Fast Divorce Law," *New York Times,* December 27, 1995; Galston was a social policy adviser

to President Clinton. For a comparison of the promise keeping in marriage contracts with the promise keeping in other contracts that is reminiscent of the comparisons made by E. D. E. N Southworth and Harriet Beecher Stowe, see Maggie Gallagher, "Why Make Divorce Easy?" *New York Times,* February 20, 1996.

2. On the importance of the moral and symbolic freight carried by divorce, see Lawrence M. Friedman, "Divorce Law in Historical Perspective," *Oregon Law Review* 63 (1984): 651.

3. See Rosin, "Separation Anxiety," 16.

4. On liberal market values and Protestant republican ambivalence, see Dorothy Ross, *The Origins of American Social Science* (New York: Cambridge University Press, 1991), xvii.

5. Lynn Hunt, *The Family Romance of the French Revolution* (Berkeley: University of California Press, 1992), 204; Carole Patemen, *The Sexual Contract* (Stanford: Stanford University Press, 1988).

Index

Abortion, 159, 222n19

Adultery as grounds: cited with desertion, in New York, 105, 114, 217n34; English equivalent of, 23–24; male versus female defendants of, 202n8; and prohibited remarriage, 40, 106, 134, 216n16; in Puritan model, 48; in 1787 New York statute, 40; in 1795 territorial statute, 23; undermined by slavery, 49

Adultery by men, form/immorality of, 49, 165, 170–71

Adultery by women: children's corroboration of, 134; during Civil War, 128; as consequence of romantic love, 126, 174, 176; female insubordination tied to, 124, 125, 130, 131, 153; flirtation distinguished from, 155–57; and loss of custody, 133, 134–35, 137; and paternity dilemma, 133, 136–37, 159; retribution for, in sentimental fiction, 179, 181; "scandalous" court trials on, 149; as test of marital authority, 171–72; urbanization's role in, 130, 158, 162, 222n17; and woman-as-victim role, 153–55, 162–63. *See also* Chastity of women; Contested divorce trials

Advice columns, 34–35

Affinities, doctrine of, 82

Alimony: basis/evolution of, 109; female plantiff's legal pursuit of, 105, 106, 107; husband's defenses against, 112–13; in Indiana versus New York, 109, 217n22; Monroe County records of, 101; New York County records of, 101; and risk of retaliation, 113–14; during separation, 109–11

Amelia; or, The Faithless Briton, 35

American divorce law: Christian assault on, 87–90, 211n49; dilemma of justification for, 27–28; English divorce policy versus, 22, 23–24; gender issues and, 60–61, 188–91; Judeo-Christian components of, 4–5; legal prototypes for, 46–48; linked to national destiny, 16; morality issues and, 40–41, 49–50, 58, 59, 63–65, 204n17; punitive component of, for adulterous wives, 133–34, 154; regional variations in, 6, 7, 9–10, 23, 47–49; Revolutionary foundations of, 15, 20–21. *See also* Divorce; Grounds for divorce; Legitimation of divorce

American Revolution: antipatriarchal dimensions of, 26; dilemma of justification for, 28; and legitimation of divorce, 15, 20–21, 27, 29–30, 82, 93, 190; severed family imagery of, 25–26. *See also* Post-Revolutionary era

American Woman Suffrage Association, 72

Anderson, Sabrina, 110

Anderson, Thomas, 110

Andrews, Stephen Pearl, 85, 211nn40, 41

Androgyne legend of perfect union, 32

Indexer:	Patricia Deminna
Compositor:	Braun-Brumfield, Inc.
Text:	10/13 Sabon
Display:	Centaur
Printer and binder:	Braun-Brumfield, Inc.